The Probation and Parole
Treatment Planner,
with DSM-5 Updates

Practice*Planners*® Series

Treatment Planners
The Complete Adult Psychotherapy Treatment Planner, Fifth Edition
The Child Psychotherapy Treatment Planner, Fifth Edition
The Adolescent Psychotherapy Treatment Planner, Fifth Edition
The Addiction Treatment Planner, Fifth Edition
The Continuum of Care Treatment Planner
The Couples Psychotherapy Treatment Planner, with DSM-5 Updates, Second Edition
The Employee Assistance Treatment Planner
The Pastoral Counseling Treatment Planner
The Older Adult Psychotherapy Treatment Planner, with DSM-5 Updates, Second Edition
The Behavioral Medicine Treatment Planner
The Group Therapy Treatment Planner, with DSM-5 Updates, Second Edition
The Gay and Lesbian Psychotherapy Treatment Planner
The Family Therapy Treatment Planner, with DSM-5 Updates, Second Edition
The Severe and Persistent Mental Illness Treatment Planner, with DSM-5 Updates, Second Edition
The Intellectual and Developmental Disability Treatment Planner, with DSM 5 Updates
The Social Work and Human Services Treatment Planner, with DSM-5 Updates
The Crisis Counseling and Traumatic Events Treatment Planner, with DSM-5 Updates, Second Edition
The Personality Disorders Treatment Planner
The Rehabilitation Psychology Treatment Planner
The Special Education Treatment Planner
The Juvenile Justice and Residential Care Treatment Planner, with DSM-5 Updates
The School Counseling and School Social Work Treatment Planner, with DSM-5 Updates, Second Edition
The Sexual Abuse Victim and Sexual Offender Treatment Planner, with DSM-5 Updates
The Probation and Parole Treatment Planner, with DSM-5 Updates
The Psychopharmacology Treatment Planner
The Speech-Language Pathology Treatment Planner
The Suicide and Homicide Risk Assessment and Prevention Treatment Planner, with DSM-5 Updates
The College Student Counseling Treatment Planner
The Parenting Skills Treatment Planner, with DSM-5 Updates
The Early Childhood Intervention Treatment Planner
The Co-occurring Disorders Treatment Planner, with DSM-5 Updates
The Complete Women's Psychotherapy Treatment Planner
The Veterans and Active Duty Military Psychotherapy Treatment Planner, with DSM-5 Updates

Progress Notes Planners
The Child Psychotherapy Progress Notes Planner, Fifth Edition
The Adolescent Psychotherapy Progress Notes Planner, Fifth Edition
The Adult Psychotherapy Progress Notes Planner, Fifth Edition
The Addiction Progress Notes Planner, Fifth Edition
The Severe and Persistent Mental Illness Progress Notes Planner, Second Edition
The Couples Psychotherapy Progress Notes Planner, Second Edition
The Family Therapy Progress Notes Planner, Second Edition
The Veterans and Active Duty Military Psychotherapy Progress Notes Planner

Homework Planners
Couples Therapy Homework Planner, Second Edition
Family Therapy Homework Planner, Second Edition
Grief Counseling Homework Planner
Group Therapy Homework Planner
Divorce Counseling Homework Planner
School Counseling and School Social Work Homework Planner, Second Edition
Child Therapy Activity and Homework Planner
Addiction Treatment Homework Planner, Fifth Edition
Adolescent Psychotherapy Homework Planner, Fifth Edition
Adult Psychotherapy Homework Planner, Fifth Edition
Child Psychotherapy Homework Planner, Fifth Edition
Parenting Skills Homework Planner
Veterans and Active Duty Military Psychotherapy Homework Planner

Client Education Handout Planners
Adult Client Education Handout Planner
Child and Adolescent Client Education Handout Planner
Couples and Family Client Education Handout Planner

Complete Planners
The Complete Depression Treatment and Homework Planner
The Complete Anxiety Treatment and Homework Planner

PracticePlanners®

Arthur E. Jongsma, Jr., Series Editor

The Probation and Parole Treatment Planner, with DSM-5 Updates

Brad M. Bogue

Anjali Nandi

Arthur E. Jongsma, Jr.

WILEY

To my wife, Andrea, my daughter, Beccah and my son, Sam, for their continuous ability to make my life meaningful and wonderful

—B.M.B.

To Elbert Gibford, my husband, my best friend, my source of endless love and support; to my family, Margaret Fraser, Jennifer Nandi, Sanjay Nandi, and Aarathi Bhat for their unconditional love; and, to my father for being here in spirit

—A.N.

To Beccah Bogue, one of God's marvelous lights, strong then weak, now becoming strong again and looking for her perfect place to shine. Watch for her brightness. It will not be denied.

—A.E.J.

CONTENTS

PRACTICE*PLANNERS*® SERIES PREFACE

Accountability is an important dimension of the practice of psychotherapy. Treatment programs, public agencies, clinics, and practitioners must justify and document their treatment plans to outside review entities in order to be reimbursed for services. The books in the Practice*Planners*® series are designed to help practitioners fulfill these documentation requirements efficiently and professionally.

The Practice*Planners*® series includes a wide array of treatment planning books including not only the original *Complete Adult Psychotherapy Treatment Planner*, *Child Psychotherapy Treatment Planner*, and *Adolescent Psychotherapy Treatment Planner*, all now in their fifth editions, but also *Treatment Planners* targeted to specialty areas of practice, including:

Addictions
- Co-occurring disorders
- Behavioral medicine
- College students
- Couples therapy
- Crisis counseling
- Early childhood education
- Employee assistance
- Family therapy
- Gays and lesbians
- Group therapy
- Juvenile justice and residential care
- Mental retardation and developmental disability
- Neuropsychology
- Older adults
- Parenting skills
- Pastoral counseling
- Personality disorders
- Probation and parole
- Psychopharmacology

- Rehabilitation psychology
- School counseling and school social work
- Severe and persistent mental illness
- Sexual abuse victims and offenders
- Social work and human services
- Special education
- Speech-language pathology
- Suicide and homicide risk assessment
- Veterans and active military duty
- Women's issues

In addition, there are three branches of companion books that can be used in conjunction with the *Treatment Planners*, or on their own:

- ***Progress Notes Planners*** provide a menu of progress statements that elaborate on the client's symptom presentation and the provider's therapeutic intervention. Each *Progress Notes Planner* statement is directly integrated with the behavioral definitions and therapeutic interventions from its companion *Treatment Planner*.
- ***Homework Planners*** include homework assignments designed around each presenting problem (such as anxiety, depression, substance use, anger control problems, eating disorders, or panic disorder) that is the focus of a chapter in its corresponding *Treatment Planner*.
- ***Client Education Handout Planners*** provide brochures and handouts to help educate and inform clients on presenting problems and mental health issues, as well as life skills techniques. The handouts are included on CD-ROMs for easy printing from your computer and are ideal for use in waiting rooms, at presentations, as newsletters, or as information for clients struggling with mental illness issues. The topics covered by these handouts correspond to the presenting problems in the *Treatment Planners*.

The series also includes adjunctive books, such as *The Psychotherapy Documentation Primer* and *The Clinical Documentation Sourcebook*, contain forms and resources to aid the clinician in mental health practice management.

The goal of our series is to provide practitioners with the resources they need in order to provide high-quality care in the era of accountability. To put it simply: We seek to help you spend more time on patients, and less time on paperwork.

ARTHUR E. JONGSMA, JR.
Grand Rapids, Michigan

ACKNOWLEDGMENTS

We would like to acknowledge Jim Bonta, Don Andrews, Ken Wanberg, Harvey Milkman, Robert Ross, Arnie Goldstein, Alan Marlatt, William Miller, Stephen Rollnick, Carlo DiClemente, Delbert Elloitt, Bill Woodward, Roger Lauen, Tom O'Connor, and Dave Dillingham for their wisdom, clarity, commitment, and vision of what treatment/intervention in an evolving corrections program can look like.

We also want to thank Sami Halbert, Matt Merrion, Bill Woodward, David Tinken, and Tom O'Connor for their support and contribution to chapters in this Planner.

Brad Bogue and Anjali Nandi are extremely grateful to Art Jongsma and Jen Byrne, Dr. Jongsma's manuscript assistant, for their patience and understanding throughout this process. Without their support, encourage-ment, and faith in us, this book would not have been possible.

Anjali Nandi is grateful to Brad Bogue for mentoring her, challenging her, supporting her, and for giving her endless opportunities to grow.

Art Jongsma would like to take this opportunity to thank Brad Bogue and Anjali Nandi who have completed this project under extremely trying circumstances that intervened midstream. Although progress came to a necessary halt for several weeks while all their energies went in directions they were needed and belonged, true grit and determination brought them back to focus on writing this book. Dark days have lifted and the book has emerged as a tribute to the strength of the human spirit—their spirit. I offer you my gratitude and admiration for hanging on and creating a gift to your profession—*The Probation and Parole Treatment Planner*.

The Probation and Parole Treatment Planner, with DSM-5 Updates

INTRODUCTION

Gradually, since the early 1960s, formalized treatment planning has become a vital aspect of the healthcare delivery system, whether it is treatment related to physical health, mental health, child welfare, or substance abuse. What started in the medical sector in the 1960s spread to the mental health sector in the 1970s as clinics, psychiatric hospitals, agencies, and so on, began to seek accreditation from bodies such as the Joint Commission on Accreditation of Healthcare Organizations (JCAHO) to qualify for third-party reimbursements. With the advent of managed care in the 1980s, treatment planning became even more important. Managed care systems *insisted* that clinicians move rapidly from problem assessment to formulation and implementation of the treatment plan. The goal of most managed care companies is to expedite the treatment process by prompting the client and treatment provider to focus on identifying and changing behavioral problems as quickly as possible. Treatment plans must specifically address presenting problems, behaviorally-defined symptoms, treatment goals and objectives, and interventions. Treatment plans must be individualized to meet the client's needs and goals, and the observable objectives must set milestones that can be used to chart the client's progress. Pressure from third-party payers, accrediting agencies, and other outside parties has increased the need for clinicians to produce effective, high-quality treatment plans in a short time frame. However, many mental health providers have little experience in treatment-plan development. This book will clarify, simplify, and accelerate the treatment planning process.

PLANNER FOCUS

The Probation and Parole Treatment Planner is written for practitioners in the field of corrections and related treatment areas (addictions, domestic violence, sex offender treatment, etc.). It serves as a guide with a comprehensive menu of case plan ingredients from which the officer or clinician may select offender objectives and/or practitioner interventions for addressing the criminogenic needs of offenders on their caseloads. Appropriate offender assessment to determine actuarial risk (for recidivism) and to identify each offender's most prominent criminogenic needs is a critical function that must precede the case planning protocols elaborated in this text.

The field of community corrections (e.g., probation, parole, residential halfway houses, day reporting) is dynamic and complex, involving a number of different *critical event cycles* within any agency. Research in the past 10 to 15 years, sometimes referred to as "What Works," highlights the significance of effective intervention strategies in terms of potential reductions in recidivism and criminal victimization. As policy-makers listen to their constituencies on the one hand and their analysts and researchers on the other, the "What Works" literature and evidence has become a driving force for reengineering community corrections to have a greater accountability and emphasis on outcomes. This trend plays a significant role in shaping the demand for more efficient and effective offender case plans.

Case plans, long considered the linchpins for accountability in case management, have languished for 20 years, not evolving in corrections until recently. Given the advent of so-called third-generation risk/need offender assessment tools (LSI-R; Compas, etc.), the means for identifying offender criminogenic needs now mandates case plans that are tailored to these same critical factors. The chapters in the *Planner* can each be logically subsumed or identified with the primary dynamic risk factors (e.g., antisocial peers, antisocial values, dysfunctional family relations, substance abuse, and self-control deficits) that have the most research evidence as being criminogenic. Therefore, the *Planner* should readily serve as a bridge between the offender needs identified in assessment and individualized plans of action to address those specific (and criminogenic) needs. This linkage is crucial for operationalizing the need and responsivity principles described throughout the "What Works" literature.

Many of the case plan short-term objectives in each of the problem-oriented *Planner* chapters are commonly found in a variety of cognitive behavioral skills training curriculum and adhere to cognitive behavioral training paradigms. Cognitive behavioral interventions are clearly indicated in the research as the preferred treatment strategy when working with corrections populations. This book emphasizes the suggestion of interventions that involve skill training with directed practice.

We assume that the monitoring and necessary surveillance of the client will be driven by the policies in each agency. Nevertheless, it is our recommendation that monitoring and necessary surveillance correspond to the risk principle, which is to provide services in proportion to risk levels: the greater the risk, the greater the level of surveillance services. Treatment or case plans for the client developed from this book should be consistent with the needs principle; that is, the provider must target those criminogenic need areas of the client with a sequential plan of treatment action. *The Probation and Parole Treatment Planner* is an ambitious guide for developing individual offender action plans in accordance with current research and demonstrated effectiveness.

USING QUANTIFIABLE LANGUAGE IN TREATMENT PLANS

Appendix A contains the Criminal Peers chapter, which has been revised using more measurable, quantifiable language than in previous editions. In today's clinical-economic marketplaces of both managed care/third-party payors and accrediting bodies—JCAHO, NCQA, and CARF—there is an increased emphasis on behaviorally observable and/or quantifiable aspects of treatment plans. One reason for this is a general and national movement toward shorter inpatient stays (public and private hospitals and residential facilities) and briefer managed outpatient treatment, with the focus on specific symptom resolution. If you are experiencing such pressure, you may need to alter our *Treatment Planner* observable behavioral criteria into language that is more measurable and quantifiable.

Clinicians may want to look for the opportunity to craft measurable/quantifiable aspects of the patient's behaviors into their treatment plans. You may introduce measurability at the symptomatic level (e.g., behavioral definitions) and/or at the treatment outcome level (e.g., short-term objectives). Behavioral definition terms such as *repeated, frequent, tendency, pattern consistent, excessive, high-level, persistent, displays, heightened, recurrent,* and the like, and even words like *verbalizes, displays, demonstrates, refuses, unable, avoids, seeks, difficulty, increasing,* or *declining* can have frequencies or circumstances added to quantify the item. For example, the definition item "Verbalizes having suicidal ideation" can be made more quantifiably measurable by changing it to "Verbalizes having suicidal ideation once to twice daily for the past two weeks."

Clinicians may add aspects of severity to symptom definition statements, in addition to frequency, to introduce greater measurability. For example, "Verbalizes having sad thoughts four to five times daily for the past two weeks and, on a scale from 1 to 10 (10 being the worst), were judged to be at an 8." Or, alternatively, the clinician may list quantified psychometric data as a criterion measure, such as scores from symptoms screening instruments such as the BPRS, BDI, Ham-D, BSI, SCL-90-R, or GAF, to reduce subjectivity.

The short-term objective language found in the *Treatment Planner* can also be modified to follow the more quantified approach; thus, "Engage in physical and recreational activities that reflect increased energy and interest" becomes "Engage in physical and recreational activities within one week's time (by 1/20/2004)." Also, "Verbally express an understanding of the relationship between depressed mood and repression of sadness and anger" becomes "Verbally express an understanding of the relationship between depressed mood and repression of sadness and anger (by 1/18/2004)." A sample treatment plan containing quantified language is located at the end of this Introduction. This "Sample Quantitative Treatment Plan" exactly mirrors the "Sample Standard Treatment Plan" in terms of the items that have been selected from the "Criminal Peers" chapter.

DEVELOPING A TREATMENT PLAN

The process of developing a treatment plan involves a logical series of steps that build on one another much like constructing a house. The foundation of any effective treatment plan is the gathering of data in a thorough biopsychosocial assessment. As the client presents himself or herself for treatment, the clinician must sensitively listen to and understand what the client struggles with in terms of family-of-origin issues, current stressors, emotional status, social network, physical health, coping skills, interpersonal conflicts, self-esteem, and so on. Assessment data may be gathered from a social history, physical exam, clinical interview, psychological testing, or contact with a client's significant others. The integration of the data by the clinician or the multidisciplinary treatment team members is critical for understanding the client, as is an awareness of the basis of the client's struggle. We have identified six specific steps for developing an effective treatment plan based on the assessment data.

STEP ONE: PROBLEM SELECTION

Although the client may discuss a variety of issues during the assessment, the clinician must focus the treatment process on the most significant problems. Usually a *primary* problem will surface, and *secondary* problems may also be evident. *Other* problems may have to be set aside as not urgent enough to require treatment at this time. An effective treatment plan can deal only with a few selected problems or the treatment will lose its direction. This *Planner* offers 30 problems that you can use to select those that most accurately represent your client's presenting issues.

As the problems to be selected become clear to the clinician or the treatment team, it is important to include opinions from the client about his or her prioritization of issues for which help is being sought. A client's motivation to participate in and cooperate with the treatment process depends, to some extent, on the degree to which treatment addresses his or her greatest needs.

STEP TWO: PROBLEM DEFINITION

Each individual client presents with unique nuances about how a problem behaviorally reveals itself in his or her life. Therefore, each problem that is selected for treatment focus requires a specific definition on how it is evidenced in that particular client. The symptom pattern should be associated with diagnostic criteria and codes such as those found in the *Diagnostic and Statistical Manual (DSM)* or the *International Classification of Diseases (ICD)*. The *Planner,* following the pattern established by *DSM-5,* offers behaviorally specific definition statements to choose from or to serve as a model for your own personally crafted statements. You will find several behavior symptoms or syndromes listed that may characterize one of the 30 presenting problems.

STEP THREE: GOAL DEVELOPMENT

The next step in treatment plan development is to set broad goals for the resolution of the target problem. Although not crafted in measurable terms, these statements are global, long-term goals that indicate a desired positive outcome to the treatment procedures. The *Planner* suggests several possible goal statements for each problem, but only one statement is required in a treatment plan.

STEP FOUR: OBJECTIVE CONSTRUCTION

In contrast to long-term goals, objectives must be stated in behaviorally measurable language. It must be clear when the client has achieved the established objectives; therefore, vague, subjective objectives are not acceptable. Accrediting agencies, HMOs, and managed care organizations insist on measurable psychological treatment outcomes. The objectives presented in this *Planner* are designed to meet this demand for accountability. Alternatives are presented to allow construction of a variety of treatment plan possibilities for the same presenting problem. The clinician must exercise professional judgment concerning the appropriateness of objectives for a given client.

Each objective should be developed as a step toward attaining the broad treatment goal. In essence, objectives can be thought of as a series of steps that, when completed, result in the achievement of the long-term goal. There should be at least two objectives for each problem, but the clinician may construct as many as necessary for goal achievement. Target attainment dates may be listed for each objective. New objectives should be added to the plan as the individual's treatment progresses. When all the necessary objectives have been achieved, the client should have resolved the target problem successfully.

STEP FIVE: INTERVENTION CREATION

Interventions are the actions of the clinician designed to help the client complete the objectives. There should be at least one intervention for every objective. If the client does not accomplish the objective after the initial intervention, new interventions should be added to the plan.

Interventions should be selected on the basis of the client's needs and the treatment provider's full therapeutic repertoire. This *Planner* contains interventions from a broad range of therapeutic approaches, including cognitive, dynamic, behavioral, pharmacologic, family-oriented, and solution-focused brief therapy. Other interventions may be written by the provider to reflect his or her own training and experience. The addition of new problems, definitions, goals, objectives, and interventions to those found in the *Planner* adds to the database for future reference and use.

Some suggested interventions listed in the *Planner* refer to specific books that can be assigned to the client for adjunctive bibliotherapy. Appendix B contains a full reference list of these bibliotherapy materials. The books are arranged by the problem for which they are appropriate as assigned reading for clients. When a book is used as part of an intervention plan, it should be reviewed with the client after it is read, enhancing the application of the content of the book to the specific client's circumstances. For further information about self-help books, mental health professionals may wish to consult *The Authoritative Guide to Self-Help Resources in Mental Health* by Norcross, Santrock, Campbell, Smith, Sommer, and Zuckerman (New York: Guilford Press, 2000).

Assigning an intervention to a specific provider is most relevant if the client is being treated by a team in an inpatient, residential, or intensive outpatient setting. Within these settings, personnel other than the primary clinician may be responsible for implementing a specific intervention. Accrediting agencies require that the responsible provider's name be stipulated for every intervention.

STEP SIX: DIAGNOSIS DETERMINATION

The determination of an appropriate diagnosis is based on an evaluation of the client's complete clinical presentation. The clinician must compare the behavioral, cognitive, emotional, and interpersonal symptoms that the client presents to the criteria for diagnosis of a mental illness condition as described in *DSM-5*. The issue of differential diagnosis is a difficult one that research has shown to have rather low inter-rater reliability. Psychologists have also been trained to think more in terms of maladaptive behavior than in disease labels. In spite of these factors, diagnosis is a reality that exists in the world of mental health care and it is a necessity for third-party reimbursement. (Recently, managed care agencies are more interested in behavioral indices that are exhibited by the client than in the actual diagnosis.) It is the clinician's thorough knowledge of *DSM-5* criteria and a complete understanding of the client assessment data that contribute to the most reliable, valid diagnosis. An accurate assessment of behavioral indicators also contributes to more effective treatment planning.

HOW TO USE THIS PLANNER

Learning the skills of effective case management plan writing can be a tedious and difficult process for many clinicians. It is even more stressful to try to develop this expertise when under the pressure of increased client load and short time frames placed on clinicians today by managed care systems. The documentation demands can be overwhelming when moving quickly from assessment to case plan to progress notes. In the process, we must be specific about how and when objectives can be achieved and how progress is exhibited in each client. *The Probation and Parole Treatment Planner* was developed as a tool to aid clinicians in writing a case plan that is clear, specific, and highly individualized according to the following progression:

1. Choose one presenting problem (Step One) you have identified through your assessment process. Locate the corresponding page number for that problem in the *Planner's* table of contents.
2. Select two or three of the listed behavioral definitions (Step Two) and record them in the appropriate section on your case management plan form. Feel free to add your own defining

statement if you determine that your client's behavioral manifestation of the identified problem is not listed. (Note that while our design for case planning is vertical, it will work equally well on plan forms formatted horizontally.)

3. Select a single long-term goal (Step Three) and write the selection, exactly as it is written in the *Planner* or in some appropriately modified form, in the corresponding area of your own form.

4. Review the listed objectives for this problem and select the ones you judge to be clinically indicated for your client (Step Four). Remember, it is recommended that you select at least two objectives for each problem. Add a target date or the number of sessions allocated for the attainment of each objective.

5. Choose relevant interventions (Step Five). The *Planner* offers suggested interventions related to each objective in the parentheses following the objective statement, but do not limit yourself to those interventions. The entire list is eclectic and may offer options that are more tailored to your theoretical approach or preferred way of working with clients. Also, just as with definitions, goals, and objectives, there is space allowed for you to enter your own interventions into the *Planner*. This allows you to refer to these entries when you create a plan around this problem in the future. You will have to assign responsibility for implementation of each intervention to a specific person if the treatment is being carried out by a multidisciplinary team.

6. Several *DSM-5* diagnoses are listed at the end of each chapter that are commonly associated with a client who has this problem. These diagnoses are meant to be suggestions for clinical consideration. Select a diagnosis listed or assign a more appropriate choice from the *DSM-5* (Step Six).

To accommodate those practitioners who tend to plan case management in terms of diagnostic labels rather than presenting problems, Appendix C lists all of the *DSM-5* diagnoses that have been presented in various presenting problem chapters as suggestions for consideration. Each diagnosis is followed by the presenting problem that has been associated with that diagnosis. Providers may look up the presenting problems for a selected diagnosis to review definitions, goals, objectives, and interventions that may be appropriate for their clients with that diagnosis.

Congratulations! You should now have a complete, individualized case management plan that is ready for immediate implementation and presentation to the client. It should resemble the format of the first example: "Sample Standard Treatment Plan."

A FINAL NOTE

One important aspect of effective case management planning is that each plan should be tailored to the individual client's problems and needs. Plans should not be mass produced, even if clients have similar problems. The individual's strengths and weaknesses, unique stressors, social network, family circumstances, and symptom patterns *must* be considered in developing a treatment strategy. Drawing on our own years of clinical experience, we have assembled a variety of case choices. These statements can be combined in thousands of permutations to develop detailed case plans. Relying on their own good judgment, clinicians can easily select the statements that are appropriate for the individuals they are treating. In addition, we encourage readers to add their own definitions, goals, objectives, and interventions to the existing samples. It is our hope that *The Probation and Parole Treatment Planner* will promote effective, creative case planning—a process that will ultimately benefit the client, clinician, and criminal justice community.

SAMPLE STANDARD TREATMENT PLAN

PROBLEM: CRIMINAL PEERS

Definitions: Currently associates with friends and acquaintances who are involved in criminal behavior.

Admires or identifies with others who are pro-crime and sees their lifestyle as desirable.

Willing to protect, cover-up, and accept responsibility for peers' deviant behavior.

Inability to establish and maintain meaningful pro-social peer support group.

Goals: Significantly reduce or eliminate association with criminal friends.

Develop a meaningful, pro-social support network.

OBJECTIVES

1. List all friends and acquaintances; placing an asterisk next to those who have been involved in criminal behavior.

2. Describe the history and consequences of criminal behavior with peers.

3. List the positive and negative consequences of yielding to peer pressure.

INTERVENTIONS

1. Assign the client to list all his/her friends and acquaintances; denoting criminal peers with an asterisk.

2. Review the client's list of peers, exploring his/her feelings and thoughts about the number of pro-crime peers compared to pro-social peers.

1. Explore the client's history and consequences of his/her involvement in criminal behavior with friends and acquaintances.

1. Explain the dynamics of peer pressure to the client (e.g., wanting to fit in) and the

positive (e.g., feeling of belongingness, having fun, avoiding conflict) and negative (e.g., going against one's better judgment, getting caught, conflict with peers) consequences of yielding to peer pressure.

4. Identify factors that have led to the development of relationships with deviant peers.

1. Teach the client the various factors that can lead to developing relationships with criminal peers (e.g., low self-esteem, desire to belong, curiosity, thrill seeking).

2. Assist the client in generating a list of personal factors that have led him/her to develop relationships with deviant peers; review and process this list, reinforcing the client's increased understanding of himself/herself.

5. Identify, practice, and implement new strategies for distancing self from criminal peers.

1. Teach the client new strategies (e.g., setting clear boundaries, telling peers his/her goal of avoiding criminal behavior, saying no) for distancing himself/herself from criminal peers.

2. Role play with the client the use of the new distancing techniques; provide him/her with positive feedback for effort, as well as suggestions for improvement in implementation.

3. Assign the client the task of choosing one deviant friend or acquaintance that he/she feels comfortable distancing himself/herself from and implement the new distancing techniques with that person.

4. Debrief with client about how new distancing techniques worked with chosen person; provide positive reinforcement and feedback for improvement.

6. Make a list of the values, traits, attributes, and attitudes that are seen as important to look for when making a new, supportive, pro-social friend.

1. Help the client generate a list of values and attitudes that he/she sees as important to look for when making a new, supportive, pro-social friend; highlight the differences between this set of values and attitudes and those values and attitudes associated with his/her criminal peers.

7. Implement new ways to go about making supportive friendships.

1. Use role playing, modeling, and behavior rehearsal to teach the client new social skills to be used in making new, supportive friendships (e.g., active sharing, using "I" statement, listening to feedback, asking open questions, listening to nonverbal communication).

Diagnosis: F60.2   Antisocial Personality Disorder

SAMPLE QUANTITATIVE TREATMENT PLAN

PROBLEM: CRIMINAL PEERS

BEHAVIORAL DEFINITIONS

1. Currently associates 95% of the time with friends and acquaintances who are involved in criminal behavior.
2. Admires or identifies with others who are pro-crime and sees their lifestyle as desirable as evidenced by verbalizing this view five times per week.
3. Willing to protect, cover-up, and accept responsibility for peers' deviant behavior 100% of the time that the opportunity arises.
4. Inability to establish and maintain meaningful pro-social peer support group as evidenced by 5% of the available time being spent with pro-social people.

LONG-TERM GOALS

1. Significantly reduce or eliminate association with criminal friends.
2. Develop a meaningful, pro-social support network.

SHORT-TERM OBJECTIVES	THERAPEUTIC INTERVENTIONS
1. By 2/20/2004 list all friends and acquaintances; placing an asterisk next to those who have been involved in criminal behavior.	1. Assign the client to list all his/her friends and acquaintances; denoting criminal peers with an asterisk.

2. By 2/27/2004 describe the history and consequences of criminal behavior with peers.

3. By 3/15/2004 list the positive and negative consequences of yielding to peer pressure as defined by friends inviting his inclusion in a planned criminal activity.

4. By 3/30/2004 identify factors that have led to the development of relationships with deviant peers.

5. By 4/15/2004 identify, practice, and implement new strategies (i.e., setting clear boundaries, sharing goal of avoiding criminal activity, assertively saying no to offers of criminal activity) for distancing self from criminal peers.

2. Review the client's list of peers, exploring his/her feelings and thoughts about the number of pro-crime peers compared to pro-social peers.

1. Explore the client's history and consequences of his/her involvement in criminal behavior with friends and acquaintances.

1. Explain the dynamics of peer pressure to the client (e.g., wanting to fit in) and the positive (e.g., feeling of belongingness, having fun, avoiding conflict) and negative (e.g., going against one's better judgment, getting caught, conflict with peers) consequences of yielding to peer pressure.

1. Teach the client the various factors that can lead to developing relationships with criminal peers (e.g., low self-esteem, desire to belong, curiosity, thrill seeking).

2. Assist the client in generating a list of personal factors that have led him/her to develop relationships with deviant peers; review and process this list, reinforcing the client's increased understanding of himself/herself.

1. Teach the client new strategies (e.g., setting clear boundaries, telling peers his/her goal of avoiding criminal behavior, saying no) for distancing himself/herself from criminal peers.

2. Role-play with the client the use of the new distancing

techniques; provide him/her with positive feedback for effort, as well as suggestions for improvement in implementation.

3. Assign the client the task of choosing one deviant friend or acquaintance that he/she feels comfortable distancing himself/herself from and implement the new distancing techniques with that person.

4. Debrief with client about how new distancing techniques worked with chosen person; provide positive reinforcement and feedback for improvement.

6. By 4/30/2004 make a list of the values, traits, attributes, and attitudes that are seen as important to look for when making a new, supportive, pro-social friend.

1. Help the client generate a list of values and attitudes that he/she sees as important to look for when making a new, supportive, pro-social friend; highlight the differences between this set of values and attitudes and those values and attitudes associated with his/her criminal peers.

7. By 5/15/2004 implement new ways (i.e., active listening, active sharing of thoughts and feelings, using "I" statements, asking open-ended questions) to go about making supportive friendships.

1. Use role-playing, modeling, and behavior rehearsal to teach the client new social skills to be used in making new, supportive friendships (e.g., active sharing, using "I" statement, listening to feedback, asking open questions, listening to nonverbal communication).

DIAGNOSTIC SUGGESTIONS:

F60.2   Antisocial Personality Disorder

ANGER

BEHAVIORAL DEFINITIONS

1. History of explosive, aggressive outbursts out of proportion to any precipitating stressors leading to assaultive acts or destruction of property.
2. Overreaction of hostility to insignificant irritants.
3. Swift and harsh judgment statements made to or about others.
4. Body language of tense muscles (e.g., clenched fist or jaw, glaring looks, or refusal to make eye contact).
5. Use of passive-aggressive patterns (e.g., social withdrawal due to anger, lack of complete or timely compliance in following directions or rules, complaining about authority figures behind their backs, or nonparticipation in meeting expected behavioral norms).
6. Anger intensity that leads to mental confusion (e.g., all or nothing thinking, progressive use of abusive language expressed to self or others).
7. Hypersensitivity to perceived disapproval, rejection, or criticism that causes angry communication breakdowns.
8. Passive avoidance of conflict and irritations that contribute ultimately to a rapid (and often inappropriate), intense expression of anger.
9. Uses aggression as a means to achieve needed power and control.

—. _____

_____

LONG-TERM GOALS

1. Decrease frequency and intensity of expression of angry feelings.

2. Increase ability for coping with angry feelings in a constructive way that enhances daily functioning.
3. Improve awareness and understanding of anger: How it is triggered and its consequences.
4. Access and accept a greater range of emotions with more flexibility and ability to express these emotions constructively.

—. _____

_____

SHORT-TERM OBJECTIVES	THERAPEUTIC INTERVENTIONS
1. Describe history of what triggers anger and how it is expressed. (1, 2)	1. Explore the client's history of situations that trigger anger and how anger is expressed (e.g., verbal, threats of violence, assaults, damage to property).
	2. Confront the client's attempts to minimize his/her poor management of anger to project blame on to others, or to discount the harmful consequences.
2. Verbalize where anger comes from (antecedents), how it manifests (behavior), and what results (consequences) are likely to be produced by it. (3, 4, 5)	3. Teach the client a basic objective perspective on anger that minimally includes instruction on the Antecedents of anger, Behavior and physical features associated with anger, and Consequences of anger (i.e., the ABCs of anger).
	4. Assign reading from anger management curriculum (e.g., *The* Prepare *Curriculum* by Goldstein; *Reasoning and Rehabilitation* by Ross, Fabiano, and Ross; *Controlling Anger and Learning to Manage [CALM] Program* by Winogron, VanDieten, and Gauzas; or *The EQUIP Program: Teaching Youth to Think and Act Responsibly Through a Peer Helping Approach*

by Gibbs, Potter, and Goldstein) that addresses and provides an overview of a social learning, behaviorally-based perspective on anger.

5. Assign the client to read *Of Course You're Angry* by Rosellini and Worden or *Anger: How to Live With and Without It* by Ellis.

3. Attend anger management or assertiveness training didactic sessions. (6, 7)

6. Assign the client to anger management or assertiveness training classes.

7. Process principles the client has learned in the didactic sessions focused on anger management or assertiveness training; apply these principles to his/her daily life through role-playing or modeling.

4. Complete a self-administered anger/aggression assessment instrument and accept feedback of results. (8, 9)

8. Administer to the client a validated anger/aggression assessment test (e.g., Aggression Inventory (AI) by Gladue, Aggression Questionnaire (AQ) by Buss and Perry, State-Trait Anger Scale (STAS) by London and Spielberger).

9. Provide the client with an objective interpretation and normative feedback of his/her scores and profile on the validated anger/aggression test administered.

5. Verbalize common triggers people experience that provoke anger. (10, 11, 12)

10. Teach and explore with the client the insidious aspects of anger that displace other feelings (e.g., pain, guilt) and reinforce ignorance through projection.

11. Assign specific exercises from an established curriculum and

workbook that teaches the causes and consequences of anger (e.g., *The Prepare Curriculum* by Goldstein; *Reasoning and Rehabilitation* by Ross, Fabiano, and Ross; *Controlling Anger and Learning to Manage [CALM] Program* by Winogron, VanDieten, and Gauzas; *Anger Workout Book* by Weisinger; *Treating Alcohol Dependence* by Monti, Abrams, Kadden, and Coney; *Criminal Conduct and Substance Abuse Treatment* by Wanberg and Milkman).

12. Guide the client in a brainstorming session that identifies common triggers that instigate anger in people; ask the client to compile a written list of potential triggers.

6. Sort generic anger triggers into those that are internal versus external. (12, 13)

12. Guide the client in a brainstorming session that identifies common triggers that instigate anger in people; ask the client to compile a written list of potential triggers.

13. Ask the client to sort potential triggers into those that are internal or originate from within the client (e.g., jealousy, perceived rejection, guilt) and those that are external or originate from the environment (e.g., threatened, rights trampled on, belittled).

7. Verbalize what arousal is and how it affects human functioning negatively and positively. (11, 14)

11. Assign specific exercises from an established curriculum and workbook that teaches the causes and consequences of anger (e.g., *The Prepare Curriculum* by Goldstein; *Reasoning and Rehabilitation* by

Ross, Fabiano, and Ross; *Controlling Anger and Learning to Manage [CALM] Program* by Winogron, VanDieten, and Gauzas; *Anger Workout Book* by Weisinger; *Treating Alcohol Dependence* by Monti, Abrams, Kadden, and Coney; *Criminal Conduct and Substance Abuse Treatment* by Wanberg and Milkman).

14. Teach the client how emotional/physical arousal influences performance using the notion of a distribution or bell curve to show how it occurs at various levels or elevations (e.g., low arousal leads to less than optimal performance, medium levels are associated with optimal performance, high arousal leads to decreased performance).

8. List common cues for identifying arousal and the process for how angry feelings generally emerge for people. (11, 14, 15)

11. Assign specific exercises from an established curriculum and workbook that teaches the causes and consequences of anger (e.g., *The Prepare Curriculum* by Goldstein; *Reasoning and Rehabilitation* by Ross, Fabiano, and Ross; *Controlling Anger and Learning to Manage [CALM] Program* by Winogron, VanDieten, and Gauzas; *Anger Workout Book* by Weisinger; *Treating Alcohol Dependence* by Monti, Abrams, Kadden, and Coney; *Criminal Conduct and Substance Abuse Treatment* by Wanberg and Milkman).

14. Teach the client how emotional/physical arousal influences per-

formance using the notion of a distribution or bell curve to show how it occurs at various levels or elevations (e.g., low arousal leads to less than optimal performance, medium levels are associated with optimal performance, high arousal leads to decreased performance).

15. Guide the client in a brainstorming session that identifies common cues that can potentially alert people to when they are becoming angry (e.g., tight tummy, dry mouth, heart rate increases, blood pressure increases, shallower breathing, clenched fists, perceived threats).

9. Sort anger cues into those that occur in the early, middle, and late stage of escalation. (11, 15, 16)

11. Assign specific exercises from an established curriculum and workbook that teaches the causes and consequences of anger (e.g., *The Prepare Curriculum* by Goldstein; *Reasoning and Rehabilitation* by Ross, Fabiano, and Ross; *Controlling Anger and Learning to Manage [CALM] Program* by Winogron, VanDieten, and Gauzas; *Anger Workout Book* by Weisinger; *Treating Alcohol Dependence* by Monti, Abrams, Kadden, and Coney; *Criminal Conduct and Substance Abuse Treatment* by Wanberg and Milkman).

15. Guide the client in a brainstorming session that identifies common cues that can potentially alert people to when they are becoming angry (e.g., tight tummy, dry mouth, heart rate

increases, blood pressure increases, shallower breathing, clenched fists, perceived threats).

16. Ask the client to organize a generic list of anger cues into logical, chronological order as they would be apt to occur in a typical experience with anger (e.g., early stage: perceive a threat, shallower breathing; middle: hear rate increases, dry mouth; late: blood pressure increases, tight tummy, fists clenched).

10. List five of the best personal consequences for anger expression and the five worst personal consequences. (4, 11, 17)

4. Assign reading from anger management curriculum (e.g., *The Prepare Curriculum* by Goldstein; *Reasoning and Rehabilitation* by Ross, Fabiano, and Ross; *Controlling Anger and Learning to Manage [CALM] Program* by Winogron, VanDieten, and Gauzas; or *The EQUIP Program: Teaching Youth to Think and Act Responsibly Through a Peer Helping Approach* by Gibbs, Potter, and Goldstein) that addresses and provides an overview of a social learning, behaviorally-based perspective on anger.

11. Assign specific exercises from an established curriculum and workbook that teaches the causes and consequences of anger (e.g., *The Prepare Curriculum* by Goldstein; *Reasoning and Rehabilitation* by Ross, Fabiano, and Ross; *Controlling Anger and Learning to Manage [CALM] Program* by Winogron, VanDieten, and Gauzas; *Anger*

Workout Book by Weisinger;
Treating Alcohol Dependence by
Monti, Abrams, Kadden, and
Coney; *Criminal Conduct and
Substance Abuse Treatment* by
Wanberg and Milkman).

17. Ask the client to list the five best
and worst consequences for him-
self/herself that have resulted
from his/her expression of anger;
process these consequences.

11. Monitor and record anger
episodes, degree of escalation,
and the related context and
time of day they occurred.
(11, 18)

11. Assign specific exercises from an
established curriculum and
workbook that teaches the causes
and consequences of anger (e.g.,
The Prepare Curriculum by
Goldstein; *Reasoning and
Rehabilitation* by Ross, Fabiano,
and Ross; *Controlling Anger and
Learning to Manage [CALM]
Program* by Winogron,
VanDieten, and Gauzas; *Anger
Workout Book* by Weisinger;
Treating Alcohol Dependence by
Monti, Abrams, Kadden, and
Coney; *Criminal Conduct and
Substance Abuse Treatment* by
Wanberg and Milkman).

18. Provide the client with a
standard form for recording
his/her episodes with anger that
notes the situation or trigger, the
rating of the degree of anger
felt, how anger was expressed,
the outcome, assessment of how
he/she responded, as well as date
and time.

12. Share the results of
monitoring anger and
verbalize lessons learned from
the data. (11, 18, 19)

11. Assign specific exercises from
an established curriculum and
workbook that teaches the
causes and consequences of
anger (e.g., *The Prepare
Curriculum* by Goldstein;

Reasoning and Rehabilitation by Ross, Fabiano, and Ross; *Controlling Anger and Learning to Manage [CALM] Program* by Winogron, VanDieten, and Gauzas; *Anger Workout Book* by Weisinger; *Treating Alcohol Dependence* by Monti, Abrams, Kadden, and Coney; *Criminal Conduct and Substance Abuse Treatment* by Wanberg and Milkman).

18. Provide the client with a standard form for recording his/her episodes with anger that notes the situation or trigger, the rating of the degree of anger felt, how anger was expressed, the outcome, assessment of how he/she responded, as well as date and time.

19. Process with the client the results of his/her anger monitoring, concentrating on what can be learned from that personal behavior information.

13. List several techniques that could be used to reduce anger quickly. (20, 21)

20. Instruct the client in a technique for progressive muscle relaxation that enables him/her to relax his/her entire body within 5 to 10 minutes and have him/her practice this technique daily for at least one week.

21. Teach the client simple, quick techniques (e.g., deep breathing, counting backward, engaging in pleasant imagery, using a worry stone) to immediately help reduce anger elevations in a variety of situations.

14. Write an inventory of personal triggers (external and internal)

12. Guide the client in a brainstorming session that

for anger and prioritize them in terms of strength and frequency. (12, 13, 22)

identifies common triggers that instigate anger in people; ask the client to compile a written list of personal triggers.

13. Ask the client to sort potential triggers into those that are internal or originate from within the client (e.g., jealousy, perceived rejection, guilt) and those that are external or originate from the environment (e.g., threatened, rights trampled on, belittled).

22. Review and help the client inventory and prioritize his/her own personal anger triggers.

15. Verbalize the importance of self-statements and the role they play in either escalating or reducing anger. (23)

23. Explain the role of self-talk and how it can lead to either negative or positive reaction to anger triggers; demonstrate how this Mental process modifies the Antecedent condition, Behavioral reaction, and Consequences model by the interjection of a subjective element between Antecedents and Behavior (thus, the A-M-B-C model).

16. Identify instances of engaging distorted self-talk and the consequences of this on anger management. (24, 25)

24. Assist the client in identifying and inventorying his/her distorted self-talk in response to recent triggers and cues.

25. Process what the consequences might be for the client reacting to his/her most common distorted self-talk statements.

17. List and implement alternative, positive, realistic self-talk in response to internal and external anger trigger situations. (26, 27)

26. Facilitate a brainstorming inventory of alternative positive and realistic self-statements to the cues and trigger situations that the client finds most frequently (or intensively)

associated with his/her anger experiences.

27. Teach the client how to substitute positive and realistic self-statements in response to triggers.

18. Implement a self-evaluation process for assessing anger management. (11, 25, 28)

11. Assign specific exercises from an established curriculum and workbook that teaches the causes and consequences of anger (e.g., *The Prepare Curriculum* by Goldstein; *Reasoning and Rehabilitation* by Ross,Fabiano, and Ross; *Controlling Anger and Learning to Manage [CALM] Program* by Winogron, VanDieten, and Gauzas; *Anger Workout Book* by Weisinger; *Treating Alcohol Dependence* by Monti, Abrams, Kadden, and Coney; *Criminal Conduct and Substance Abuse Treatment* by Wanberg and Milkman).

25. Process what the consequences might be for the client reacting to his/her most common distorted self-talk statements.

28. Instruct the client in a basic self-evaluation process that is simple, but geared to increase his/her objectivity in assessing his/her anger expression and its consequences surveying antecedents, behavioral expressions of anger, and consequences.

19. Implement new alternative skills for altering interpersonal expressions of anger. (29, 30)

29. Teach the client to implement a thought-stopping technique(e.g., thinking of a stop sign and then a pleasant scene, or snapping a rubber band on the wrist) that cognitively interferes with distorted

cognitive messages that fuel anger; monitor and encourage the client's use of this technique in daily life between sessions.

30. Use role-playing, modeling, and empty chair techniques to teach the client interpersonal expressions of anger that are constructive and assertive, rather than alienating and aggressive.

20. Write an inventory of resentments and old anger targets that continue to recycle and facilitate engaging current triggers. (22, 31)

22. Review and help the client inventory and prioritize his/her own personal anger triggers.

31. Assign the client the task of listing all the resentments he/she experiences, especially those that recycle over time in his/her life.

21. Verbalize how resentments lead to negative expressions of anger. (31, 32)

31. Assign the client the task of listing all the resentments he/she experiences, especially those that recycle over time in his/her life.

32. Show the client how to dissect resentments he/she has identified according to either a 12-step model or a cognitive/behavioral (A-M-B-C) model and encourage him/her to apply these principles to his/her resentment.

22. Verbalize an action plan for coping with and resolving old resentments. (4, 5, 11, 33, 34)

4. Assign reading from anger management curriculum (e.g., *The Prepare Curriculum* by Goldstein; *Reasoning and Rehabilitation* by Ross, Fabiano, and Ross; *Controlling Anger and Learning to Manage [CALM] Program* by Winogron, VanDieten, and Gauzas; or *The EQUIP Program: Teaching Youth to Think and Act Responsibly Through a Peer*

Helping Approach by Gibbs, Potter, and Goldstein) that addresses and provides an overview of a social learning, behaviorally-based perspective on anger.

5. Assign the client to read *Of Course You're Angry* by Rosellini and Worden or *Anger: How to Live With and Without It* by Ellis.

11. Assign specific exercises from an established curriculum and workbook that teaches the causes and consequences of anger (e.g., *The Prepare Curriculum* by Goldstein; *Reasoning and Rehabilitation* by Ross, Fabiano, and Ross; *Controlling Anger and Learning to Manage ([CALM] Program* by Winogron, VanDieten, and Gauzas; *Anger Workout Book* by Weisinger; *Treating Alcohol Dependence* by Monti, Abrams, Kadden, and Coney; *Criminal Conduct and Substance Abuse Treatment* by Wanberg and Milkman).

33. Assign the client to write an action plan for each of his/her recurring resentments that addresses the triggers, cues, anger reducers, self-statements, and self-evaluation.

34. Ask the client to write a letter of forgiveness to each individual associated with significant resentments.

23. Verbalize how influential people in growing up have modeled anger expressions. (5, 35)

5. Assign the client to read *Of Course You're Angry* by Rosellini and Worden or *Anger:*

How to Live With and Without It by Ellis.

35. Assist the client in identifying ways key life figures (e.g., father, mother, and teachers) have expressed angry feelings and how positively or negatively these experiences have influenced the way he/she handles anger.

24. Identify pain and hurt of past or current life that fuels anger. (5, 36, 37)

5. Assign the client to read *Of Course You're Angry* by Rosellini and Worden or *Anger: How to Live With and Without It* by Ellis.

36. Assign the client to list the experiences of life that have hurt and led to anger.

37. Empathize and clarify feelings of hurt and anger tied to traumas of the past.

25. Verbalize recognition of how holding on to angry feelings freezes you and hands control over to other and cite the advantages of forgiveness. (34, 38, 39)

34. Ask the client to write a letter of forgiveness to each individual associated with significant resentments.

38. Discuss forgiveness of perpetrators of pain as process of letting go of anger.

39. Assign the client to read the book *Forgive and Forget* and/or *The Art of* Forgiving by Smedes.

26. Complete a reassessment with a valid anger/aggression instrument and accept feedback of results. (40, 41)

40. Reassess the client with a validated anger/aggression assessment test (e.g., Aggression Inventory (AI) by Gladue, Aggression Questionnaire (AQ) by Buss and Perry, State-Trait Anger Scale (STAS) by London and Spielberger).

41. Provide the client with an objective interpretation and

27. Receive normative feedback regarding reassessment scores on an anger/aggression instrument that includes presentation of "gain scores" (i.e., the difference between pretest and posttest). (40, 41)

normative feedback of his/her reassessment scores and profile of the validated anger/aggression test administered.

40. Reassess the client with a validated anger/aggression assessment test (e.g., Aggression Inventory (AI) by Gladue, Aggression Questionnaire (AQ) by Buss and Perry, State-Trait Anger Scale (STAS) by London and Spielberger).

41. Provide the client with an objective interpretation and normative feedback of his/her reassessment scores and profile of the validated anger/aggression test administered.

—. _____   —. _____

_____   _____

DIAGNOSTIC SUGGESTIONS:

ICD-9-CM	*ICD-10-CM*	*DSM-5* Disorder, Condition, or Problem
312.34	F63.81	Intermittent Explosive Disorder
296.xx	F31.xx	Bipolar I Disorder
296.89	F31.81	Bipolar II Disorder
312.82	F91.2	Conduct Disorder, Adolescent-Onset Type
312.81	F91.1	Conduct Disorder, Childhood-Onset Type
310.1	F07.0	Personality Change Due to Another Medical Condition
309.81	F43.10	Posttraumatic Stress Disorder
301.83	F60.3	Borderline Personality Disorder
301.7	F60.2	Antisocial Personality Disorder
301.0	F60.0	Paranoid Personality Disorder
301.81	F60.81	Narcissistic Personality Disorder
301.9	F60.9	Unspecified Personality Disorder

_____ _____   _____

_____ _____   _____

ASSERTIVENESS DEFICITS

BEHAVIORAL DEFINITIONS

1. Reluctant to express dissatisfaction or verbalize unmet needs or desires.
2. Frequently fails to refuse a request to do something undesirable for or with someone.
3. Avoids expressing views that are in conflict with others' opinions.
4. Expresses thoughts aggressively.
5. Utilizes a passive-aggressive or indirect style of communication that alienates others.
6. Excessive tolerance of unpleasant situations.
7. Inability to directly express feelings appropriately to others.
8. Overly anxious in social situations.
9. Pattern of suppressing bad feelings until one single event triggers explosion of resentment.

__. _____
_____
__. _____
_____
_____
__. _____
_____

LONG-TERM GOALS

1. Improve ability to effectively express personal opinions, desires, and feelings without antagonizing or alienating others.
2. Maintain a clearer perception and appreciation for the rights and boundaries of self and others.

3. Increase sense of ease and confidence in different social situations.
4. Learn to differentiate and exhibit assertive communication from that which is passive and aggressive.

—. _____
   _____
—. _____
   _____
—. _____
   _____

SHORT-TERM OBJECTIVES

1. Describe situations in which it has been difficult to express thoughts or feelings assertively. (1)

2. Verbalize a greater understanding of the principal elements of assertiveness versus passivity or aggression. (2, 3)

THERAPEUTIC INTERVENTIONS

1. Explore the client's history of lack of assertiveness, noting the early development of this pattern and current situations that trigger assertiveness anxiety.

2. Teach the client the differences between passive, passive-aggressive, aggressive, and assertive styles of interpersonal communication that minimally includes: (1) tactics associated with each style, (2) short-term consequences, and (3) long-term consequences associated with each style.

3. Assign the client to read a book on assertiveness (e.g., *Your Perfect Right: A Guide to Assertive Living* by Alberti and Emmons; *Asserting Yourself: A Practical Guide for Positive Change* by Bower, Bower, and Bower; *Managing Assertively: How to Improve Your People Skills* by Burley; or *The Assertiveness Workbook: How to Express*

Your Ideas and Stand Up for Yourself at Work and in Relationships by Paterson).

3. Complete an objective assertiveness assessment and receive feedback of results. (4, 5)

4. Administer to the client a validated assertiveness assessment test (e.g., Assertion Inventory [AI] by Grambrill and Richey or Assertion Self-Statement Test Revised by Heimberg, Chiauzzi, Becker, and Madrazo-Peterson).

5. Provide the client with an objective interpretation and feedback of his/her scores and profile on the validated assertiveness test completed.

4. Implement active listening skills. (6, 7, 8)

6. Teach the client the fundamental skills of active listening (e.g., asking open-ended questions, affirming the speaker with eye contact and nodding, reflecting the feelings behind the communication, summarizing the content, and eliciting self-motivating statements) and how to implement these skills in everyday communication.

7. Model active listening skills showing how they are apt to vary within the four classic interpersonal styles (e.g., passive, passive-aggressive, aggressive, and assertive).

8. Assign specific exercises from an established curriculum and workbook for effective communication skills (e.g., *The Prepare Curriculum* by Goldstein; *Reasoning and Rehabilitation* by Ross, Fabiano, and Ross; *Controlling Anger and Learning to*

Manage [CALM] Program by Winogron, VanDieten, and Gauzas; *Anger Workout Book* by Weisinger; *Treating Alcohol Dependence* by Monti, Abrams, Kadden, and Coney; *Criminal Conduct and Substance Abuse Treatment* by Wanberg and Milkman).

5. Identify own interpersonal communication style and techniques. (1, 5, 9)

1. Explore the client's history of lack of assertiveness, noting the early development of this pattern and current situations that trigger assertiveness anxiety.

5. Provide the client with an objective interpretation and feedback of his/her scores and profile on the validated assertiveness test completed.

9. Assist the client in identifying the composition of the various communication styles he/she tends to use in routine interactions.

6. List the relationship consequences that are most likely to result from passive, passive-aggressive, aggressive, and assertive interpersonal styles. (2, 3, 8, 10)

2. Teach the client the differences between passive, passive-aggressive, aggressive, and assertive styles of interpersonal communication that minimally includes: (1) tactics associated with each style, (2) short-term consequences, and (3) long-term consequences associated with each style.

3. Assign the client to read a book on assertiveness (e.g., *Your Perfect Right: A Guide to Assertive Living* by Alberti and Emmons; *Asserting Yourself: A Practical Guide for Positive Change* by Bower, Bower, and Bower;

Managing Assertively: How to Improve Your People Skills by Burley; or *The Assertiveness Workbook: How to Express Your Ideas and Stand Up for Yourself at Work and in Relationships* by Paterson).

8. Assign specific exercises from an established curriculum and workbook for effective communication skills (e.g., *The Prepare Curriculum* by Goldstein; *Reasoning and Rehabilitation* by Ross, Fabiano, and Ross; *Controlling Anger and Learning to Manage [CALM] Program* by Winogron, VanDieten, and Gauzas; *Anger Workout Book* by Weisinger; *Treating Alcohol Dependence* by Monti, Abrams, Kadden, and Coney; *Criminal Conduct and Substance Abuse Treatment* by Wanberg and Milkman).

10. Assist the client in generating a list of personal consequences most likely to result from passive, passive-aggressive, aggressive, and assertive interpersonal communication styles.

7. List three recent situations where having better communication skills might have been helpful. (1, 11)

1. Explore the client's history of lack of assertiveness, noting the early development of this pattern and current situations that trigger assertiveness anxiety.

11. Review with the client recent situations in which he/she could have benefited from more assertive communication skills.

8. Identify the benefits of assertive communication. (12)

12. Guide the client in a brainstorming session that

identifies the common benefits resulting from assertive communication skills (e.g., get needs or desires met, promotes understanding, clarifies feelings to others, establishes boundaries for self and others).

9. Describe specific personal goals for improving interpersonal communication skills and why they are important. (13, 14)

13. Assist the client in identifying and prioritizing specific goals for improving his/her interpersonal communication skills.

14. Process with the client the decisional balance (e.g., pros and cons) of the payoffs for his/her present interpersonal communication style versus implementing a healthier, more assertive style.

10. Verbalize and implement the essential steps for effectively expressing criticism or complaint to another person. (15, 16)

15. Instruct the client in a technique for expressing a complaint or providing another criticism (e.g., specifically decide what the issue is; decide if he/she should express anything; when, to whom, and what should be done; state complaint and suggested solution in a friendly manner; ask for reaction; indicate he/she understands others' view; discuss alternative solutions; reach agreement).

16. Use role-playing, modeling, and behavioral rehearsal to apply the effective, assertive technique for expressing complaints and criticism to real-life situations.

11. Verbalize and implement the essential steps for effectively receiving a complaint or criticism from another person. (17, 18)

17. Instruct the client in a technique for responding to complaints or criticism (e.g., listen carefully to the complaints, ask for more

information, decide if the complaint is justified, decide if he/she should accept or deny responsibility and what should be done, express his/her view and suggested solution, ask for other person's view).

18. Use role-playing, modeling, and behavioral rehearsal to apply the assertive technique for responding to complaints and criticism to real-life situations.

12. Report success at giving and receiving complaints and criticism. (19)

19. Review the client's implementation of giving and receiving complaints and criticism; reinforce success and redirect for failure experiences.

13. Identify three new conflict communication skills that would improve interpersonal communications. (20)

20. Describe and model for the client several conflict communication skills (e.g., double-sided reflections, partially agreeing, agreeing with a twist, "I" statements) that could improve his/her communication.

14. Describe how new communication skills could have been employed in recent situations. (20, 21)

20. Describe and model for the client several conflict communication skills (e.g., double-sided reflections, partially agreeing, agreeing with a twist, "I" statements) that could improve his/her communication.

21. Assign the client to list specifically how three new communication skills could have been employed in recent situations where he/she experienced a need for a better communication outcome.

15. Implement new conflict communication skills and receive feedback. (20, 22, 23)

16. Make daily recordings of any interpersonal conflicts experienced or avoided due to interpersonal communication skills. (24, 25)

17. Identify and describe in writing the typical interaction skills of one person known that has superior interpersonal communication skills compared to others. (26)

20. Describe and model for the client several conflict communication skills (e.g., double-sided reflections, partially agreeing, agreeing with a twist, "I" statements) that could improve his/her communication.

22. Facilitate client skill rehearsals for three new communication skills, utilizing his/her own recent situations where better communication skills would have improved the outcome.

23. Review the client's implementation of new conflict communication skills in daily life; reinforce success and redirect for failure.

24. Introduce and instruct the client in the use of an assertiveness problem log (e.g., see CALM curriculum by Winogron, VanDieten, and Gauzas) which documents: (1) location, (2) who was there, (3) what happened, (4) what was the response to the situation, (5) self-assessment of outcome, and (6) what the degree of difficulty was for using the new skill.

25. Process with the client the results of his/her weekly assertiveness problem log; reinforce success and redirect for failure.

26. Direct the client to identify someone he/she knows that has superior interpersonal skills compared to others and write a description of those skills.

18. Interview someone with respectable interpersonal skills to learn how they acquired and maintain these skills. (27, 28)

27. Assign the client to interview someone with respectable interpersonal skills to learn more about how he/she acquired and maintains those skills.

28. Process the client's experience interviewing someone with relatively good interpersonal skills; list lessons learned.

19. Implement positive self-talk relative to new assertive communication skills. (29)

29. Assist the client in reviewing and inventorying some of the self-statements he/she recently made in response to implementing communication skills and provide helpful reframing of distorted, disparaging self-talk.

20. Complete a reassessment with a valid assertiveness instrument and receive feedback regarding progress compared to first testing. (30, 31)

30. Reassess the client with a validated assertiveness assessment test he/she completed.

31. Provide the client with an objective interpretation and feedback of his/her reassessment scores and profile on validated assertion test he/she completed.

21. Attend an assertiveness training group. (32, 33)

32. Assign the client to attend assertiveness training or interpersonal communication classes.

33. Process the content the client has learned from attending an assertiveness group and reinforce implementation of new assertiveness skills.

22. Identify the fears associated with being assertive versus passive. (29, 34, 35)

29. Assist the client in reviewing and inventorying some of the self-statements he/she made recently in response to implementing communication

skills and provide helpful reframes of distorted, disparaging self-talk.

34. Explore the client's fears associated with being assertive and the origin of these fears in early development.

35. Explore the client's physical, sexual, or psychological abuse experience that could have contributed to low self-esteem and adoption of a passive communication style (see Childhood Trauma/Abuse/Neglect chapter in this *Planner*).

23. Identify aggressive role models. (36)

36. Ask the client to identify aggressive role models that have been influential in his/her life and may have led to his/her adoption of any aggressive communication style.

24. Identify the negative impact on others of communicating in an aggressive manner. (2, 10, 37, 38)

2. Teach the client the differences between passive, passive-aggressive, aggressive, and assertive styles of interpersonal communication that minimally includes: (1) tactics associated with each style, (2) short-term consequences, and (3) long-term consequences associated with each style.

10. Assist the client in generating a list of personal consequences most likely to result from passive, passive-aggressive, aggressive, and assertive interpersonal communication styles.

37. Ask the client to explore his/her feelings when he/she was the target of aggressive communication; relate these

feelings to others who have been the target of the client's aggressive communication.

38. Confront the client's insensitivity to the feelings of others who are the targets of his/her aggression (see Callousness (Lack of Empathy/Honesty) chapter in this *Planner*).

—. _____   —. _____
   _____   _____
—. _____   —. _____
   _____   _____
—. _____   —. _____
   _____   _____

DIAGNOSTIC SUGGESTIONS:

ICD-9-CM	*ICD-10-CM*	*DSM-5* Disorder, Condition, or Problem
300.00	F41.9	Unspecified Anxiety Disorder
300.23	F40.10	Social Anxiety Disorder (Social Phobia)
296.xx	F32.x	Major Depressive Disorder, Single Episode
296.xx	F33.x	Major Depressive Disorder, Recurrent Episode
300.4	F34.1	Persistent Depressive Disorder
301.82	F60.6	Avoidant Personality Disorder
301.7	F60.2	Antisocial Personality Disorder
301.6	F60.7	Dependent Personality Disorder
_____	_____	_____
_____	_____	_____

AUTHORITY CONFLICTS

BEHAVIORAL DEFINITIONS

1. Rejects, resists, or opposes rules, instruction, direction, or feedback from authority figures.
2. Typically blames others rather than taking any responsibility for conflicts.
3. Frequently harbors feelings of victimization and resentment toward others.
4. Has a limited definition of self, based on defying authority.
5. Negatively prejudges others in a manner that maintains continued isolation and ignorance.
6. Inability to effectively communicate needs to authority figures.
7. Perceived liberties are easily threatened, causing reactive hostility or oppositional behavior.
8. Commonly perceives the world from a fear-based or distrustful mentality.
9. Deliberately annoys other people.

___. _____

_____

LONG-TERM GOALS

1. Learn to accept direction from authority figures without hostility or opposition.
2. Develop sensitivity to reactance patterns that precede conflict with authority figures.
3. Maintain a more balanced and useful perspective of authority figures that is not resentful and distrustful.

4. Increase ability to communicate needs effectively to authority figures and others.
5. Increase personal options and skills that will promote harmony within power relations.

—. _____

_____

SHORT-TERM OBJECTIVES

THERAPEUTIC INTERVENTIONS

1. Describe a history of conflicts with authority figures beginning in childhood or adolescence. (1, 2)

2. Identify factors that have led to development of an attitude of opposition to authority. (2, 3)

3. List ways in which beliefs influence emotions and behavior. (4)

1. Explore the client's history of resistance to authority figures.

2. Explore family dynamics that contributed to the client's anger and distrust of authority figures, including broken promises, abuse, neglect, exposure to violence, and role models of oppositional behavior.

2. Explore family dynamics that contributed to the client's anger and distrust of authority figures, including broken promises, abuse, neglect, exposure to violence, and role models of oppositional behavior.

3. Assist the client in identifying the historical factors that have shaped his/her negative attitude toward authority figures (e.g., family criminal history, abuse or neglect experiences, early street life experiences, discrimination).

4. Instruct the client in how personal judgment and the real world are not the same, but the interaction between them is important: thus, beliefs

and thoughts influence our actions more than events; people see the world differently because of their beliefs and attitudes; automatic thinking can become more and more distorted; behavior, thoughts, and feelings affect each other; events trigger different emotional and behavioral reactions in people.

4. Write out a list of beliefs about authorities. (5)

5. Assign the client the task of generating a list of 10 statements (each prefaced by "Authority is. . . .") that describe his/her beliefs about authority.

5. Monitor and record episodes of authority conflict or personal reactance. (6)

6. Instruct the client in how to maintain a four-column daily log (e.g. location, who was there, what happened internally and externally, what the outcome was) for monitoring his/her authority conflicts and reactance episodes.

6. Debrief and share the results of authority conflict and reactance log at least once a week with one other supportive person. (7)

7. Assist the client in inventorying and debriefing the results of maintaining a daily "authority conflicts log" and reinforce his/her progress.

7. Identify negative, distorted self-talk regarding authority figures and list more realistic, positive reframed thoughts. (8)

8. Assist the client in reviewing and explaining some of the distorted self-statements he/she was prone to making regarding authority figure interactions and provide helpful, realistic reframes.

8. List all frequently contacted people who might be personally perceived as authority figures. (9, 10)

9. Ask the client to list all the people he/she comes into routine contact with that might be perceived as authority figures.

10. Coach the client to prioritize the top five personal authority

figures in terms of frequency of contact and magnitude of perceived authority.

9. Preface authority interactions with thinking enhancement techniques. (8, 11, 12, 13)

8. Assist the client in reviewing and explaining some of the distorted self-statements he/she was prone to making regarding authority figure interactions and provide helpful, realistic reframes.

11. Teach the client thinking enhancement techniques that reduce automatic thinking in relation to authority figures (e.g., *C.O.R.T. Thinking Program* by deBono, *Reasoning and Rehabilitation* by Ross, *Controlling Anger and Learning to Manage* by Winogron, *Criminal Conduct and Substance Abuse Treatment: Strategies for Self-Improvement and Change* by Wanberg).

12. Ask the client to deliberately exercise at least two new thinking enhancement techniques every day for one week.

13. Discuss and debrief with the client his/her experience with new thinking enhancement techniques.

10. Verbalize positive interactions with authority figures. (14, 15)

14. Ask the client to monitor and record his/her interactions with the top five authority figures in his/her life as he/she tries to apply new thinking skills to the interaction.

15. Debrief the client's monitoring of his/her attempts to apply new skills to authority figure interaction and reinforce any improvements.

11. Implement assertiveness skills and reduce aggressive reactions to authority figures. (16, 17)

16. Teach the client the difference between passivity, aggression, and assertiveness; assign books on assertiveness (e.g., *Your Perfect Right* by Alberti and Emmons).

17. Assign the client to assertiveness training or anger management classes.

12. Complete an authority conflict assessment instrument. (18, 19)

18. Administer to the client and score a validated assertiveness assessment test (e.g., Authority Inventory by Rigby or Victim Profile by Dyer).

19. Provide the client with an objective interpretation and normative feedback of his/her scores and profile on validated authority test he/she completed.

13. Read material on how to resolve conflicts with people without aggression and list new concepts learned. (16, 20)

16. Teach the client the difference between passivity, aggression, and assertiveness; assign books on assertiveness (e.g., *Your Perfect Right* by Alberti and Emmons).

20. Assign the client to read a self-help book that teaches authority conflict resolution skills (e.g., *It Takes Two: Managing Yourself When Working with Bosses and Other Authority Figures* by Boccialetti, *Pulling Your Own Strings: Dynamic Techniques for Dealing with Other People and Living Life as You Choose* by Dyer, *Thank You for Being Such a Pain: Spiritual Guidance for Dealing with Difficult People* by Rosen, *The Art and Skill of Dealing with People* by Toropov) and list helpful concepts learned; process these new ideas.

14. Verbalize how reactance affects interaction with authority figures and how certain people are more prone to this dynamic. (21, 22, 23, 24)

21. Give the client a description of an authority conflict pattern (e.g., inability to receive criticism) and examples of how this syndrome plays out in work, love, and play.

22. Explain the dynamics of projection, (e.g., attributing to another person what is actually within oneself) defensive avoidance (e.g., a defective conflict resolution strategy involving diminished information-gathering and appraisal), and reactance (e.g., perceived threats to a given liberty that result in increased sense of protection over that liberty) and how these mechanisms serve to promote authority conflicts.

23. Demonstrate to the client how having clear boundaries, avoiding comparisons, between self and others, and operating from his/her strength are positive alternatives to projections, defensive avoidance, and reactance.

24. Teach the client how reactance effects operate (e.g., perceptions of threatened liberties engender stronger attachments to the associated behavior) and can vary across people and circumstances in terms of strength and frequency.

15. Describe some interactions with people, where reactance effects are commonly triggered. (25, 26)

25. Explore with the client what the common costs (e.g., defective decisions, anxiety episodes, interpersonal and institutional conflicts) and benefits (e.g., sense of autonomy and

freedom) of strong reactance effects might typically be.

26. Ask the client to generate a list of five recent personal experiences with reactance in authority conflicts, including the outcomes.

16. Identify three examples of media portrayals of reactance effects. (27, 28)

27. Discuss different examples of reactance effects in the popular media (e.g., the movie *Cool Hand Luke,* National Rifle Association campaigns).

28. Direct the client to identify a minimum of three examples of reactance or authority conflict in the current media (e.g., news, press, and film) and discuss his/her assessment of the related cost/benefits in each examples.

17. Identify what aspects of life can be controlled and those that must be accepted. (29, 30)

29. Ask the client to list the people, places, and things (e.g., institutions, laws) that periodically affect his/her quality of life.

30. Discuss with the client his/her inventory of people, places, and things and assist him/her in delineating what part of the inventory he/she can or cannot control or influence, emphasizing his/her ability to only control his/her reactions to people, places, and things.

18. Debrief and inventory recent personal experiences with authority conflicts. (26, 31)

26. Ask the client to generate a list of five recent personal experiences with reactance in authority conflicts, including the outcomes.

31. Debrief the client of his/her most recent experiences with authority conflict and review if he/she was: (1) operating from

19. List some specific personal goals for managing reactance and authority conflicts and why they are important. (32)

20. Observe and learn the essential steps for effectively expressing a complaint or providing another person criticism. (33, 34)

21. Observe and learn the essential steps for effectively receiving criticism from another person. (35, 36)

strength, (2) accepting something that could not be changed, or (3) avoiding comparing himself/herself to others.

32. Discuss goals for managing reactance and authority conflicts and assign the client to write a prioritized list of goals.

33. Instruct the client in a technique for expressing a complaint or providing another person criticism (e.g., specifically decide what the issue is; decide if he/she should express anything; when, to whom, and what should be done; state complaint and suggested solution in a friendly manner; ask for reaction; indicate he/she understands other's view; discuss alternative solutions; reach an agreement).

34. Model for the client examples of how the technique for expressing complaints and criticism is used in real life.

35. Instruct the client in a technique for responding to a complaint (e.g., actively listen to the complaint, ask for more information, determine if the complaint is valid, decide if he/she should accept or deny responsibility and what should be done, express his/her view and suggested solution, ask for his/her reaction).

36. Model for the client examples of how the technique for responding to complaints and criticism is used in real life.

22. Rehearse giving and receiving complaints and criticism with another person utilizing recent situations where personal authority conflicts emerged. (37)

37. Facilitate client skill rehearsals for giving and receiving complaints and criticism using client inventory of recent situations where authority conflicts requiring better communication skills would have helped him/her.

23. Complete a reassessment with a valid authority conflict instrument. (38, 39)

38. Reassess the client with a validated authority conflict assessment test (e.g., Authority Inventory by Rigby or Victim Profile by Dyer).

39. Provide the client with an objective interpretation and normative feedback of his/her reassessment scores and profile on validated authority conflict test he/she completed.

DIAGNOSTIC SUGGESTIONS:

ICD-9-CM	*ICD-10-CM*	*DSM-5* Disorder, Condition, or Problem
313.81	F91.3	Oppositional Defiant Disorder
312.82	F91.2	Conduct Disorder, Adolescent-Onset Type
312.81	F91.1	Conduct Disorder, Childhood-Onset Type
296.xx	F31.xx	Bipolar I Disorder
296.89	F31.81	Bipolar II Disorder
312.34	F63.81	Intermittent Explosive Disorder
312.30	F91.9	Unspecified Disruptive, Impulse-Control, and Conduct Disorder
309.4	F43.25	Adjustment Disorder, With Mixed Disturbance of Emotions and Conduct
301.0	F60.0	Paranoid Personality Disorder
301.7	F60.2	Antisocial Personality Disorder
301.83	F60.3	Borderline Personality Disorder
301.81	F60.81	Narcissistic Personality Disorder
_____	_____	_____
_____	_____	_____

CALLOUSNESS (LACK OF EMPATHY/HONESTY)

BEHAVIORAL DEFINITIONS

1. Demonstrates little genuine sympathy or respect for the feelings of others.
2. Shows no remorse or concern for the negative consequences his/her actions have had on others.
3. Frequently deceives and manipulates others for personal gain.
4. Lying and fabrications are an integral part of interactions with others.
5. Interpersonal style or interactions are insincere and superficial.
6. Overinflated sense of abilities and self-worth.
7. Does not accept responsibility for own actions.
8. Displays an extremely shallow and narrow range of emotions.

—. _____
   _____
—. _____
   _____
   _____
—. _____
   _____

LONG-TERM GOALS

1. Become more sensitive to the feelings and rights of others.
2. Acknowledge a lack of empathy that frequently results in harm to other people.
3. Develop perspectives and relationships that are less self-focused.

4. Reduce the frequency and magnitude of deceptions, lies, and conning behavior.
5. Adopt a lifestyle based more on giving than getting.

—. _____
   _____

—. _____
   _____

—. _____
   _____

SHORT-TERM OBJECTIVES	**THERAPEUTIC INTERVENTIONS**
1. Verbalize an understanding of callousness and how it is revealed in many areas of life. (1, 2)	1. Give the client a description of the key elements of callousness (see Behavioral Definitions section) and examples of how this syndrome is demonstrated in work, love, and play.
	2. Explain how intertwining cycles related to issues of power, control, and absence of feelings promote callousness (e.g., how lack of feelings can lead to compensatory control and power issues).
2. Acknowledge the presence of callousness in own life and how it is demonstrated. (3, 4)	3. Explore the signs of callousness in the client's life and confront his/her denial of responsibility for evidence of it.
	4. Ask the client to list at least five instances in which callousness has affected his/her behavior toward others.
3. Complete a self-administered assessment instrument that measures selfishness and narcissistic tendencies. (5, 6)	5. Administer to the client a validated self-orientation assessment test (e.g., Selfism by Phares and Erskine or Paulhus Deception Scales by Paulhus).

6. Provide the client with an objective interpretation and feedback regarding scores and profile on validated self-orientation test he/she completed.

4. Verbalize an understanding of grandiosity and its causes. (7, 8, 9)

7. Explain the dynamics of grandiosity (e.g., an overinflated sense of ability that masks a low self-esteem) and how it serves to fill a vacuum in one's self-concept.

8. Provide the client with a range of materials (e.g., cardboard, scissors, glue, tape, string, magazine pictures, feathers) and instructions in building a personal mask.

9. Discuss with the client the various functions a mask serves and how the mask might be a metaphor for his/her grandiosity.

5. List people, places, and things apt to trigger grandiose self-assessment. (10, 11)

10. Assist the client in generating a list of people, places, and things that might provoke false pride in him/her (e.g., people that are either threatening or vulnerable, places that make one stand apart or appear different, things that enhance one's sense of power).

11. Review the client's list of possible triggers (e.g., people, places, things) for grandiosity and positively reinforce his/her efforts to achieve better understanding of himself/herself.

6. Identify several of the negative and positive consequences of grandiose portrayals of self. (12, 13)

12. Explore with the client what common costs (e.g., credibility problems, false security, less motivation for change) and

benefits (e.g., immediate relief, protective camouflage, delay of responsible action) he/she experiences in making grossly inflated self-assessments.

13. Ask the client to identify three recent personal experiences in which he/she portrayed himself/herself with grandiosity; explore the consequences of this grandiosity behavior.

7. Describe the various feelings and emotions people are capable of having for others along a continuum, from very little to considerable feelings. (14)

14. Discuss the range of feeling people are capable (or incapable) of having for others and portray this range along a continuum (e.g., extremely sensitive and empathic to very calloused and detached).

8. Explain how shallow feelings, no remorse, and no empathy are alike and different. (15, 16)

15. Define shallow feelings, (e.g., glib, superficial, charming, and sentimental) no empathy, (e.g., total lack of understanding for other's feelings) and no remorse (e.g., no conscience or feelings of guilt) using examples.

16. Teach the client how shallow feelings, no empathy, and no remorse are similar, but different.

9. List three benefits and three disadvantages of having encapsulated feelings. (17)

17. Assign the client to list three benefits (e.g., appear in control, easier to be independent from other people, less distracting information to process) and three disadvantages (e.g., incomplete experience of the present moment, harder to connect with others, incomplete view of reality) for having encapsulated feelings.

10. Acknowledge that human relations are critical in order to meet basic human emotional needs. (18, 19)

18. Teach the client the difference between human wants (e.g., money or power) and human needs (e.g., security, love, affirmation).

19. Assign the client to write a paper that explains how human relationship are necessary to meet basic human emotional needs.

11. List methods for trying to get human emotional needs met. (20)

20. Assign the client to list several fundamentally different methods (e.g., coerce, manipulate, trade off, persuade, collaborate, inspire) for obtaining what he/she needs emotionally from other people.

12. List the short- and long-term consequences of each method of trying to get emotional needs met. (21)

21. Assist the client in identifying short- and long-term consequences for each of the six fundamental strategies (e.g., coerce, manipulate, trade off, persuade, collaborate, inspire) for meeting his/her needs through other people.

13. Describe and review the different kinds and levels of honesty that are possible. (22)

22. Teach the client the different types and levels of honesty (e.g., not directly sharing feelings; not directly sharing content or meaning, white lies; flattery not felt, wishful thinking; exaggerating; total misrepresentation).

14. Describe feelings when successful at telling a lie. (23)

23. Explore the client's feelings when he/she successfully dupes someone and explore how that reaction might vary under different circumstances (e.g., the person they are fooling is normally hard to fool, the lie involves not saying something, the lie involves fabrication).

15. List the negative and positive consequences for utilizing different levels or types of honesty. (24, 25)

24. Assign the client to list several different positive and negative consequences for various types and levels of honesty.

25. Review the client's list of honesty consequences and instruct him/her in how to extend his/her decisional balance (e.g., exploring the short-term versus long-term consequences for becoming more honest or less honest).

16. Monitor and record experiences with different levels or types of dishonesty for one full day. (26, 27)

26. Instruct the client to monitor and record throughout an entire day his/her use of different levels of dishonesty (e.g., not directly sharing feelings; not directly sharing content or meaning; white lies, flattery not felt, wishful thinking; exaggerating; total misrepresentation).

27. Review the client's honesty monitoring and positive reinforce new and emerging effort at honesty and self-examination.

17. List specific goals for improving honesty. (28)

28. Discuss the client's goals for increasing his/her quality of honesty; ask him/her to list prioritized goals.

18. Develop an inventory of high-risk situations for lies of omission, exaggeration, and complete fabrication. (29, 30)

29. Assign the client to maintain a log formatted in three columns of types of dishonesty (e.g., not directly sharing feelings; not directly sharing content or meaning; white lies, flattery not felt, wishful thinking; exaggerating; total misrepresentation) and three rows (e.g., with person, place/time, circumstance) to

track and record his/her honesty progress and high-risk situations.

30. Review with the client his/her honesty log in order that he/she might better identify high-risk situations for his/her dishonesty (e.g., social pressure, intrapersonal extreme moods, interpersonal conflicts).

19. Rehearse and implement alternative ways of responding to high-risk situations with greater honesty. (31, 32)

31. Utilize role-play and modeling to teach the client skills for responding to identified personal high-risk situations with greater honesty.

32. Review the client's experience with implementing greater honesty; recognize and reinforce the client's efforts, even minimal ones, to become more honest.

20. Verbalize an understanding of the relationship between thoughts, beliefs, feelings, and actions. (33)

33. Instruct the client in the relationship between thoughts, beliefs, feelings, and actions and how "automatic thinking" is manufactured (see *Cognitive Therapy of Personality Disorders* by Beck and Freeman).

21. List the ways that "automatic thinking" might be related to problems with lack of power, feelings for others, and control over others. (34, 35)

34. Explain to the client how "automatic thinking" might interact and exacerbate problems with lack of power, feelings for others, and control "over" others (e.g., making the issues related to power, feelings and control unconscious and therefore "invisible").

35. Assign the client to empathy training or cognitive restructuring classes.

22. Attend group sessions focused on teaching empathy. (35)

23. Complete a reassessment for personal selfishness with a valid instrument. (36, 37)

24. Identify conditions and personal boundaries necessary to maintain acceptable levels of honesty and integrity with other people. (38)

35. Assign the client to empathy training or cognitive restructuring classes.

36. Reassess the client with a validated self-orientation assessment test (e.g., Selfism by Phares and Erskine or Paulhus Deception Scales by Paulhus).

37. Provide the client with an objective interpretation and normative feedback of his/her reassessment and profile on the validated self-orientation test he/she completed.

38. Discuss and assist the client in defining acceptable levels of honesty in his/her interactions with other people and the conditions necessary for maintaining this level of honesty.

__. _____

_____

__. _____

_____

__. _____

_____

__. _____

_____

__. _____

_____

__. _____

_____

DIAGNOSTIC SUGGESTIONS:

ICD-9-CM	*ICD-10-CM*	*DSM-5* Disorder, Condition, or Problem
301.81	F60.81	Narcissistic Personality Disorder
301.7	F60.2	Antisocial Personality Disorder
301.9	F60.9	Unspecified Personality Disorder
_____	_____	_____
_____	_____	_____

CHEMICAL DEPENDENCE

BEHAVIORAL DEFINITIONS

1. Functioning in fundamental life areas (e.g., family, vocation, health, finances, social) is impaired or significantly disrupted as a result of alcohol and other drug (AOD) dependence.
2. Increased tolerance for alcohol and other drugs has resulted in a repeating cycle of biopsychosocial negative consequences.
3. Tendency to engage in criminal behavior increases when under the influence of mood-altering substances.
4. Tendency to engage in criminal activity to procure mood-altering substances.
5. Feelings, attitudes, and perspectives are frequently distorted as a result of AOD abuse.
6. Pattern of unsuccessful attempts to reduce and/or terminate the use of mood-altering substances.
7. Diminished social support, fulfillment, and/or contact as a result of prolonged involvement with mood-altering substances.
8. Pattern of interpersonal conflict and/or personal isolation because of AOD abuse.
9. Repeated use of alcohol and other drugs to deal with the mental and physical pain of withdrawal from a drug.
10. Significant loss of freedom, friendships, property, and respect due to chemical dependence.
11. Inability to achieve a balance in responsibly meeting personal obligations and satisfying desires due to chemical dependence.

—. _____

_____

—. _____

_____

LONG-TERM GOALS

1. Significantly reduce or eliminate the amount of frequency of alcohol and other drugs consumed.
2. Establish a reliable social network that shares and supports a healthy, drug-free lifestyle and self-respect.
3. Balance lifestyle with responsibly meeting comparable levels of obligations and desires routinely fulfilled or gratified.
4. Minimize or eliminate the negative consequences that result from prolonged AOD abuse.
5. Attain greater serenity, acceptance, and personal self-regulation skills.
6. Experience greater self-potential and stability while being present, one moment to the next.

—. _____

_____

SHORT-TERM OBJECTIVES

1. Describe the history and current patterns of AOD abuse. (1, 2, 6)

THERAPEUTIC INTERVENTIONS

1. Explore the client's history and current abuse of AOD; evaluate the influence of family of origin experiences and current peer group on substance abuse patterns.

2. Administer or refer the client for structured, objective assessment testing for AOD dependence (e.g., Michigan Alcohol Screening Test, Alcohol Severity Index, Substance Abuse Subtle Screening Inventory).

6. Provide the client with an objective interpretation of his/her chemical dependence assessment that includes normative feedback regarding how he/she compares to other people or groups on relevant

2. Cooperate with a referral and short-term placement in a detoxification center. (3)

3. Engage in and complete an AOD abuse assessment. (4, 5, 6)

4. Cooperate with a physician evaluation of physical health and medical consequences of AOD dependence. (7, 8)

5. Comply with taking prescribed medications as directed by physician and report as to their effectiveness and side effects. (9)

6. Initiate and engage in a contract for therapy with a professional AOD abuse counselor. (10)

measures of AOD abuse and dependence.

3. Refer the client and arrange for his/her placement in an appropriate detoxification center, if medically indicated.

4. Refer the client to an agency or professional qualified in treating AOD dependence.

5. Conduct an in-depth chemical dependence assessment.

6. Provide the client with an objective interpretation of his/her chemical dependence assessment that includes normative feedback regarding how he/she compares to other people or groups on relevant measures of AOD abuse and dependence.

7. Refer the client for a medical evaluation of physical health and the necessity of pharmacological intervention to aid in AOD dependence recovery (e.g., antabuse, naltrexone, valium, lithium).

8. Refer the client and arrange for him/her to have blood tests for HIV and sexually transmitted diseases as well as liver enzyme elevation.

9. Conduct or arrange for monitoring of the client's medication compliance, effectiveness, and side effects.

10. Refer the client to a therapeutic process (individual and/or group therapy, depending on the needs of the client, his/her

7. List eight positive and eight negative consequences resulting from AOD involvement. (11)

8. Describe in writing the costs and benefits of terminating the AOD abuse pattern. (12)

9. Verbalize a short-term goal related to modifying AOD involvement. (13, 14)

10. Identify ways that others have achieved their goal of modifying AOD involvement. (15, 16, 17)

temperament, and available resources) with professional AOD abuse counselor(s).

11. Guide the client in listing eight positive and eight negative consequences resulting from his/her AOD involvement.

12. Assign the client to describe in writing the costs and benefits of terminating his/her pattern of AOD abuse.

13. Assist the client in identifying his/her short-term goal (e.g., within six months) related to modifying AOD involvement.

14. Review and provide constructive feedback to the client regarding short-term plans for modifying AOD use/abuse.

15. Describe for the client at least four different ways (e.g., "cold turkey," tapering off, trying moderation, trying sobriety) other people have achieved their goals related to modifying their AOD involvement.

16. Arrange to have someone from the addiction recovering community meet with the client and discuss his/her experience, hope, and strength in developing a recovery lifestyle.

17. Direct the client to attend three different local 12-step meetings (e.g., AA, NA, CA, Rational Recovery) and list three different ways other people have achieved their goals related to modifying their AOD involvement.

11. Verbalize the potential benefits of attending self-help recovery group meetings. (17, 18)

17. Direct the client to attend three different local 12-step meetings (e.g., AA, NA, CA, Rational Recovery) and list three different ways other people have achieved their goals related to modifying their AOD involvement.

18. Assign the client to read at least three different chapters in *Alcoholics Anonymous: The Big Book.*

12. Identify the strengths and weaknesses related to changing AOD abuse. (19)

19. Discuss with the client what things are apt to help him/her change his/her AOD abuse and what things are apt to hold him/her back from achieving any successful modifications.

13. Identify how to increase confidence in achieving goal of terminating AOD abuse. (20, 21)

20. Explore with the client any discrepancies existing between the importance of a given goal related to recovery from AOD abuse and the confidence he/she has for achieving that given goal and show him/her how this information is valuable for refining strategies for change to increase his/her confidence level.

21. Periodically review the client's progress in achieving specific AOD-related goals and help him/her modify his/her approach if failure is occurring.

14. Read material on the topic of overcoming AOD dependence and discuss important points discovered from the reading. (22)

22. Provide the client with a selection of reading options for learning more about AOD abuse and dependence (e.g., *Alcoholics Anonymous Big Book* [Anonymous]; *Kicking Addictive Habits Once and For All: A Relapse Prevention Guide* by Daley; *Overcoming Destructive*

Beliefs, Feelings, and Behaviors by Ellis; *The Addiction Workbook: A Step Guide to Quitting Alcohol and Drugs* by Fanning and O'Neil; *Overcoming Addiction* by Hardiman; *Sex, Drugs, Gambling, and Chocolate: A Workbook for Overcoming Addictions* by Harvath; *Addictions and Trauma Recovery* by Miller and Guidry; *The Truth about Addiction and Recovery* by Peele and Brodsky; *Addiction Is a Choice* by Schaler).

15. Make necessary social/environmental adjustments essential for terminating AOD abuse. (23)

23. Assist the client in identifying significant living situations, recreational activities, peer group loyalties, and/or employment changes necessary to support recovery from AOD abuse and dependence; support him/her in taking steps to implement these changes.

16. Demonstrate healthy communication skills. (24)

24. Instruct the client in established methods or curriculums (e.g., *Aggression Reduction Training* by Goldstein and Glick; *The Prepare Curriculum* by Goldstein; *Reasoning and Rehabilitation* by Ross, Fabiano, and Ross; *Treating Alcohol Dependence* by Monti, Abrams, Kadden, and Cooney) for attaining healthy communication and social skills.

17. Contact someone daily that understands and supports goals for modifying AOD involvement. (25, 26, 27)

25. Direct the client to establish at least one clean and sober confidant that he/she can contact every day to discuss whatever issues are arising related to modifying AOD abuse/dependence.

26. Encourage the client to expand his/her network of sober, supportive groups or individuals available for routine interaction (e.g., 12-step groups, church or faith community, sports or fitness groups).

27. Affirm the client for any progress in expanding his/her social network that is supportive of recovery from AOD abuse.

18. List the specific situations, feelings, and attitudes that interfere with progressing in successfully modifying AOD involvement. (28)

28. Review the client's progress toward AOD-related goals, communication skills, and social support and direct him/her to write in a journal all situations, beliefs, and attitudes that are interfering with his/her progress.

19. Formulate, in writing, several alternatives or ways to reframe each of the feelings or attitudes that represent obstacles to modifying AOD involvement. (29, 30, 31)

29. Discuss the client's inventory of progress obstacles and demonstrate how adapting different perspectives reframes various conditions and circumstances to make them more manageable (e.g., "I can't stand that guy" versus "I'm not going to let that guy upset me").

30. Assign the client to list two or three alternative ways of looking at or reframing each of the conditions or circumstances inventoried as current obstacles.

31. Read the client's alternative perspectives for obstacles to AOD modification and provide him/her with feedback and affirmations for effort and insights made.

20. Maintain a written log for one week, recording all strong negative emotions and attitudes experienced. (32, 33)

32. Assign the client to maintain an emotions log for one week, recording all the strong, difficult, or negative emotions (e.g., fear, anxiety, anger, depression, uncontrollable hilarity) that he/she experiences on a day-to-day basis.

33. Discuss and review with the client his/her emotion log at the end of one-week assignment and delineate interpersonal from intrapersonal emotional experiences; identify conflict resolution or stress reduction skills that are needed as alternatives to AOD abuse to cope.

21. Maintain a written log for one week recording all strong, difficult conflicts experienced with other people. (34, 35)

34. Assign the client to maintain an interpersonal conflict log for one week to record when the conflict attains an agreed threshold.

35. Discuss and review with the client interpersonal conflict log at the end of one-week assignment; teach conflict resolution skills (see Problem-Solving Skill Deficits chapter in this *Planner*).

22. Describe how urges and cravings for AOD manifest themselves. (36, 37)

36. Assign the client to maintain an urges (e.g., physical sensations and impulses) and cravings (e.g., mental obsessions) for AOD log for one week, recording when the urge or craving attains an agreeable threshold, and noting the tine, place, and circumstance.

37. Discuss and review with the client urges and cravings log at the end of one-week assignment and delineate those

that appeared to result from interpersonal conflict, internal mood states, social pressure, or external physical cues.

23. Identify distorted cognitive messages encourage AOD abuse and define and implement more adaptive messages. (38, 39)

38. Assist the client in identifying distorted cognitive messages that are maladaptive in responding to cravings ("I have to have a drink to feel better" or "If I snort some cocaine then I can relax").

39. Teach the client positive, realistic cognitive messages to replace his/her distorted messages (e.g., "If I delay fulfilling this urge, it will dissipate" or "If I use constructive relaxation skills, I'll relax without the drug").

24. Learn and practice deep relaxation techniques to cope with conflict and stress. (40, 41)

40. Instruct or refer the client for instruction in stress-reduction techniques (e.g., *Learn to Relax* by Walker; *Stress Relief and Relaxation Techniques* by Lazarus; *The Relaxation Response* by Benson; *The Stress Management Sourcebook* by Cunningham; *Five Weeks to Healing Stress: The Wellness Option* by O'Hara; *The Relaxation and Stress Reduction Workbook* by Davis, Eshelman, and McKay; *Chop Wood, Carry Water* by Fields, Taylor, Weyler, and Ingrasci).

41. Refer the client to possible resources for achieving greater relaxation and peace of mind (e.g., health club membership, acupuncture, aerobic sports, church, yoga, martial arts, having pets and hobbies).

25. Practice thinking about and helping others more over time. (42)

42. Challenge the client to think about themselves less (as opposed to thinking less of themselves) and to think and do more for others by making some small commitments in that direction (e.g., cleaning up a general living, work, or meeting area before leaving; introducing himself/herself to others that might be experiencing social inhibition; offering assistance when not required).

26. Identify and list in writing personal high-risk situations for AOD relapse. (43, 44)

43. Assign the client to review his/her inventory resulting from urges and craving log to identify his/her ten highest risk situations for relapse.

44. Review the client's high-risk situation inventory and compare it to 37-relapse symptom checklist (*Staying Sober: A Guide for Relapse Prevention* by Gorski and Miller) to see if he/she has overlooked any of his/her triggers.

27. Formulate a written plan for relapse prevention that includes personal high-risk situations, thinking, and feeling triggers for urges and cravings. (45, 46)

45. Direct the client to formulate a complete relapse plan that incorporates all personally identified high-risk situations, cues for urges and cravings, and new communication and coping skills.

46. Review the client's draft relapse prevention plan and provide affirmations and suggestions when appropriate.

28. Acknowledge the connection between criminal behavior and AOD dependence. (47, 48)

47. Explore the client's tendency to engage in criminal behavior subsequent to AOD abuse or to procure AOD.

48. Emphasize to the client the need for him/her to maintain sobriety to reduce or eliminate legal conflicts.

DIAGNOSTIC SUGGESTIONS:

ICD-9-CM	*ICD-10-CM*	*DSM-5* Disorder, Condition, or Problem
305.00	F10.10	Alcohol Use Disorder, Mild
305.70	F15.10	Amphetamine Use Disorder, Mild
305.70	F15.20	Amphetamine Use Disorder, Moderate or Severe
305.20	F12.10	Cannabis Use Disorder, Mild
305.60	F14.10	Cocaine Use Disorder, Mild
305.30	F16.10	Other Hallucinogen Use Disorder, Mild
305.30	F16.20	Other Hallucinogen Use Disorder, Moderate or Severe
305.90	F18.10	Inhalant Use Disorder, Mild
305.90	F18.20	Inhalant Use Disorder, Moderate or Severe
304.00	F11.20	Opioid Use Disorder, Moderate or Severe
304.00	F11.10	Opioid Use Disorder, Mild
305.50	F16.10	Phencyclidine Use Disorder, Mild
305.50	F16.20	Phencyclidine Use Disorder, Moderate or Severe
304.10	F13.10	Sedative, Hypnotic, or Anxiolytic Use Disorder, Mild
304.10	F13.20	Sedative, Hypnotic, or Anxiolytic Use Disorder, Moderate or Severe
305.90	F19.10	Other (or Unknown) Substance Use Disorder, Mild
305.90	F19.20	Other (or Unknown) Substance Use Disorder, Moderate or Severe
305.00	F10.20	Alcohol Use Disorder, Moderate or Severe
304.30	F12.20	Cannabis Use Disorder, Moderate or Severe
304.20	F14.20	Cocaine Use Disorder, Moderate or Severe
301.7	F60.2	Antisocial Personality Disorder
_____	_____	_____
_____	_____	_____

CHILDHOOD TRAUMA/ABUSE/ NEGLECT

BEHAVIORAL DEFINITIONS

1. Reported memories of childhood physical, sexual, or emotional abuse.
2. Confirmed history of abusive or neglectful parenting.
3. Describes parents/caregivers as neglectful, absent, chemically dependent, and so on.
4. Inability to recall childhood.
5. Irrational fears, rage, low self-esteem, depression, or insecurity related to painful childhood memories or when in contact with family members.
6. Pervasive pattern of abusive, neglectful, or promiscuous intimate relationships.
7. Disturbing thoughts or dreams about the traumatic events.
8. Inability to experience a wide range of emotions.
9. Repeating the pattern of abuse, violence, and neglect that was experienced in childhood.
10. Dissociative phenomena experienced as maladaptive coping mechanism resulting from childhood trauma.

—. _____
_____

—. _____
_____

—. _____
_____

LONG-TERM GOALS

1. Reduce the negative impact that child abuse/trauma/neglect has on quality of life and functioning.
2. Terminate destructive coping mechanisms and implement healthy coping strategies that promote healing and responsible living.
3. Develop the ability to express a wide range of emotions like fear, joy, compassion, anger, and hurt.
4. Develop awareness of how past childhood trauma affects current relationships, self-care, or parenting skills.
5. Increase ability to form and maintain meaningful, healthy intimate relationships.

—. _____

_____

—. _____

_____

SHORT-TERM OBJECTIVES

THERAPEUTIC INTERVENTIONS

1. Cooperate with a psychiatric evaluation. (1)

1. Refer the client for a psychiatric evaluation to assess him/her for suicidal ideation, PTSD, depression, dissociative identity disorder, or other serious mental illness and to prescribe psychotropic medication.

2. Take psychotropic medications as prescribed and report as to effectiveness and side effects. (2)

2. Monitor the client for psychotropic medication prescription compliance, effectiveness, and side effects.

3. Accept referral for voluntary admission to an inpatient psychiatric facility. (3)

3. Refer the client to short-term placement in a psychiatric hospital if he/she is potentially harmful to self or others.

4. Accept a referral for individual psychotherapy with a focus on trauma resolution. (4)

4. Recommend that the client participate in therapy with a professional trained in modalities that focus on trauma (e.g., Eye Movement

5. List ways that other people have coped successfully with an abusive, neglectful, or traumatic childhood. (5, 6)

6. Create a family genogram, verbalizing emotions that arise as a result. (7, 8)

7. Describe what it was like to grow up within the family system, noting family roles and patterns. (9, 10)

Desensitization and Reprocessing (EMDR), Gestalt, Hakomi).

5. Instruct the client to attend three different community self-help groups (e.g., Adult Children of Alcoholics, AlAnon) and list three successful ways other people have coped with childhood trauma, abuse, or neglect.

6. Provide the client with a selection of reading materials on the topic of emotional healing from abuse and neglect (e.g., *The Right to Innocence* by Engel, *Outgrowing the Pain* by Gil, *Trapped in the Mirror* by Golomb, *Grow Up!* by Pittman, *Forgive and Forget* by Smedes, *Healing the Child Within* by Whitfield).

7. Support the client in developing a family genogram that lists family members and indicates depth of relationships and feelings about each member.

8. Encourage the client to go as slow as necessary and process with the client any emotions that arise as a result of developing a family genogram.

9. Facilitate a discussion with the client about the genogram and what it was like to grow up in the family system; assist him/her in identifying and clarifying feelings.

10. Identify with the client any roles or patterns that existed in the family (e.g., roles such as

victim, persecutor, rescuer, scapegoat, hero, or enabler; patterns such as narcissism, alcohol/drug abuse, violence).

8. Inventory how childhood experiences affect current lifestyle. (11, 12)

11. Help the client to differentiate between healthy and unhealthy behavior and relationships in the family while supporting any of the client's current coping behavior that helps him/her survive.

12. Assist the client in identifying how childhood experiences have affected, both positively and negatively, his/her current lifestyle (e.g., unable to maintain an intimate relationship; constant sense of fear, anger, or hurt; lack of self-esteem).

9. Implement techniques to reduce emotional arousal. (13, 14, 15)

13. Assist the client in developing an awareness of cues (e.g., shaky hands, begins to dissociate, tightness in the stomach, distractedness, eyes lose focus) that presage overwhelming emotions associated with traumatic experiences.

14. Brainstorm with the client ways to self-regulate intense emotions (e.g., stop and breathe deeply, practice grounding exercises, repeating a self-affirming statement); role-play application of these techniques to the client's daily life.

15. Teach the client simple, quick, relaxation techniques (e.g., breathing deeply, counting backwards, imagining pleasant

scenes, manipulating a worry stone); encourage the client to implement these techniques to reduce emotional arousal.

10. Identify and "reframe" the specific negative self-talk that has resulted from childhood abuse, trauma, or neglect. (16, 17)

16. Assist the client in reviewing and inventorying some of the negative self-talk that has resulted from childhood abuse, trauma, or neglect (e.g., "Everything is my fault," "I am unlovable," "I will always be hurt").

17. Facilitate a brainstorming inventory of possible positive ways to "reframe" self-talk that has resulted from childhood abuse, trauma, or neglect (e.g., "I am not to blame for others' actions," "I am lovable and capable," "I am a survivor").

11. Identify any patterns of repeating in own current life the abandonment, neglect, or abuse that was experienced as a child. (18)

18. Explore with the client how he/she may be repeating the pattern of abandonment, neglect, or abuse that he/she experienced as a child (e.g., involvement in abusive relationships, perpetrating abuse, neglectful toward own family or children).

12. Impose healthy relationship boundaries in daily life. (19, 20)

19. Teach the client about boundaries, emphasizing that he/she has the choice of when to exercise strong boundaries (e.g., saying no) and when to be flexible.

20. Facilitate a role-play with the client setting boundaries in different situations; give feedback as to the client's implementation of boundaries in his/her daily life.

13. Implement healthy communication skills. (21, 22, 23)

21. Instruct the client in healthy communication skills (e.g., feelings talk, listening skills, asking for help, refusing request, "I" statements).

22. Facilitate the client's skill rehearsal for three new communication skills, focusing on communicating anger, fear, or hurt.

23. Review the client's implementation of new conflict communication skills in daily life; reinforce success and redirect for failure.

14. Verbalize a plan to fulfill unmet needs of childhood. (24)

24. Assist the client in expressing grief, hurt, and anger associated with the unmet needs of childhood; formulate a plan for the client to fulfill these unmet needs.

15. Write an action plan for dealing with resentments toward perpetrators of abuse. (25, 26)

25. Assign the client the task of making an inventory of resentments toward the perpetrators of childhood abuse, neglect, or trauma; use a structured debriefing format (e.g., a 12-step model of listing the target of anger, the cause of the anger, the effect of the pain, my role in the abusive situation).

26. Instruct the client to write an action plan for overcoming each of his/her resentments that addresses the triggers, cues, anger reducers, self-statements, and self-evaluation.

16. Identify relationships that are supportive of the goal of overcoming the effects of childhood trauma, abuse, or neglect. (27)

27. Assist the client in identifying validation relationships that are supportive of his/her work toward reducing the negative effects that childhood abuse,

17. Evaluate progress made in reducing the negative effects that childhood abuse, trauma, or neglect have had on present lifestyle and reset new short-term goals. (28)

28. Evaluate with the client his/her progress made in reducing the negative effects that childhood abuse, trauma, or neglect have had on present lifestyle and reset new short-term goals.

__. _____
_____

__. _____
_____

__. _____
_____

trauma, or neglect have on present lifestyle.

__. _____
_____

__. _____
_____

__. _____
_____

DIAGNOSTIC SUGGESTIONS:

ICD-9-CM	_ICD-10-CM_	_DSM-5_ Disorder, Condition, or Problem
303.90	F10.20	Alcohol Use Disorder, Moderate or Severe
300.4	F34.1	Persistent Depressive Disorder
296.xx	F32.x	Major Depressive Disorder, Single Episode
296.xx	F33.x	Major Depressive Disorder, Recurrent Episode
300.02	F41.1	Generalized Anxiety Disorder
300.14	F44.81	Dissociative Identity Disorder
300.15	F44.89	Other Specified Dissociative Disorder
995.53	T74.22XA	Child Sexual Abuse, Confirmed, Initial Encounter
995.53	T74.22XD	Child Sexual Abuse, Confirmed, Subsequent Encounter
312.34	F63.81	Intermittent Explosive Disorder
301.82	F60.6	Avoidant Personality Disorder
301.6	F60.7	Dependent Personality Disorder
_____	_____	_____
_____	_____	_____

CONSEQUENTIAL THINKING DEFICITS

BEHAVIORAL DEFINITIONS

1. Lack of control over impulsive, irrational, and/or emotional behavior regardless of consequences.
2. Loss of personal freedoms due to presence in criminal justice system as a result of consequential thinking deficits.
3. Remorse for past behavior that resulted from acting without thought of consequences.
4. Does not develop and incorporate long-term problem-solving strategies, resulting in an inability to attain personal goals.
5. Dissatisfaction with self due to inability to attain desired quality of life because of poor decision making.
6. Inability to maintain meaningful employment due to capricious and cavalier lack of regard for performance outcomes.
7. Loss of meaningful relationships as a result of impulsive, aggressive, and/or thoughtless behavior.

—. _____
_____
—. _____
_____
—. _____
_____

LONG-TERM GOALS

1. Acquire greater self-control by improving decision-making ability through consideration of consequences.

2. Enjoy close personal relationships based on mutual respect and thoughtful consideration of each other's feelings.
3. Progressively fulfill more personal commitments, obligations, and goals by means of behavior that is deliberate and circumspect.
4. Experience self-confidence and mastery in terms of career or livelihood because of engaging in more thoughtful behavior.

—. _____
   _____
—. _____
   _____
—. _____
   _____

SHORT-TERM OBJECTIVES

THERAPEUTIC INTERVENTIONS

1. Identify personal history of impulsive thinking, decision making, and acting and their consequences. (1, 2)

1. Explore with the client his/her history of impulsive thinking, decision making, and acting (e.g., always reacting to every situation with hostility, doing the first thing that comes to mind).

2. Assist the client in listing the consequences for self and others of his/her past impulsive actions (e.g., hurt feelings, physical pain, arrests, loss of relationships and/or jobs).

2. List the pros and cons of making a decision impulsively, without thinking through the consequences. (3, 4)

3. Brainstorm with the client the pros (e.g., decisions are made quickly) and cons (e.g., loss of opportunities, monetary costs) of making a decision impulsively without thinking through the consequences.

4. Ask the client to identify which of the negative outcomes of impulsivity he/she has experienced.

3. Recognize how anger or aggression can influence decision making. (5, 6)

5. Assist the client in exploring the role of anger and aggression in poor decision making (e.g., anger interferes with logical thinking, anger energizes immediate reactions, anger seeks revenge, not justice).

6. Assign the client to list and described at least five incidents in which anger contributed to his/her poor decision-making and include the negative consequences of these actions.

4. List common cues for identifying arousal and the process for how angry feelings generally emerge for people. (7, 8)

7. Teach the client to recognize the arousal cues (e.g., muscle tension, throat tightness, dry mouth, shallow breathing, voice level increases, agitation) and how it relates to performance (e.g., recognize when arousal is escalating to a degree where it will impair judgment).

8. Guide the client discussion in a brainstorming session that identifies common cues that can potentially alert people to when they are becoming angry (e.g., tight tummy, dry mouth, heart rate increases, blood pressure increases, shallower breathing, clenched fists, perceived threats).

5. Verbalize where anger comes from (antecedents), how it manifests (behavior), and what results (consequences) are likely to be produced by it. (9)

9. Teach the client a basic objective perspective on anger that minimally includes instruction on the Antecedents of anger, Behavior and physical features associated with anger, and Consequences of anger (i.e., the ABCs of anger).

6. List several techniques that could be used to reduce anger quickly. (10, 11)

10. Teach the client tools of anger management using anger management curriculum (see *In Control* by Kellner or *Problem-Solving Skills for Offenders* by Taymans and Parese available from National Institute of Corrections [www.nicic.org]).

11. Teach the client simple, quick techniques (e.g., deep breathing, counting backward, engaging in pleasant imagery, using a worry stone) to immediately help reduce anger elevations in a variety of situations.

7. Critically examine past behavior and brainstorm alternate more deliberate courses of action and alternate outcomes thereof. (12, 13)

12. Explore with the client examples of his/her impulsive behavior and brainstorm alternate, more deliberate courses of action and the positive outcomes thereof.

13. Assign the client to write a description of two impulsive incidents from his/her past including the negative consequences and then write a description of these same incidents substituting a deliberate, thoughtful problem-solving approach and the probable consequences.

8. Verbalize an acceptance of responsibility for the negative consequences of past behavior. (14)

14. Encourage and support the client in taking responsibility for negative consequences of his/her past impulsive behavior.

9. Implement the steps that aid in consequential thinking. (15, 16, 17, 18)

15. Assign the client to list some steps that would aid in consequential thinking (e.g., pausing-to-think, stating the situation clearly, stating the desired outcome, listing the

alternative ways of achieving the desired outcome, sorting out the pros and cons for each alternative, implementing one option, evaluating the outcome).

16. Use role-playing and modeling to teach the client how to think consequentially (e.g., pausing-to-think, stating the situation clearly, stating the desired outcome, listing the alternative ways of achieving the desired outcome, sorting out the pros and cons for each alternative); provide him/her with supportive feedback on his/her performance on the role-play, reinforcing any attempt to think through a situation before reacting.

17. Instruct the client to describe in writing the role pausing-to-think has in aiding consequential thinking (e.g., increases the space between the incident and action taken, gives emotions a chance to dissipate).

18. Assign the client physical exercises (e.g., rock climbing) to practice his/her decision-making skills and emphasize potential consequences of bad decisions.

10. Keep a daily journal of how problems and stressors are reacted to impulsively or deliberately and thoughtfully. (19, 20)

19. Instruct the client to keep a journal of problems and stressors that arise daily, recording how they were handled, the outcome of the situation, the desired outcome, and the alternate courses of action that could have been

taken to achieve desired outcome.

20. Process the client's journal material to reinforce the need for and payoffs of more deliberate reactions.

11. List the value and responsibility of having freedom in decision-making. (21, 22)

21. Brainstorm with the client the value of having freedom in decision-making (e.g., a sense of autonomy and empowerment, builds confidence, develops individuality, fosters creativity), emphasizing the tremendous responsibility to himself/herself, others, and the environment that comes with it.

22. Instruct the client to list the people who have been affected or hurt by his/her impulsive, irresponsible behavior.

12. Examine past relationship failures and consider how a different outcome could have been achieved. (22, 23)

22. Instruct the client to list the people who have been affected or hurt by his/her impulsive, irresponsible behavior.

23. Explore the client's past relationship failures and assist him/her in discovering how a different outcome could have been achieved through more thoughtful actions.

13. Contact those who have been affected/hurt by irresponsible behavior to gain feedback and/or make amends. (24, 25, 26)

24. Encourage the client to contact, if appropriate, those who have been affected or hurt by his/her irresponsible behavior to gain feedback and make amends.

25. Ask the client to list how the loss of decision-making freedom due to his/her legal restrictions has affected him/her.

26. Debrief with the client any contact he/she made with those affected or hurt by the client's irresponsible behavior; support or redirect the client as necessary.

14. Verbalize an understanding of past failures as experiences that can be learned from. (27)

27. Support the client in understanding his/her past failures as experiences that can be learned from, rather than an immutable, inescapable pattern of behavior.

15. Implement new conflict communication skills and receive feedback. (28, 29, 30)

28. Describe and model for the client several conflict communication skills (e.g., double-sided reflections, partially agreeing, agreeing with a twist, "I" statements) that could improve his/her communication (see *The Prepare Curriculum* by Goldstein or *Motivational Interviewing* by Miller and Rollnick).

29. Use role-play and modeling to facilitate client skill rehearsals for three new communication skills, utilizing his/her own recent situations where better communication skills would have improved the outcome.

30. Assign the client to implement new conflict communication skills in his/her daily life; review and process the experience, reinforcing success, and redirecting for failure.

16. Maintain a journal of own thoughts and emotions, and critically examine for the purpose of developing a better understanding of self. (31)

31. Instruct the client to maintain a journal of thoughts and emotions related to interpersonal communication for better understanding of impulsive patterns.

17. Set concrete goals that can be met within two months regarding improving consequential thinking skills. (32)

32. Guide the client in setting some concrete goals that can be met within two months regarding improving consequential thinking skills (e.g., increase awareness of impulsive thoughts, pause to think and weighing the pros and cons before making any decisions, fulfill commitments with thoughtful behavior).

__. _____   __. _____

   _____   _____

__. _____   __. _____

   _____   _____

DIAGNOSTIC SUGGESTIONS:

ICD-9-CM	_ICD-10-CM_	_DSM-5_ Disorder, Condition, or Problem
314.01	F90.2	Attention-Deficit/Hyperactivity Disorder, Combined Presentation
314.9	F90.1	Attention-Deficit/Hyperactivity Disorder, Predominately Hyperactive/Impulsive Presentation
296.xx	F31.xx	Bipolar I Disorder
296.89	F31.81	Bipolar II Disorder
312.30	F91.9	Unspecified Disruptive, Impulse-Control, and Conduct Disorder
312.34	F63.81	Intermittent Explosive Disorder
301.83	F60.3	Borderline Personality Disorder
301.7	F60.2	Antisocial Personality Disorder
_____	_____	_____
_____	_____	_____

CRIMINAL PEERS

BEHAVIORAL DEFINITIONS

1. Currently associates with friends and acquaintances who are involved in criminal behavior.
2. Verbalizes acceptance of peers' criminal behavior.
3. Admires or identifies with others who are pro-crime and sees their lifestyle as desirable.
4. Encouraged and easily influenced by peers to participate in criminal behavior.
5. Participates in criminal behavior with friends.
6. Willing to protect, cover-up, and accept responsibility for peers' deviant behavior.
7. Verbalizes a sense of loyalty to and identification with a gang.
8. Prior attempts to distance self from criminal peers have been unsuccessful.
9. Inability to establish and maintain meaningful pro-social peer support group.

—. _____
   _____

—. _____
   _____

LONG-TERM GOALS

1. Significantly reduce or eliminate association with criminal friends.
2. Learn to manage existing pro-criminal relationships by reestablishing boundaries to reduce risk for relapse or recidivism.

3. Develop a greater understanding about peer group; how peers influence and interact with personal behavior to effect lifestyle quality.
4. Develop a meaningful, pro-social support network.
5. Terminate all criminal behavior, even if it results in peer conflict.

—. _____
_____
_____

—. _____
_____

SHORT-TERM OBJECTIVES

THERAPEUTIC INTERVENTIONS

1. List all friends and acquaintances; placing an asterisk next to those who have been involved in criminal behavior. (1, 2)

1. Assign the client to list all his/her friends and acquaintances; denoting criminal peers with an asterisk.

2. Review the client's list of peers, exploring his/her feelings and thoughts about the number of pro-crime peers compared to pro-social peers.

2. Map all friends and acquaintances according to how frequently interactions with them occur. (3)

3. Instruct the client to draw three concentric rings, each two inches apart, the center a circle representing himself/herself, the next band representing friends and acquaintances seen almost daily; the next band representing those seen almost every week. Insert small circles (with initials) depicting all friends and acquaintances, and shade each initialed small circle according to how criminally involved he/she is; process this graph's meaning and implication.

3. Describe the history and consequences of criminal behavior with peers. (4, 5)

4. Explore the client's history and consequences of his/her involvement in criminal

behavior with friends and acquaintances.

5. Ask the client to write an autobiography focusing the history of involvement in and consequences of criminal behavior with friends and acquaintances beginning in childhood or adolescence.

4. List the positive and negative consequences of yielding to peer pressure. (6)

6. Explain the dynamics of peer pressure to the client (e.g., wanting to fit in) and the positive (e.g., feeling of belongingness, having fun, avoiding conflict) and negative (e.g., going against one's better judgment, getting caught, conflict with peers) consequences of yielding to peer pressure.

5. Identify the feelings that are experienced when pressured by peers to participate in criminal behavior. (7)

7. Explore the client's feelings that are generated by being subjected to peer pressure.

6. Identify factors that have led to the development of relationships with deviant peers. (8, 9)

8. Teach the client the various factors that can lead to developing relationships with criminal peers (e.g., low self-esteem, desire to belong, curiosity, thrill seeking).

9. Assist the client in generating a list of personal factors that have led him/her to develop relationships with deviant peers; review and process this list, reinforcing the client's increased understanding of himself/herself.

7. List 10 positive and 10 negative consequences of having friends and acquaintances that are involved in criminal behavior. (10)

10. Ask client to list 10 positive (e.g., excitement, adventure, familiarity) and ten negative (e.g., anxiety, being pressured into criminal behavior, getting

8. List the costs and benefits of changing versus not changing the prevailing personal pattern of involvement with criminal peers. (11)

9. Compare the values, traits, attributes, and attitudes of criminal peers with those of self. (12)

10. Identify needs that are being met with peer-approved criminal behavior that could be met with pro-social behavior. (13)

11. Verbalize a resolution of resistant feelings associated with ending relationships with friends and acquaintances who are involved in criminal behavior. (14)

12. List the reasons past attempts to end relationships with criminal friends were unsuccessful. (15)

caught) consequences of having friends and acquaintances that are involved in criminal behavior.

11. Assign client to list in writing the costs and benefits of changing versus not changing the prevailing personal pattern of involvement with criminal peers.

12. Assign the client to list the values, traits, attributes, and attitudes his/her deviant peers possess; review the list, exploring the similarities and differences between his/her values and attitudes and those of his/her friends and acquaintances.

13. Explore the client's feelings that occur when he/she participates in criminal behavior with friends and acquaintances; note if there are needs being met through this behavior that could be met pro-socially.

14. Explore the client's feelings about ending his/her relationships with criminal friends and acquaintances; process ambivalent or resistant feelings.

15. Explore the client's past attempts to distance himself/herself from deviant friends and acquaintances, assessing the reasons the past attempts were unsuccessful, and identifying triggers (e.g., people, places, things), ambivalence, and unclear boundaries that led to failure.

13. Identify, practice, and implement new strategies for distancing self from criminal peers. (16, 17, 18, 19)

16. Teach the client new strategies (e.g., setting clear boundaries, telling peers his/her goal of avoiding criminal behavior, saying no) for distancing himself/herself from criminal peers.

17. Role-play with the client the use of the new distancing techniques; provide him/her with positive feedback for effort, as well as suggestions for improvement in implementation.

18. Assign the client the task of choosing one deviant friend or acquaintance that he/she feels comfortable distancing himself/herself from and implement the new distancing techniques with that person.

19. Debrief with client about how new distancing techniques worked with chosen person; provide positive reinforcement and feedback for improvement.

14. Implement activities designed to meet pro-social people. (20)

20. Advise the client to make efforts to get more involved with other pro-social people; suggest activities that might facilitate that process (e.g., joining a community or church group, inviting someone from work to a recreational activity, become a volunteer, take an educational class).

15. Describe ways to maintain relationships with friends and acquaintances involved in criminal behavior without participating in such behavior. (21)

21. Assist the client in identifying ways he/she can maintain his/her relationships with some of his/her criminal peers without engaging in deviant behavior (e.g., setting clear

boundaries, expressing his/her goal, saying no). However, if the client is unable to prevent engaging in deviant behavior as a result, instruct him/her to distance himself/herself from criminal peers.

16. Identify high-risk situations that could lead to participating in criminal behavior and develop a written prevention plan for these high-risk situations. (22)

22. Highlight with the client some high-risk situations that may lead to relapse (e.g. criminal behaviors, alcohol or other drug use); develop a written prevention plan for becoming involved in deviant behavior in such high-risk situations.

17. Review high-risk situations and determine if the primary triggers are social pressure, problems managing emotions, or conflicts with others. (23)

23. Explain to the client how criminal behavior relapse triggers tend to fall into one of three categories (e.g., social pressure, problems managing moods and emotions, or hassles and conflicts with others) and ask him/her to determine which category his/her primary trigger fits into.

18. Practice healthy communication skills to establish boundaries with deviant friends and acquaintances. (24, 25, 26, 27)

24. Teach the client how to establish boundaries with friends and acquaintances using healthy communication skills such as assertiveness techniques, distancing practices, and refusal skills (e.g., saying no; stating needs in a clear, friendly manner; stating complaints in a clear, friendly manner; using "I" messages).

25. Role-play with the client using healthy communication skills (e.g., refusing requests, drug/ alcohol refusal skills) to practice establishing boundaries with deviant friends and acquaintances; provide

him/her with positive reinforcement as well as suggestions for improvement.

26. Assign the client to choose one criminal peer and practice using new communication skills with that person.

27. Debrief with client about how new communication skills worked with chosen person; provide him/her with positive reinforcement and feedback for improvement.

19. Identify personal values, traits, feelings, and attitudes that may be preventing pro-social relationships from developing. (28)

28. Assist the client in identifying personal values, attitudes, and feelings that may be preventing him/her from developing meaningful, pro-social relationships (e.g., they won't like me, those people are boring).

20. Formulate several ways to reframe each of the feelings and attitudes that represent obstacles to making new friendships. (29)

29. Assist the client in formulating several ways to reframe each of the feelings and attitudes that represent obstacles to making new friendships (e.g., once they get to know me, they will like me; everyone has something interesting to share).

21. Make a list of the values, traits, attributes, and attitudes that are seen as important to look for when making a new, supportive, pro-social friend. (30)

30. Help the client generate a list of values and attitudes that he/she sees as important to look for when making a new, supportive, pro-social friend; highlight the differences between this set of values and attitudes and those values and attitudes associated with his/her criminal peers.

22. Implement new ways to go about making supportive friendships. (31)

31. Use role-playing, modeling, and behavior rehearsal to teach the client new social skills to be

used in making new, supportive friendships (e.g., active sharing, using "I" statement, listening to feedback, asking open questions, listening to nonverbal communication).

23. Evaluate past attempts to establish pro-social friendships, looking at what went wrong and how to replace old patterns with new techniques. (32)

32. Explore the client's past attempts to establish and maintain meaningful, pro-social friends and acquaintances; evaluate what went wrong and how the client can replace old patterns with new social skills.

24. Attend three different clubs, groups in three weeks. (33)

33. Advise the client to attend three different clubs, groups, or organizations (e.g., 12-step groups, church or faith community, sports, or fitness groups) in three weeks to initiate contact with pro-social people.

25. Participate in a club, group, or organization for at least nine continuous weeks, using new social skills to initiate and maintain pro-social relationships. (34, 35, 36)

34. Direct the client to become involved in a club, group, or organization of interest (e.g., sports league, church, charity organization, AA/NA) for at least nine consecutive weeks to give himself/herself a chance to build relationships.

35. Encourage client to practice new social skills with other members of a club, group, or organization in an effort to develop new friends and acquaintances.

36. Debrief with client about how new techniques worked; provide him/her with positive reinforcement for effort and feedback for improvements.

26. Remap and compare all friends and acquaintances according to how frequently interactions with them occur. (37)

37. Instruct the client to draw three concentric rings, each two inches apart, the center circle representing himself/herself, the next band representing friends and acquaintances seen almost daily, the next band representing those seen almost every week. Insert small circles (with initials) depicting all friends and acquaintances, and shade each initialed small circle according to how criminally involved he/she is; reinforce him/her for any difference between the first map drawn and this current map.

—. _____   —. _____

_____   _____

—. _____   —. _____

_____   _____

DIAGNOSTIC SUGGESTIONS:

ICD-9-CM	_ICD-10-CM_	_DSM-5_ Disorder, Condition, or Problem
300.23	F40.10	Social Anxiety Disorder (Social Phobia)
312.34	F63.81	Intermittent Explosive Disorder
300.4	F34.1	Persistent Depressive Disorder
301.20	F60.1	Schizoid Personality Disorder
301.7	F60.2	Antisocial Personality Disorder
301.82	F60.6	Avoidant Personality Disorder
301.6	F60.7	Dependent Personality Disorder
_____	_____	_____
_____	_____	_____

DECEITFUL

BEHAVIORAL DEFINITIONS

1. Frequently takes delight in duping or deceiving others.
2. Fabricates information when defensive.
3. Routinely embellishes or exaggerates to impress others.
4. Deceives others to hurt, manipulate, or use them.
5. Lies and practices deception routinely.
6. Frequently omits sharing information to avoid accountability.
7. Thinking distortions impair honesty with self.
8. Significant discrepancies between emotions experienced and emotions expressed.
9. Often involved in secretive behaviors and communications.

—. _____

  _____

—. _____

  _____

LONG-TERM GOALS

1. Establish a clear and unambiguous goal for greater truthfulness.
2. Achieve greater self-congruence, confidence, and ability to be truthful.
3. Fully recognize discrepancies between current practice of and actual potential for honesty.
4. Increase awareness and understanding of the underlying motives for specific types of dishonesty.
5. Develop a precise understanding of various levels and types of honesty.

—. _____
   _____
   _____
—. _____
   _____
   _____
—. _____
   _____

SHORT-TERM OBJECTIVES

1. Acknowledge the practice of deceitfulness in personal life and how it is demonstrated. (1, 2)

2. Complete a self-administered assessment instrument that measures deceitfulness and deception tendencies. (3)

3. Enroll in a therapeutic process focusing on overcoming deceitfulness. (4)

4. Describe and review the different kinds and levels of honesty that are possible. (5)

THERAPEUTIC INTERVENTIONS

1. Explore the practice of deceitfulness in the client's life and confront his/her denial of responsibility for evidence of it.

2. Assign the client to list at least five instances in which he/she has been consciously deceitful toward others.

3. Administer to the client a validated test of deception (e.g., Paulhus Deception Scales by Paulhus, Defensiveness Scale on the ASUS by Wanberg); provide the client with an objective interpretation and feedback regarding test scores.

4. Refer the client to a therapeutic process that focuses on deceitfulness; process issues that arise during the therapeutic process.

5. Teach the client the different types and levels of honesty (e.g., not directly sharing feelings; not directly sharing content or meaning, white lies; flattery not felt; wishful thinking; exaggerating; total misrepresentation).

5. Identify and reframe feelings or self-statements of "duping delight." (6, 7)

6. Explore the client's feelings (e.g., powerful, clever, proud) when he/she successfully dupes someone and explore how that reaction might vary under different circumstances (e.g., the person they are fooling is normally hard to fool, the lie involves not saying something, the lie involves fabrication).

7. Brainstorm with the client different reframes for his/her "duping delight" thoughts and feelings (e.g., I did not represent myself honestly which is a disservice to myself and demonstrates a lack of respect for myself and my opinion).

6. List the negative and positive consequences for utilizing different levels or types of honesty. (8, 9)

8. Ask the client to list several positive (e.g., feeling powerful, clever; ability to manipulate a situation to one's advantage) and negative (e.g., misrepresenting oneself, not getting one's needs met) consequences for various types and levels of dishonesty; process the list.

9. Review the client's list of dishonesty consequences and instruct him/her in how to extend his/her decisional balance (e.g., exploring the short-term versus long-term consequences for becoming more honest or less honest).

7. Monitor and record experiences with different levels or types of dishonesty for one full day. (10, 11)

10. Instruct the client to monitor and record throughout an entire day his/her use of different levels of dishonesty (e.g., not directly sharing feelings; not directly sharing content or meaning; white lies,

flattery not felt, wishful thinking; exaggerating; total misrepresentation).

11. Review the client's honesty monitoring and positive reinforce new and emerging effort at honesty and self-examination.

8. List specific goals for improving honesty. (12)

12. Discuss the client's goals for increasing his/her quality of honesty; ask him/her to list prioritized goals (e.g., reducing the number of exaggerations, presenting situations as honestly as possible without omission or fabrication, increasing the frequency of being honest about feelings).

9. Develop an inventory of high-risk situations for lies of omission, exaggeration, and complete fabrication. (13, 14)

13. Instruct the client to develop an inventory of high-risk situations for the three levels or types of dishonesty: lies of omission, exaggeration, and total misrepresentation.

14. Assign the client to maintain a daily log formatted in three columns of types of dishonesty (e.g., lies of omission—not directly sharing feelings or not directly sharing content or meaning; exaggerating—white lies, flattery not felt, wishful thinking; complete fabrications—total misrepresentation) and three rows (e.g., who present, place/time, circumstance) to track and record his/her honesty progress and high-risk situations.

10. Rehearse and implement alternative ways of responding to high-risk

15. Review with the client his/her honesty log in order that he/she might better identify high-risk

situations with greater honesty. (15, 16, 17)

situations for his/her dishonesty (e.g., social pressure, intra-personal extreme moods, interpersonal conflicts).

16. Utilize role-play and modeling to teach the client skills (e.g., acknowledging the high-risk situation, using reframes to self-talk to support honesty, reinforcing that one's opinion will be heard when spoken truthfully) for responding to identified personal high-risk situations with greater honesty; encourage implementation of these skills in daily living.

17. Review the client's experience with implementing greater honesty; recognize and reinforce the client's efforts, even minimal ones, to become more honest.

11. List the ways that deceitful "automatic thinking" might be related to problems with a lack power, feelings for others, and control over others. (18, 19)

18. Instruct the client in the relationship between thoughts, beliefs, feelings, and actions and how "automatic thinking" is manufactured (see *Cognitive Therapy of Personality Disorders* by Beck and Freeman).

19. Explain to the client how "automatic thinking" might interact and exacerbate problems with a need for power, feelings for others, and control "over" others (e.g., making the issues related to power, feelings, and control unconscious and therefore "invisible").

12. Share information reducing amounts of fabrication even though feelings of vulner-ability are present. (20, 21)

20. Rehearse the client's sharing in-formation that makes him/her feel vulnerable (e.g., embarrass-ing moments, worst thing I've

done, biggest fear) with as little fabrication as possible.

21. Recognize and reinforce the client's efforts to reduce fabrications and increase an honest representation of the situation.

13. Identify conditions and personal boundaries necessary to maintain acceptable levels of honesty and integrity with other people. (22)

22. Assist the client in defining acceptable levels of honesty in his/her interactions with other people and the conditions necessary for maintaining this level of honesty.

14. Complete a retest on a self-administered assessment instrument that measures deceitfulness and deception tendencies. (23)

23. Reassess the client with a validated test of deception (e.g., Paulhus Deception Scales by Paulhus, Defensiveness Scale on the ASUS by Wanberg); provide the client with an objective interpretation and normative feedback of his/her reassessment and profile.

—. _____   —. _____

_____   _____

DIAGNOSTIC SUGGESTIONS:

ICD-9-CM	*ICD-10-CM*	*DSM-5* Disorder, Condition, or Problem
296.2x	F32.x	Major Depressive Disorder, Single Episode
296.3x	F33.x	Major Depressive Disorder, Recurrent Episode
300.4	F34.1	Persistent Depressive Disorder
301.81	F60.81	Narcissistic Personality Disorder
301.50	F60.4	Histrionic Personality Disorder
301.7	F60.2	Antisocial Personality Disorder
301.83	F60.3	Borderline Personality Disorder
301.13	F34.0	Cyclothymic Disorder
301.9	F60.9	Unspecified Personality Disorder

_____   _____   _____

_____   _____   _____

DEPRESSION/SUICIDAL IDEATION

BEHAVIORAL DEFINITIONS

1. Depressed affect every day.
2. Insomnia or hypersomnia.
3. Loss of appetite.
4. Diminished interest and enjoyment in activities.
5. Resignation from groups, organizations, or activities.
6. Feelings of helplessness, hopelessness, and worthlessness.
7. Low self-esteem and feelings of inappropriate guilt.
8. Psychomotor agitation or retardation.
9. Inability to concentrate.
10. History of chronic or recurrent depression for which the client has received treatment.
11. Previous attempts at suicide.
12. Recurrent thoughts of or preoccupation with death.
13. Specific plan for committing suicide.
14. Sudden, unexplained change from being depressed to being upbeat and putting personal affairs in order.

—. _____
_____
—. _____
_____
—. _____
_____

LONG-TERM GOALS

1. Alleviate depressed mood/suicidal ideation and return to previous level of effective functioning.
2. Increase ability for coping with depression in a way that enhances daily functioning.
3. Improve awareness, acceptance and understanding of depression.
4. Develop healthy cognitive patterns and beliefs about self and the world that lead to the alleviation of symptoms of depression and/or suicidal ideation.
5. Resolve the grief or emotional conflicts that underlie depression or suicidal patterns.

—. _____
_____
—. _____
_____
—. _____
_____

SHORT-TERM OBJECTIVES	**THERAPEUTIC INTERVENTIONS**
1. Verbalize the strength of suicidal feelings and the details of the plan. (1, 2)	1. Explore with the client the strength of suicidal feelings and the details of the plan.
	2. Determine the client's suicide risk level by assessing his/her strength of verbalized intent and motive, the deadliness and availability of the method, past attempts at suicide, and family history of suicide.
2. Sign a suicide contract that states that contact will be made with a crisis center, a therapist, or a family member if the urge for self-harm increases. (3, 4, 5, 6)	3. Establish a contract with the client, stipulating that he/she will contact a crisis/help line, a therapist, a staff member, or a family member if a serious urge to harm himself/herself arises.

4. Provide the client with the telephone number of a 24-hour crisis/help line.

5. Contact family members and significant others regarding the suicidal ideation and ask them to form a suicide watch until the crisis subsides.

6. Contact corrections staff regarding the suicidal ideation and ask them to form a suicide watch until the crisis subsides.

3. Cooperate with a short-term placement in supervised and secure setting. (7, 8)

7. Arrange for psychiatric hospitalization if the client is assessed to be capable of serious harm to himself/herself.

8. Arrange for the client to be put on the strictest of suicide precautions and supervision, as well as moved to a highly secure setting within the facility.

4. Cooperate with a complete psychiatric evaluation. (9)

9. Refer and arrange for a complete psychiatric evaluation to assess for a prescription for psychopharmacological intervention.

5. Comply with medication recommendations. (10)

10. Monitor the client for psychotropic medication prescription compliance, effectiveness, and side effects.

6. Complete an assessment instrument to assess the depth of depression and suicide potential. (11, 12)

11. Refer and arrange for the client to complete an assessment instrument (e.g., the Beck Depression Inventory or Modified Scale for Suicidal Ideation) to evaluate the depth of depression and suicide potential.

12. Provide the client with objective interpretation of the

depression/suicide risk assessment.

7. Initiate and engage in a psychotherapeutic process. (13, 19)

13. Refer the client for psychotherapy (individual and/or group therapy, depending on the needs of the client, temperament and available resources).

19. Process with the client what he/she has learned about resolution of depression and suicidal urges through participation in therapeutic or self-help treatment.

8. Read material on causes for, recovering from, and coping with depression. (14, 15)

14. Provide the client with a selection of reading options (e.g., *Change Your Brain, Change Your Life* by Amen; *Healing Depression* by Carrigan; *Relaxation and Stress Reduction Workbook* by Davis, McKay, and Robbins; *Undoing Depression* by O'Connor; *Depression: The Way Out of Your Prison* by Rowe; *Breaking the Patterns of Depression* by Yapko) for learning more about depression recovery; process material read.

15. Instruct the client to read at least three chapters from *Depressed Anonymous*; process the content in a subsequent session.

9. Attend a support group focused on depression recovery. (16, 19)

16. Instruct the client to attend a depression self-help group (e.g., Depression Anonymous, Sadness & Sorrow).

19. Process with the client what he/she has learned about resolution of depression and suicidal urges through

10. Verbalize any unresolved grief issues that may be contributing to depression. (17)

11. Attend a grief and loss group to receive support and learn how other people have worked with grief and loss. (18, 19)

12. Contact at least one supportive person daily. (20, 21)

13. List the specific negative self-talk that supports depression. (22)

14. Formulate, in writing, several positive ways to "reframe" the negative self-talk that supports depression. (23)

17. Explore with the client any unresolved grief issues that may be contributing to depression.

18. Instruct client to attend grief/loss support groups (e.g., Bereavement Groups, A Breakfast Group for Widowers, HOPE for Bereaved).

19. Process with the client what he/she has learned about resolution of depression and suicidal urges through participation in therapeutic or self-help treatment.

20. Brainstorm with the client to develop a list of seven people that he/she can reach out to for support when feeling depressed and/or suicidal.

21. Instruct the client to contact at least one supportive person daily; process the benefits of each contact.

22. Assist the client in reviewing and inventorying some of the distorted, negative self-talk that supports depression (e.g., I am no good; it will never get better; it's useless to continue to live).

23. Facilitate a brainstorming inventory of possible alternatives or ways to reframe negative self-talk that supports depression into positive, realistic thoughts (e.g., I do have good qualities; if I just hold on, things may improve; others would be hurt if I died).

15. Establish a regular sleeping and eating pattern. (24, 25)

24. Teach the client the emotional benefits of a regular pattern of sufficient sleep and a nutritious diet routinely implemented; develop a schedule of eating and sleeping regularly.

25. Follow up with the client about his/her progress on maintaining a healthy sleeping and eating pattern.

16. Journal daily about what interferes with eating or sleeping regularly, and develop coping skills. (26, 27)

26. Instruct the client to maintain a daily journal about what keeps him/her from eating or sleeping regularly, and the negative self-talk that accompanies this.

27. Process with the client material in his/her daily journal to counter negative self-statements and reinforce his/her ability to reframe these statements.

17. Identify causes for depression and suicidal ideation. (28)

28. Explore with the client his/her perceived causes for feeling so depression, sorting causes into external (e.g., conflicts with others, rejection) versus internal (e.g., critical of self, hopelessness) stressors.

18. List ways to overcome external causes of depression. (29)

29. Brainstorm ways to cope with or overcome external causes of depression (e.g., learn problem-solving techniques, reach out to others).

19. Reframe distorted self-talk that nurtures internal causes of depression. (23, 27, 30)

23. Facilitate a brainstorming inventory of possible alternatives or ways to 'reframe' negative self-talk that supports depression into positive, realistic thoughts (e.g., I do have good qualities; if I just hold on, things may improve; others would be hurt if I died).

27. Process with the client material in his/her daily journal to counter negative self-statements and reinforce his/her ability to reframe these statements.

30. Review the use of cognitive restructuring techniques to resolve internal causes of depression.

20. Participate in at least six of enjoyable activities in the next four weeks. (31, 32)

31. Engage the client in a brainstorming session of at least 10 activities that he/she might enjoy doing (e.g., painting, pottery, church, music, reading clubs, bowling).

32. Encourage the client to participate in at least six enjoyable activities in the next four weeks; ask him/her to select these activities from his/her list of enjoyable activities and commit to participation.

21. Participate in some sort of physical exercise three times per week. (33, 34, 35)

33. Engage the client in brainstorming different types of physical exercise he/she would be interested in (e.g., walking, biking, hiking, yoga, aerobics, swimming).

34. Instruct the client to read *Exercising Your Way to Better Mental Health: Fight Depression and Alleviate Stress through Exercises* by Leith.

35. Encourage the client to participate in some sort of physical exercise three times per week; schedule the time and type of exercise.

22. Implement relaxation techniques to overcome stress and tension. (36, 37, 38, 39)

36. Teach the client simple, quick relaxation techniques (e.g., deep breathing, counting

backwards, pleasant imagery, worry stone).

37. Instruct the client in a technique for progressive deep muscle relaxation that enables him or her to relax their entire body within 5 to 10 minutes and have them practice this technique daily for at least one week.

38. Instruct the client to read material on relaxation and stress management (e.g., *Relaxation and Stress Reduction Workbook* by Davis, McKay, and Robbins).

39. Refer the client to possible sources for achieving greater relaxation and peace of mind (e.g., health club membership, acupressure, church, yoga, martial arts, pets, hobbies).

23. Learn and implement healthy communication skills that support the expression of thoughts, feelings and needs. (40, 41, 42)

40. Instruct the client in healthy assertive communication skills (e.g., feelings talk, listening skills, asking for help, refusing request).

41. Use modeling, role-playing, and behavior rehearsal to teach the client several conflict communication skills that could improve his/her communication (e.g., double-sided reflections, partially agreeing, agreeing with a twist, "I" statements).

42. Review the client's implementation of new conflict communication skills in daily life; reinforce success and redirect for failure.

24. Retake an assessment instrument to assess the depth of depression and suicide potential. (43, 44)

43. Reassess the client with an assessment instrument (e.g., the Beck Depression Inventory or Modified Scale for Suicidal Ideation) to evaluate depth of depression and suicide potential.

44. Provide the client with an objective interpretation of his/her reassessment scores.

—. _____

_____

—. _____

_____

—. _____

_____

—. _____

_____

—. _____

_____

DIAGNOSTIC SUGGESTIONS:

ICD-9-CM	_ICD-10-CM_	_DSM-5_ Disorder, Condition, or Problem
309.0	F43.21	Adjustment Disorder, With Depressed Mood
296.xx	F31.xx	Bipolar I Disorder
296.89	F31.81	Bipolar II Disorder
300.4	F34.1	Persistent Depressive Disorder
301.13	F34.0	Cyclothymic Disorder
296.2x	F32.x	Major Depressive Disorder, Single Episode
296.3x	F33.x	Major Depressive Disorder, Recurrent Episode
295.70	F25.0	Schizoaffective Disorder, Bipolar Type
295.70	F25.1	Schizoaffective Disorder, Depressive Type
V62.82	Z63.4	Uncomplicated Bereavement
301.7	F60.2	Antisocial Personality Disorder
301.81	F60.81	Narcissistic Personality Disorder
301.83	F60.3	Borderline Personality Disorder
_____	_____	_____
_____	_____	_____

DRIVING-RELATED OFFENSES

BEHAVIORAL DEFINITIONS

1. Drives while under the influence of a mood altering substance (e.g., alcohol, drugs, prescription medicines).
2. Drives with a suspended or revoked license.
3. History of more than five arrests and convictions for traffic violations (e.g., speeding, moving violations).
4. Exhibits a blatant disregard for traffic laws.
5. History of driving with debilitating physical disorders (e.g., epilepsy, hypertension, significant auditory problems, significant visual problems, immobility).
6. History of driving with debilitating cognitive, mood, anxiety or sleep disorders (e.g., brain/head injury, dementia, schizophrenia, anxiety, depression, narcolepsy).
7. Explosive, aggressive outbursts in reaction to stressors while driving (i.e., "road rage" incidents).
8. History of taking undue risks while driving; at times causing accidents for self or others.

—. _____

 _____

—. _____

 _____

LONG-TERM GOALS

1. Eliminate driving while under the influence of mood altering substances.
2. Increase understanding of and compliance with driving/traffic laws.
3. Terminate high-risk driving behavior.

4. Increase responsible monitoring of health and medication concerns that may influence driving safety.
5. Increase ability to cope with angry feelings in a constructive way while driving.

—. _____
_____

—. _____
_____

SHORT-TERM OBJECTIVES

THERAPEUTIC INTERVENTIONS

1. Complete a self-administered driving risk assessment instrument. (1)

1. Administer and score a validated driving risk assessment test (e.g., Driving Assessment Survey [DAS] or Adult Substance Use and Driving Survey [ASUDS]) with the client.

2. Receive normative feedback (objective personal score comparisons with established normative data for related populations) regarding scores on a driving risk assessment instrument. (2)

2. Provide the client with an objective interpretation and feedback (e.g., objective personal score comparisons with established normative data for related populations) of his/her scores and profile on the validated driving risk assessment instrument.

3. Describe history of driving-related infractions. (3)

3. Explore the client's history of driving-related infractions.

4. Visit the state Department of Motor Vehicles (DMV) information on what the requirements are to get license back. (4)

4. Instruct the client to visit the State Department of Motor Vehicles (DMV) for information on what the requirements are for him/her to get his/her license back.

5. Design a plan to meet DMV requirements to get driver's license back. (5, 6)

5. Assist the client in prioritizing DMV requirements to get driver's license reinstated.

	6. Guide the client in designing a plan to meet DMV requirement for license reinstatement (e.g., complete treatment requirements; install interlock device that prevents a car from starting without the driver blowing a clean breathalyzer, as evidence that the driver has not consumed any alcohol; obtain SR-22—special risk insurance required by the DMV in case of a DUI).
6. Identify the feelings that arise due to loss of the privilege to drive. (7)	7. Facilitate a discussion with the client to identify the feelings that arise due to the loss of his/her driving privilege (e.g., guilt, anger, frustration, hopelessness).
7. Brainstorm ways of getting around without driving. (8)	8. Guide the client in a brainstorming session to list alternative ways of getting around without driving (e.g., taking the bus, contacting car pooling programs, asking friends, moving closer to work to allow for walking or riding a bike).
8. Attend and complete an alcohol and other drug (AOD) assessment. (9)	9. Refer the client to an agency or professional qualified in AOD assessment, to conduct an initial screening assessment, and if deemed appropriate, a full differential assessment.
9. Cooperate with a psychiatric referral. (10, 11)	10. Refer and arrange for the client to participate in a psychiatric evaluation if indicated; include an assessment of emotional, cognitive, physical, or medication factors that may influence driving safety.

11. Arrange for any necessary monitoring of the client's compliance with medication prescriptions.

10. Attend and complete an auditory, visual, or medical examination if indicated. (11, 12)

11. Arrange for any necessary monitoring of the client's compliance with medication prescriptions.

12. Refer and arrange for an auditory, visual, or medical examination if indicated.

11. Comply with recommended treatment as directed by the professionals. (11, 13)

11. Arrange for any necessary monitoring of the client's compliance with medication prescriptions.

13. Review with results of all assessments with the client and assign him/her to comply with treatment as recommended by the professionals.

12. Verbalize a clear understanding of traffic/driving laws. (14)

14. Assign the client to read about traffic/driving laws (e.g., *Responsible Driving* by American Automobile Association); process his/her understanding of the material.

13. Attend a highway safety and alcohol and drug education program. (15, 24)

15. Assign the client to attend a highway safety program that includes an alcohol and drug education program.

24. Instruct the client to attend a Victim Impact Panel where driving accident victims or their family members describe their grief and anger caused by injury or death.

14. Attend a defensive driving course. (16, 17)

16. Assign the client to attend a defensive driving course.

17. Process principles the client has learned in the didactic sessions and assist him/her in applying

these principles to his/her daily life through role-playing or modeling.

15. Verbalize an understanding of the causes of and remedies for road rage and aggressive driving. (18, 19, 20, 21)

18. Assign the client to read about road rage and aggressive driving (e.g., *Road Rage and Aggressive Driving: Steering Clear of Highway Warfare* by James and Nahl; *Drive Right* by Johnson, Crabb, and Opfer; *Road Rage to Road-Wise* by Larson and Rodriguez; *Bullies Behind the Wheel: How Your Reactions to Aggressive Drivers Can Cause Road Rage, or Prevent It!* by Shorey).

19. Teach the client a basic objective perspective on anger that minimally includes instruction on the Antecedents of anger, Behavior and physical features associated with anger, and Consequences of anger (i.e., the ABCs of anger); apply these concepts to his/her road rage problem.

20. Assign specific exercises from an established curriculum and workbook for anger (e.g., *The Prepare Curriculum* by Goldstein; *Reasoning and Rehabilitation* by Ross, Fabiano, and Ross; *Controlling Anger and Learning to Manage [CALM] Program* by Winogron, VanDieten, and Gauzas; *The EQUIP Program: Teaching Youth to Think and Act Responsibly Through a Peer Helping Approach* by Gibbs, Potter, and Goldstein; *Treating Alcohol Dependence* by Monti, Abrams, Kadden, and Cooney;

or *Criminal Conduct and Substance Abuse Treatment: Strategies for Self-Improvement and Change* by Wanberg and Milkman).

21. Teach the client the insidious aspects of anger that displace or cover up other feelings (e.g., pain, worry, guilt) and reinforce ignorance through projection; explore for the presence of feelings beneath his/her anger.

16. Demonstrate an understanding of the use of quick anger reducers. (22, 23)

22. Teach the client simple techniques (e.g., deep breathing, counting backwards, pleasant imagery, worry stone) for immediately reducing anger elevations in a variety of situations, including prior to or during driving.

23. Instruct the client in a technique for progressive muscle relaxation that enables him or her to relax their entire body within 5 to 10 minutes and have them practice this technique daily for at least one week; emphasize the benefits of reduced stress on safe driving.

17. Attend a Victim Impact Panel. (24)

24. Instruct the client to attend a Victim Impact Panel where driving accident victims or their family members describe their grief and anger caused by injury or death.

18. Describe, in writing, what are the elements of safe driving and its benefits. (25, 26)

25. Guide the client in defining the essential elements of his/her safe driving (e.g., being familiar with the traffic laws, driving while ability is unimpaired, paying attention to others on the road).

26. Process with the client his/her decisional balance (pros and cons) of being a safe driver; write out a list of the pros and cons.

19. List the responsibilities a driver has to the community. (27)

27. Assist the client in listing what his/her responsibilities are to the community as a driver (recognizing that driving is a privilege, recognizing the effects one's actions have on others, having a positive attitude toward others using the road).

20. Verbalize common triggers for unsafe driving that people experience that keep them from being safe drivers. (28)

28. Guide the client discussion in a brainstorming session that identifies common triggers that keep people from being safe drivers (preoccupation with emotional events, driving while under the influence of drugs and alcohol, overreacting to others on the road).

21. Sort generic triggers into those that are internal versus external. (29)

29. Ask client to sort these potential triggers for unsafe driving into internal (e.g., impatient, preoccupied, distressed) and external (e.g., being threatened, using a cell phone, using an unmaintenanced car) categories.

22. Brainstorm ways of overcoming each of these internal and external triggers. (30, 31)

30. Brainstorm ways of effectively overcoming each of these internal and external triggers (e.g., using anger reducers, not having emotion-laden conversations while driving, pulling over, using a hands-free set, cell phone).

31. Teach the client about how emotional/physical arousal influences performance by

explaining that as emotional/physical arousal increases, less attention can be paid to the activity at hand, therefore performance is affected.

23. Identify distorted self-talk that influences unsafe driving. (32, 33, 34)

32. Reinforce and elaborate on an A-B-C behavioral model by explaining the role of self-talk in influencing the implementation of either negative or positive behavior.

33. Assist the client in identifying some of the self-statements used in response to triggers (e.g., I can drive faster than the car that passed me; I can make the light even if it is yellow).

34. Probe with the client what the consequences might be for using his/her most common distorted self-statements.

24. Formulate, in writing, several ways to reframe the self-talk that represent obstacles to successfully modifying unsafe driving. (35)

35. Facilitate a brainstorming inventory of positive self-statements to the trigger situations that the client finds most frequently (or intensively) associated with unsafe driving (e.g., I'm driving fast enough; Someone's unsafe driving should not make me drive unsafely; I better stop on yellow or I might cause an accident).

25. Complete a reassessment with a valid driving risk assessment instrument. (36)

36. Reassess the client with a validated driving risk assessment (e.g., Driving Assessment Survey [DAS], Adult Substance Use and Driving Survey [ASUDS]).

26. Receive normative feedback regarding reassessment scores on a driving risk assessment instruments that includes presentation of "gain scores" (i.e., the difference between Time 1 and Time 2). (37)

37. Provide the client with an objective interpretation and feedback of his/her reassessment scores and profile on validated driving risk assessment test he/she completed.

__. _____   __. _____
   _____   _____
__. _____   __. _____
   _____   _____
__. _____   __. _____
   _____   _____

DIAGNOSTIC SUGGESTIONS:

ICD-9-CM	_ICD-10-CM_	_DSM-5_ Disorder, Condition, or Problem
305.00	F10.10	Alcohol Use Disorder, Mild
303.90	F10.20	Alcohol Use Disorder, Moderate or Severe
305.20	F12.10	Cannabis Use Disorder, Mild
304.30	F12.20	Cannabis Use Disorder, Moderate or Severe
305.60	F14.10	Cocaine Use Disorder, Mild
304.20	F14.20	Cocaine Use Disorder, Moderate or Severe
309.3	F43.24	Adjustment Disorder, With Disturbance of Conduct
312.89	F91.8	Other Specified Disruptive, Impulse Control, and Conduct Disorder
296.89	F31.81	Bipolar II Disorder
296.xx	F31.1x	Bipolar I Disorder, Manic
301.13	F34.0	Cyclothymic Disorder
301.7	F60.2	Antisocial Personality Disorder
301.81	F60.81	Narcissistic Personality Disorder
_____	_____	_____
_____	_____	_____

FAMILY CONFLICT/ALIENATION

BEHAVIORAL DEFINITIONS

1. A pattern of frequent conflicts with family members that often triggers involvement in criminal behavior.
2. Unable to establish and maintain healthy, pro-social relationships with family members due to their involvement in criminal and/or substance abuse behavior.
3. Family members are not actively supportive of the client's attempts to refrain from or terminate criminal lifestyle.
4. Current physical, emotional, or psychological abuse in the family.
5. Hypersensitivity to perceived disapproval, rejection, or criticism of family that leads to superficial or dishonest relationships with the family.
6. Lack of communication or contact with family leading to feelings of isolation, alienation, or depression.
7. Alienated from family members due to own history of criminal behavior.

—. _____
    _____
—. _____
    _____
—. _____
    _____

LONG-TERM GOALS

1. Manage relationships with pro-criminal family members by establishing boundaries to reduce risk for relapse or recidivism.

2. Gain a greater understanding about how family interactions affect behavioral choices.
3. Develop and maintain healthy, pro-social relationships with pro-social family members.
4. Communicate needs or wishes to family members in a constructive manner.
5. Terminate reacting to family conflict with criminal behavior.

—. _____
   _____

—. _____
   _____

—. _____
   _____

SHORT-TERM OBJECTIVES	THERAPEUTIC INTERVENTIONS
1. Describe current relationships with family members. (1, 2)	1. Explore the client's current relationships with family members, paying special attention to issues of dysfunction.
	2. Assist the client in identifying those family members who are involved in deviant behavior (e.g., substance abuse, domestic violence, child abuse, criminal behavior).
2. Identify, practice, and implement new techniques for distancing self from criminal family members. (3, 4, 5, 6)	3. Teach the client new strategies (e.g., setting clear boundaries, telling family his/her goal of avoiding criminal behavior, assertively saying no) for distancing himself/herself from criminal family members.
	4. Use role-play, modeling, and behavior rehearsal to teach the client how to use the new distancing techniques; provide him/her with positive feedback

for effort, as well as suggestions for improvement in implementation.

5. Ask the client to choose one deviant family member that he/she feels comfortable distancing himself/herself from and implement the new distancing techniques with that person.

6. Debrief with the client about how new distancing techniques worked with the chosen family member; provide positive reinforcement and feedback for improvement.

3. Identify ways to maintain a limited relationship with pro-criminal family members without engaging in deviant behavior. (7)

7. Assist the client in identifying ways (e.g., moving out of the house, setting clear boundaries, expressing his/her anti-crime goals, assertively saying no) he/she can maintain his/her limited relationships with some of his/her criminal family members without engaging in deviant behavior.

4. Identify causes of past or present conflict in family relationships. (8, 9)

8. Explore the causes of the client's past or present conflicts in family relationships.

9. Confront the client's attempts to minimize his/her poor management of behavior to project blame onto others, or to discount his/her contribution to conflict and the consequences of his/her behavior.

5. Identify dysfunctional roles that exist in family relationships. (10, 11)

10. Identify with the client any dysfunctional roles or patterns that exist in the family (e.g., roles: victim, persecutor, rescuer, scapegoat, hero, enabler; patterns: narcissism,

alcohol/drug abuse, violence) and what part the client plays in perpetuating these roles.

11. Encourage and support the client to be aware of and to share his/her feelings and thoughts that arise when discussing family relationships; pay special attention to interrupting patterns of dissociative behavior to prevent retraumatization.

6. Cooperate with a referral to and participate in family therapy. (12, 13)

12. Refer the client and his/her family to a family therapeutic process.

13. Process with the client any relevant issues that arose during family therapy.

7. Identify how childhood experiences and family values have influenced current lifestyle. (14)

14. Assist the client in identifying ways that his/her childhood experiences and family values have influenced his/her current lifestyle (e.g., employment, involvement in deviancy) and behavior (e.g., racism, homophobia, issues related to power and control).

8. Highlight those values or attitudes you want to change and how to do this. (15)

15. Ask the client to indicate those values or attitudes he/she wants to hold in his/her life and those he/she wants to change; write positive alternative values and indicate how they will be rein-forced (e.g., pro-social friends, church attendance, education).

9. Identify and replace the negative self-talk that has resulted from childhood experiences or family relationships. (16, 17)

16. Assist the client in identifying the negative self-talk that has resulted from childhood experiences and family relationships (e.g., everything is my fault, I will never amount to anything, I am the black sheep

of the family, aggressiveness is the only way to get what I need).

17. Facilitate a brainstorming inventory of possible positive, realistic, and pro-social alternative ways to reframe the dysfunctional self-talk that has resulted from childhood experiences and family relationships.

10. Write and verbalize an action plan for dealing with resentments toward family members. (18, 19, 20)

18. Assign the client the task of listing the resentments built toward family members using a systematic debriefing format (e.g., a 12-step model: who are you angry at, why are you angry, how the hurt affects me, my role in the situation).

19. Assist the client in writing an action plan for working with each of the resentments toward family members that addresses the triggers, cues, anger reducers, self-statements, and self-evaluation.

20. Assign the client a selection of reading materials focused on overcoming resentments and conflict in family relationships (e.g., *I Thought We'd Never Speak Again* by Davis, *Growing Up Again* by Illsley and Dawson, *Family Estrangements* by Le Bey, and *Make Peace with Anyone* by Lieberman).

11. Learn and implement healthy communication and active listening skills. (21, 22, 23)

21. Use role-play, modeling, and behavior rehearsal to teach the client the fundamental skills of active listening (e.g., asking open-ended questions, affirming the speaker with eye

contact and nodding, reflecting the feelings behind the communication, summarizing the content, and eliciting self-motivating statements) and how to implement these skills in everyday communication.

22. Describe and model for the client several conflict communication skills (e.g., double-sided reflections, partially agreeing, agreeing with a twist, "I" statements) that could improve his/her communication.

23. Assign specific exercises from a workbook to teach effective communication skills (e.g., *The Prepare Curriculum* by Goldstein; *Reasoning and Rehabilitation* by Ross, Fabiano, and Ross; *Controlling Anger and Learning to Manage [CALM] Program* by Winogron, VanDieten, and Bauzas; *Anger Workout Book* by Weisinger; *Criminal Conduct and Substance Abuse Treatment* by Wanberg and Milkman).

12. Increase the use of assertiveness versus passivity or aggression. (24, 25, 26)

24. Teach the client the differences between passive, passive-aggressive, aggressive, and assertive styles of interpersonal communication that minimally includes: tactics associated with each style, short-term consequences, and long-term consequences associated with each style.

25. Guide the client in a brainstorming session that identifies the common benefits resulting from assertive

communication skills (e.g., get needs or desires met, promotes understanding, clarifies feelings to others, establishes boundaries for self and others).

26. Use role-play, modeling, and behavior rehearsal to teach the client assertive ways of communicating his/her wants and needs; encourage implementation of assertiveness in the client's daily life.

13. Implement reflection to deepen understanding of the other person's point of view. (27)

27. Role-play with the client seeing and stating another's point of view using reflection (e.g., "You feel angry because to you it seems like I come and go in this family as I please"); encourage the client's implementation of reflection in daily communication.

14. Implement the boundaries, communication, and listening skills learned with at least one family member every day for the next three weeks. (28, 29, 30, 31)

28. Teach the client about boundaries, how they are semipermeable with the client having the choice of when to exercise strong boundaries (e.g., saying no) and when to be flexible.

29. Facilitate a role-play with the client practicing the exercise of setting boundaries in different family situations; provide the client feedback on the role-play and continued exercising of boundaries in his/her interactions with family members.

30. Instruct the client to implement the boundary, communication, and listening skills learned with at least one family member

every day for the next three weeks; advise the client to journal about what skills were used, how it affected the interaction and any thoughts/feelings that arose in the interaction.

31. Debrief with the client about his/her experience using skills learned with family members. Reinforce positive efforts and redirect for failure.

—. _____   —. _____
   _____   _____
—. _____   —. _____
   _____   _____
—. _____   —. _____
   _____   _____

DIAGNOSTIC SUGGESTIONS:

ICD-9-CM	_ICD-10-CM_	_DSM-5_ Disorder, Condition, or Problem
300.4	F34.1	Persistent Depressive Disorder
300.00	F41.9	Unspecified Anxiety Disorder
312.34	F63.81	Intermittent Explosive Disorder
303.90	F10.20	Alcohol Use Disorder, Moderate or Severe
304.20	F14.20	Cocaine Use Disorder, Moderate or Severe
301.7	F60.2	Antisocial Personality Disorder
301.6	F60.7	Dependent Personality Disorder
301.83	F60.3	Borderline Personality Disorder
301.9	F60.9	Unspecified Personality Disorder
_____	_____	_____
_____	_____	_____

FAMILY CRIMINALITY/DEVIANCE

BEHAVIORAL DEFINITIONS

1. Family members are involved in criminal behavior.
2. Demonstrates acceptance of family members' criminal behavior.
3. Looks up to pro-criminal family members and desires to emulate these individuals.
4. Encouraged by family members to participate in deviant behavior and/or reinforced for engaging in criminal behavior.
5. Participates in criminal behavior with family members.
6. Willing to protect and cover up family members' deviant behavior.
7. Prior attempts to refrain from criminal involvement with family members have been unsuccessful.
8. Unable to establish and maintain healthy, pro-social relationships with family members due to their involvement in deviancy.
9. Family members are not actively supportive of the client's attempts to refrain from or terminate criminal lifestyle.

—. _____
_____
_____
—. _____
_____
—. _____
_____

LONG-TERM GOALS

1. Eliminate involvement in criminal behavior with family members.
2. Significantly reduce or eliminate association with family members that are involved in criminal behavior.

3. Learn to manage pro-criminal relationships with family members by establishing boundaries to reduce risk for relapse or recidivism.
4. Gain a greater understanding about how family interactions effect lifestyle choices.
5. Develop and maintain healthy, pro-social relationships with pro-social family members.

—. _____

_____

—. _____

_____

—. _____

_____

SHORT-TERM OBJECTIVES

THERAPEUTIC INTERVENTIONS

1. List all family members, acknowledging those that are involved in deviant behavior. (1, 2)

1. Ask the client to list all his/her nuclear and extended family members with whom he/she has a relationship, denoting criminal family members with an asterisk.

2. Review the list of family members with the client; explore his/her feelings and thoughts about number of deviant family members compared to pro-social members.

2. Identify the history of involvement in and consequences of criminal behavior with family members beginning in childhood or adolescence. (3)

3. Explore the client's history of involvement in criminal behavior with family members; probe the consequences of such behavior and the family's reaction to such behavior.

3. Identify situations where family members have pressured or encouraged participation in criminal

4. Ask the client to share situations when he/she has felt pressured to participate in deviant activities with family

behavior and the outcome of each situation. (4)

4. Identify feelings that occur when pressured by family members to participate in criminal behavior. (5)

5. Identify factors that have led to the involvement in criminal behavior with family members. (6, 7, 8)

6. List 10 positive and 10 negative consequences of having family members who are involved in criminal behavior. (9)

members; what was the result of this pressure and why that result?

5. Explore the client's feelings associated with family pressure to participate in antisocial activities (e.g., loyalty, guilt, desire to please, need for acceptance).

6. Explain the dynamics of learning theory to the client (e.g., modeling and reinforcement); explore how his/her involvement in criminal behavior with family members can be explained using learning theory.

7. Teach the client the various factors that can lead to becoming involved in criminal behavior with family members (e.g., modeling, low self-esteem, need for acceptance, admiration of elders, loyalty).

8. Assist the client in generating a list of his/her own personal factors that have led him/her to become involved in deviant behavior with family members; review and process this list, reinforcing his/her effort to achieve a better understanding of himself/herself.

9. Ask the client to list some of the positive (e.g., excitement, adventure, familiarity) and some of the negative (e.g., anxiety, being pressured into criminal behavior, getting caught) consequences of having family members that are involved in deviant behavior.

7. List the costs and benefits of changing versus not changing the prevailing personal pattern of involvement with criminal family members. (10)

8. Compare the values, traits, attributes, and attitudes of criminal family members with those of self. (11)

9. Identify the needs that are met when participating in criminal behavior with family members which could be met with pro-social behavior. (12)

10. Verbalize a resolution of feelings associated with ending relationships with family members who are involved in criminal behavior. (13)

11. List reasons past attempts to distance self from deviant family members were unsuccessful. (14)

12. Identify, practice, and implement new techniques for distancing self from criminal family members. (15, 16, 17, 18)

10. Assist the client in listing the costs and benefits of changing versus not changing the prevailing pattern of involvement with criminal family members.

11. Assign the client to list the values, traits, attributes, and attitudes his/her deviant family members possess; review the list for completeness, exploring for any conflict between his/her values and attitudes, and those of his/her family members.

12. Explore the client's feelings that occur when he/she participates in criminal behavior with family members; note if there are needs that are met through this antisocial behavior that could be met pro-socially.

13. Explore the client's feelings about ending his/her relationships with criminal family members; process ambivalent feelings (e.g., feelings of both betrayal and relief) or resistant feelings.

14. Explore the client's past attempts to distance himself/herself from deviant family members, assessing the reasons past attempts were unsuccessful and identifying triggers (e.g., people, places, things), ambivalence, and unclear boundaries that led to failure.

15. Teach the client new strategies (e.g., setting clear boundaries, telling family his/her goal of avoiding criminal behavior, saying no) for distancing

himself/herself from criminal family members.

16. Role-play with the client using the new distancing techniques; provide him/her with positive feedback for effort, as well as suggestions for improvement in implementation.

17. Assign the client to choose one deviant family member that he/she feels comfortable distancing himself/herself from and implement the new distancing techniques with that person.

18. Debrief with the client about how new distancing techniques worked with chosen family member; provide positive reinforcement and feedback for improvement.

13. Describe ways to maintain relationships with pro-criminal family members without participating in criminal behavior. (19)

19. Assist the client in identifying ways (e.g., moving out of the house, setting clear boundaries, expressing his/her goal, saying no) he/she can maintain his/her relationships with some of his/her criminal family members without engaging in deviant behavior.

14. Identify high-risk situations that could lead to participating in criminal behavior with family members and develop a written prevention plan for these high-risk situation. (20)

20. Highlight with the client some of the high-risk situations that may lead to relapse (e.g., family pressure, alcohol or other drug use) if he/she maintains relationships with deviant family members; develop a written prevention plan for avoiding in deviant behavior in such high-risk situations.

15. Implement healthy communication skills to establish boundaries with deviant family members. (21, 22, 23, 24)

21. Teach the client how to establish boundaries with family members using healthy communication skills such as assertiveness techniques, distancing practices, and refusal skills (e.g., saying "no"; stating needs in a clear, friendly manner; stating complaints in a clear, friendly manner; using "I" messages).

22. Role-play with the client using healthy communication skills in order to practice establishing boundaries with deviant family members; provide him/her with positive reinforcement as well as suggestions for improvement.

23. Assign the client to choose one family member who he/she would like to maintain his/her relationship with and practice using new assertive communication skills with that person to establish boundaries.

24. Debrief with the client about how the new communication skills worked with chosen family member; provide him/her with positive reinforcement and feedback for improvement.

16. Identify instances of childhood abuse, neglect, and/or abandonment and the emotional consequences of these painful experiences. (25, 26)

25. Explore the client's family history for instances of abuse, neglect, and/or abandonment.

26. Probe the client's feelings of hurt, anger, and disappointment related to experiences of abuse, neglect, and/or abandonment.

17. Verbalize how criminal behavior has become a means of attaining family acceptance. (27)

18. Identify any family members who have pro-social values and lifestyle. (28)

19. Implement behaviors that will build relationships with pro-social family members. (29, 30)

20. Identify personal values, traits, feelings, and attitudes that may be preventing pro-social relationships with family members from developing. (31)

21. Formulate several ways to reframe each of the feelings and attitudes that represent

27. Explore whether the client has become desperate in his/her search for acceptance, love, and recognition from parents and family; relate this desperation to engaging in criminal behavior to prove loyalty and/or find acceptance.

28. Explore the client's nuclear and extended family for any models of pro-social values, attitudes, and behavior.

29. Ask the client to reach out to any pro-social family members to satisfy his/her need for "belonging"; assist him/her in listing ways to build relationships with these pro-social family members (e.g., writing letter, making phone call, planning for a recreational activity).

30. Ask the client to project himself/herself 10 years into the future and predict what current relationships will be most beneficial to him/her; point out the long-term probable negative consequences of aligning with pro-criminal family members.

31. Assist the client in identifying personal values and feelings that may be preventing him/her from establishing healthy, pro-social relationships with pro-social family members (e.g., they will think I don't like them, they will feel betrayed).

32. Assist the client in formulating several ways to reframe each of the feelings and attitudes that

obstacles to establishing new relationships with family members. (32)

22. Become involved in a support group for people with criminal family members and participate for at least two weeks. (33, 34)

represent obstacles to establishing healthy relationships with pro-social family members (e.g., they will respect my decision).

33. Direct the client to become involved for at least two weeks in a support group for people with family members involved in criminal behavior.

34. Debrief with the client about his/her involvement in the support group; provide him/her with positive reinforcement for effort and involvement.

—. _____   —. _____
    _____   _____
—. _____   —. _____
    _____   _____
—. _____   —. _____
    _____   _____

DIAGNOSTIC SUGGESTIONS:

ICD-9-CM	ICD-10-CM	DSM-5 Disorder, Condition, or Problem
300.23	F40.10	Social Anxiety Disorder (Social Phobia)
312.34	F63.81	Intermittent Explosive Disorder
300.4	F34.1	Persistent Depressive Disorder
301.20	F60.1	Schizoid Personality Disorder
301.7	F60.2	Antisocial Personality Disorder
301.82	F60.6	Avoidant Personality Disorder
301.6	F60.7	Dependent Personality Disorder
_____	_____	_____
_____	_____	_____

FINANCIAL MANAGEMENT PROBLEMS

BEHAVIORAL DEFINITIONS

1. Frequently overspends, resulting in bounced checks, maximized credit cards, repossessions, defaulted loans, and/or bankruptcy.
2. Fails to prioritize financial obligations to ensure that all necessary expenses are paid before optional expenses are incurred.
3. Routinely fails to adequately estimate projected budget for actual living expenses.
4. A long-term lack of discipline in money management has led to excessive indebtedness.
5. A pattern of impulsive spending that does not consider the eventual financial consequences.
6. Dependent on others for meeting own basic needs for food, clothing, and shelter.
7. Credit rating is low or nonexistent.
8. Limited financial management abilities result in frequent self-disapproval and diminished self-concept.
9. Resorts to illegal behaviors to obtain money to cover living expenses.

—. _____
_____

—. _____
_____

—. _____
_____

LONG-TERM GOALS

1. Establish a clear income and expense budget that will meet bill payment demands.
2. Develop the ability to prioritize financial obligations and the discipline to live within those limits.
3. Attain financial independence by maximizing income and terminating unnecessary spending.
4. Maintain employment as a legal means of obtaining income and responsibly manage finances to meet obligations

—. _____

_____

SHORT-TERM OBJECTIVES

1. Describe a history of inability to manage finances and the consequences of such inabilities. (1)

2. Discuss the pros and cons of not adhering to a financial management schedule. (2)

3. List the costs and benefits of changing the prevailing personal pattern of poor finance management as well as the costs and benefits of not changing the pattern. (3)

4. List the common steps and strategies for financial management that most often assure success. (4, 5)

THERAPEUTIC INTERVENTIONS

1. Explore the client's history of an inability to manage finances and the consequences he/she has experienced due to poor financial management.

2. Have the client discuss what he/she sees as the pros (e.g., more flexibility, avoid responsibility) and cons (e.g., failure to meet deadlines, not dependable) of not adhering to a financial management schedule.

3. Ask the client to list in writing the costs and benefits of changing versus not changing the prevailing personal pattern of not managing finances efficiently or effectively.

4. Explain effective strategies to improve financial management abilities (e.g., carry a day planner with them, developing a detailed daily schedule, prioritize tasks).

    5. Teach the client the ideal steps (e.g., prioritize obligations, realistically estimate time to accomplish tasks, adhere to schedule, evaluate) involved in successful financial management.

5. Attend a financial management training class. (6)

    6. Assign the client to attend some form of financial management training, skill-building programs or classes.

6. Read material about financial management. (7)

    7. Provide the client with appropriate workbooks and other reading materials (e.g., *The Money Trap: A Practical Program to Stop Self-Defeating Financial Habits So You Can Reclaim Your Grip on Life* by Gallen, *The Budget Kit: The Common Cents Money Management Workbook* by Lawrence, *The Road to Wealthy: A Comprehensive Guide to Your Money* by Orman, *Suze Orman's Financial Guidebook: Putting the 9 Steps to Work* by Orman, and *Long-Term Care: Your Financial Planning Guide* by Shelton) relevant to providing information regarding financial management skills and strategies.

7. Identify past successful and unsuccessful attempts to manage finances in a more constructive manner. (8)

    8. Ask the client to share his/her past attempts to manage finances in a more constructive manner, exploring attempts that were both successful and unsuccessful.

8. Assess reasons past attempts were either successful or unsuccessful and write out new strategies for improving financial management based on assessment. (9, 10)

    9. Assist the client in assessing reasons some of the past attempts at financial management were successful, whereas others were unsuccessful.

9. Make a list of all personal obligations that are required to be met. (11)

10. Have client write out new strategies for improving financial management based on feedback and assessment.

11. Instruct the client to make a list of all personal obligations he/she has that are required to be met.

10. Prioritize personal obligations in terms of importance. (12, 13)

12. Teach the client how to prioritize obligations based on level of importance (e.g., deadlines, needs versus wants) to help ensure that the most important obligations are met before less important ones.

13. Ask the client to prioritize his/her list of obligations; placing what he/she sees as the most important obligation at the top of the list and continuing to do so until entire list has been numbered.

11. Receive feedback about how well the personal obligation task list has been prioritized and then rework list to include feedback. (14, 15)

14. Review the client's list of personal obligations, providing him/her with feedback about how well the list has been prioritized.

15. Have the client rework list based on feedback.

12. Identify a situation where unrealistic expectations were formed regarding how long it would take to accomplish a task, including the consequences of such unrealistic expectations. (16)

16. Ask the client to describe a situation where he/she developed unrealistic expectations of how long it would take to accomplish a task, making sure he/she includes the consequences of such unrealistic expectations.

13. Estimate how much time is required to accomplish each personal obligation task. (17, 18)

17. Teach the client how to estimate the amount of time it will take to accomplish tasks (e.g., consider the scope of task, review similar experiences,

allow for transition or off-task time) to help ensure that realistic time lines are formed.

18. Ask the client to estimate how much time he/she thinks each task on his/her personal obligation list will take; review his/her estimated times, making sure the estimates are realistic.

14. Based on the prioritized list and estimated times, develop a daily schedule that can be followed in order to meet the personal obligations. (19, 20)

19. Ask the client to develop a daily schedule based on his/her list of obligations.

20. Review the client's daily schedule with him/her, providing him/her with positive reinforcement regarding effort as well as feedback about how to improve schedule.

15. Commit to following the newly developed schedule for one week. (21)

21. Solicit the client's commitment to following the newly developed schedule for one week.

16. Maintain a financial management journal, keeping track of challenges, accomplishments and failures. (22)

22. Ask the client to maintain a financial management journal, including challenges, accomplishments and failures he/she has experienced.

17. Modify financial management schedule based on personal experience and feedback. (23, 24)

23. Debrief the client about how well he/she was able to stick to the weekly financial management schedule, providing him/her with positive reinforcement for successes as well as feedback for improvements.

24. Ask the client to incorporate feedback into schedule and commit to following the schedule for at least one month, while maintaining a journal about the experience.

18. Debrief and receive feedback on a weekly basis about how well efforts to manage finances are going. (25)

25. Meet with the client weekly to discuss progress of managing finances and meeting obligations in a timely manner; provide him/her with positive support, as well as suggestions for improvement.

—. _____

—. _____

—. _____

—. _____

—. _____

—. _____

DIAGNOSTIC SUGGESTIONS:

ICD-9-CM	_ICD-10-CM_	_DSM-5_ Disorder, Condition, or Problem
308.3	F43.0	Acute Stress Disorder
309.24	F43.22	Adjustment Disorder, With Anxiety
309.0	F43.21	Adjustment Disorder, With Depressed Mood
300.02	F41.1	Generalized Anxiety Disorder
296.xx	F31.1x	Bipolar I Disorder, Manic
296.89	F31.81	Bipolar II Disorder
296.xx	F32.x	Major Depressive Disorder, Single Episode
296.xx	F33.x	Major Depressive Disorder, Recurrent Episode
301.7	F60.2	Antisocial Personality Disorder
301.83	F60.3	Borderline Personality Disorder
_____	_____	_____
_____	_____	_____

GENDER IDENTIFICATION ISSUES

BEHAVIORAL DEFINITIONS

1. Confused sexual proclivity resulting in marginalized self-concept and lifestyle.
2. Sense of inappropriateness in assigned gender role that results in significant distress or social isolation.
3. Hatred for members of the opposite sex.
4. Rebellion against gender role resulting in impairment in social, occupational, or other areas of functioning.
5. Gender or sexual proclivity discomfort leads to involvement in an environment with excessive criminogenic influences (e.g., criminal peers, substance abuse, violence).

—. _____

_____

—. _____

_____

LONG-TERM GOALS

1. Increased sense of comfort with sexual proclivity and gender.
2. Balanced lifestyle in accordance with sexual identity development.
3. Integrate a positive sexual identity into the client's total self-concept.
4. Increased respect for self, and others with different gender and/or sexual orientation.
5. Incorporate a clear definition of own gender and sexual orientation into life to resume a healthy level of functioning.

—. _____
_____
—. _____
_____

SHORT-TERM OBJECTIVES	THERAPEUTIC INTERVENTIONS
1. Describe sense of identity and struggles with gender and sexual proclivity. (1)	1. Explore the unique experiences of the client with gender and sexual proclivity to help him/her to accept the identity that is most comfortable for him/her.
2. Initiate and engage in a therapeutic process (individual and/or group therapy) with professional counselors knowledgeable in gender identification issues. (2)	2. Refer the client to a therapeutic process (individual and/or group therapy) with professional counselors knowledgeable in gender identification issues.
3. Explore the meaning of sexual identity and the thoughts, attitudes, feelings, and actions related to it. (3, 4)	3. Explore and define with the client the meaning of sexual identity (that it concerns socially contracted experiences of identity and of membership in groups that have their own cultures) and identify the thoughts (e.g., "Who am I?"), attitudes (e.g., real men don't cry), and feelings (e.g., fear, doubt, confusion) related to it.
	4. Instruct the client in understanding the relationship among thoughts, attitudes, feelings, and actions.
4. Explore the familial, social, environmental, and political factors that affect identity development. (5)	5. Explore with the client pertinent familial, social, environmental, and political factors that have influenced or affected his/her identity development.

5. Identify the nature and origin of beliefs about sexuality and gender roles. (6, 7, 8, 9)

6. Instruct the client to write a journal about the questions "Who am I?" as related to gender identity and sexual proclivity; process with the client any relevant issues that arise through the journaling process.

7. Assist the client in identifying his/her beliefs about sexuality and gender roles (e.g., anything but heterosexuality is a sin, a woman's place is at home).

8. Encourage the client to identify which beliefs about sexual identity and gender role were taught, held, or influenced by the family of origin.

9. Explore with the client which beliefs about sexual identity and gender role he/she wants to continue to hold and those that do not serve him/her in building a positive sense of self.

6. Identify and replace negative ways used to deal with discomfort around own gender identity and sexual proclivity. (10, 11)

10. Instruct the client to list some negative ways he/she uses to deal with discomfort around his/her gender identity and sexual proclivity (e.g., substance abuse, unsafe sexual behavior, self-mutilation, violence).

11. Brainstorm with the client some positive ways to deal with discomfort around his/her gender identity and sexual proclivity (e.g., using a support system, journaling, learning how others have dealt with it).

7. Acknowledge difficulty in accepting or being tolerant of others' differences. (12, 13)

12. Explore with the client his/her negative (e.g., violence, abuse) responses to disapproval of others' sexual orientation.

13. Explore with the client his/her difficulty in accepting or being tolerant of others' sexual identity differences.

8. Brainstorm ways that would help increase tolerance or acceptance of others' differences. (14)

14. Brainstorm with the client ways that would help increase tolerance or acceptance of others' differences (e.g., empathy training, educating oneself, listening skills).

9. Identify constructive coping skills to manage internalized and externalized homophobia or heterosexism. (15, 16)

15. Explore with the client constructive ways to manage (e.g., realistic self-talk, self-acceptance, using social support) his/her internalized or externalized homophobia or heterosexism to develop a positive sense of self.

16. Provide the client with a selection of reading materials to develop a positive sense of self in spite of gender role or sexual identity conflicts (e.g., *My Gender Workbook* by Bornstein, *Reclaiming Your Life: The Gay Man's Guide to Love, Self-Acceptance, and Trust* by Isensee, *A Woman Like That: Lesbian and Bisexual Writers Tell Their Coming Out Stories* by Larkin, *Maximum Self-Esteem: The Handbook for Reclaiming Your Sense of Self-Worth* by Minchinton, *Why Am I Afraid to Tell You Who I Am?* by Powell, *Ending the Struggle Against Yourself* by Taubman); process material read.

10. Attend a support group at least twice for the next two months. (17, 18)

17. Instruct the client to attend four different support groups in the next three weeks to learn how other people have worked

with gender/sexual identity issues; process with the client what was helpful about the groups and which one provided the most support.

18. Advise the client to continue to attend the most helpful support group at least twice for the next two months.

11. Implement new conflict resolution and boundary skills. (19, 20, 21, 22)

19. Teach the client new conflict resolution skills (e.g., double-sided reflections, partially agreeing, agreeing with a twist, "I" statements).

20. Teach the client how boundaries are semipermeable and how they can be used to differentiate between self and others (e.g., "I am different from others and that's okay").

21. Facilitate role-plays with the client applying new conflict resolution and boundary-setting skills to his/her daily life; encourage his/her implementation in real life.

22. Review the client's implementation of conflict resolution and boundary-setting skills; provide feedback to the client, reinforcing any effort made to implement new skills.

12. Communicate sexual identity with supportive others and family members. (23, 24)

23. Advise the client to practice communicating his/her sexual identity with supportive others and family members using communication and boundary skills learned.

24. Review the client's sexual identity revelations, providing feedback on the results of this communication.

13. Identify and replace negative self-statements about sexual identity and proclivity. (25, 26)

25. Instruct the client to list some negative self-statements, (e.g., "I am wrong to be different"; "Because I am different I have the right to hurt others"; "I am unlovable") about sexual identity and proclivity.

26. Brainstorm self-affirming statements to support sense of self (e.g., "It's okay to be me"; "I am lovable the way I am"; "I deserve to be treated well, just as I should treat others well").

__. _____   __. _____
    _____   _____
__. _____   __. _____
    _____   _____

DIAGNOSTIC SUGGESTIONS:

ICD-9-CM	_ICD-10-CM_	_DSM-5_ Disorder, Condition, or Problem
309.0	F43.21	Adjustment Disorder, With Depressed Mood
309.28	F43.23	Adjustment Disorder, With Mixed Anxiety and Depressed Mood
300.00	F41.9	Unspecified Anxiety Disorder
309.24	F43.22	Adjustment Disorder, With Anxiety
300.4	F34.1	Persistent Depressive Disorder
302.85	F64.1	Gender Dysphoria in Adolescents and Adults
300.02	F41.1	Generalized Anxiety Disorder
296.2x	F32.x	Major Depressive Disorder, Single Episode
296.3x	F33.x	Major Depressive Disorder, Recurrent Episode
_____	_____	_____
_____	_____	_____

IMPULSIVITY

BEHAVIORAL DEFINITIONS

1. History of impulsive, aggressive outbursts out of proportion to any precipitating stressors, leading to assaultive acts or destruction of property.
2. Fails to control impulsive, irrational, and/or emotional behavior regardless of consequences.
3. Loss of personal freedoms due to presence in criminal justice system as a result of impulsive behavior.
4. Remorse for the consequences of acting without thought.
5. Easily distracted from focusing or concentrating on an activity at hand, rarely completing anything that was started.
6. Failure to maintain meaningful employment due to capricious and cavalier lack of regard for performance outcomes.
7. Loss of meaningful relationships as a result of impulsive, aggressive, and/or thoughtless behavior.
8. Impulsive behavior related to use of drugs and alcohol, gambling, sex, or other self-defeating patterns that result in diminished quality of life.

—. _____

_____

—. _____

_____

—. _____

_____

LONG-TERM GOALS

1. Decrease the frequency of impulsive behavior.
2. Acquire skills and techniques for delaying acting on impulsive thoughts.
3. Cope with impulses in a constructive way that enhances daily functioning.
4. Experience progressively better health-related, financial, and social outcomes as a result of engaging in more thoughtful behavior.

—. _____

_____

—. _____

_____

SHORT-TERM OBJECTIVES	THERAPEUTIC INTERVENTIONS
1. Describe the nature and history of impulsive behavior and how it is triggered. (1, 2)	1. Explore with the client his/her history of situations that trigger impulsive behavior and his/her impulsive thoughts, decisions, and actions (e.g., always reacting to every situation with hostility, doing the first thing that comes to mind, using drugs/alcohol, engaging in gambling or sex).
	2. Confront the client's attempts to minimize his/her poor management of impulsive behavior, to project blame onto others, or to discount the harmful consequences.
2. Participate in a biopsychosocial evaluation. (3, 4)	3. Administer or refer the client for a complete biopsychosocial evaluation to assess for chemical dependence, eating disorder, or other psychiatric disorder.
	4. Refer the client to a physician for a psychotropic medication

3. Verbalize a deeper understanding of the nature of impulsivity and possible means of impulse control. (5, 6)

4. Identify and replace dysfunctional thoughts or beliefs that trigger impulsive behavior. (7, 8)

evaluation; monitor for prescription compliance, effectiveness, and side effects.

5. Teach the client a basic objective perspective on impulsive behavior that minimally includes instruction on the Antecedents of behavior, Behavioral features associated with impulsivity, and Consequences of impulsivity (i.e., the ABCs of anger).

6. Provide the client a selection of reading options on the topic of impulse control (e.g., *The 7 Habits of Highly Effective People* by Covey; *Kill the Craving: How to Control the Impulse to Use Drugs and Alcohol* by Santoro, Bergman, and Deletis; *Smart Choices: A Practical Guide to Making Better Decisions* by Hammond, Keeney, and Raiffa; *Decisions, Decisions* by Welch); process key ideas.

7. Brainstorm with the client his/her thoughts or beliefs that trigger impulsive behavior (e.g., "Everyone is out to get me," "It's cool to respond quickly to someone in my face," "The easiest way to get out of a situation with my probation officer is to say something immediately even if it is a lie").

8. Facilitate a brainstorming inventory of alternative positive and realistic self-statements to the thoughts and beliefs that the client finds most frequently (or intensively) associated with his/her impulsive behavior.

5. List and implement alternative, positive, realistic self-talk in response to feelings that trigger impulsive behavior. (9, 10)

6. Brainstorm the pros and cons of impulsively making a decision without thinking through the consequence. (11)

7. Verbalize an understanding of how strong emotions can trigger impulsivity. (12, 13, 14)

8. Learn and utilize physiological, thinking, and behavioral tools of anger and

9. Assist the client in identifying feelings that trigger his/her impulsive behavior.

10. Facilitate a brainstorming inventory of alternative positive and realistic self-statements to counteract the feelings that the client finds most frequently (or intensively) associated with his/her impulsive behavior; encourage and reinforce implementation of positive self-talk.

11. Brainstorm with the client the pros (e.g., decisions are made quickly) and cons (e.g., loss of opportunities, monetary costs) of impulsively making a decision without thinking through the consequence.

12. Assist the client in exploring the role of anger and aggression in increasing the risk of impulsive behavior.

13. Assist the client in exploring the role of anxiety in increasing the potential for impulsive behavior in an attempt to reduce the anxious feelings.

14. Guide the client in a brainstorming session that identifies common cues that can potentially alert him/her to when he/she is becoming angry or anxious (e.g., tight tummy, dry mouth, heart rate increases, blood pressure increases, shallower breathing, clenched fists, perceived threats).

15. Teach the client tools of anger management (e.g., use an anger management curriculum such

anxiety management.
(15, 16, 17)

as *In Control* by Kellner or *Problem Solving Skills for Offenders* by Taymans and Parese, available from National Institute of Corrections [www.nicic.org]).

16. Provide the client a selection of reading options for tools to deal with anxiety (e.g., *Change Your Brain, Change Your Life* by Amen; *Healing Depression* by Carrigan; *Relaxation and Stress Reduction Workbook* by Davis, McKay, and Robbins).

17. Teach the client simple, quick techniques to immediately help reduce anger or anxiety elevations in a variety of situations (e.g., deep breathing, counting backward, engaging in pleasant imagery, using a worry stone).

9. Identify and accept responsibility for the negative consequences of past impulsive behavior. (18)

18. Assist the client in identifying some of the negative consequences of his/her impulsive behavior; encourage and support the client in taking responsibility for consequences of his/her past behavior.

10. Identify cognitive steps that would aid in preventing impulsive behavior. (19, 20)

19. Teach the client steps that would aid in preventing impulsive behavior (e.g., pausing-to-think; implementing thought stopping; taking thoughts or feelings to court; using a problem-solving approach of stating the situation clearly, stating the desired outcome, listing the alternative ways of achieving the desired outcome, sorting out the pros and cons for each alternative).

20. Instruct the client to describe in writing the role pausing-to-think has in preventing impulsive actions (e.g., increases the space between the incident and action taken, allows for consideration of consequences, allows for consideration of alternative actions).

11. Implement the cognitive steps that aid in preventing impulsive behavior. (21, 22)

21. Role-play with the client the cognitive steps that can prevent impulsivity (e.g., pausing-to-think; thought stopping; taking thoughts or feelings to court; problem solving by stating the situation clearly, stating the desired outcome, listing the alternative ways of achieving the desired outcome, sorting out the pros and cons for each alternative); provide the client with supportive feedback on his/her performance on the role-play, encouraging any attempt to think before acting.

22. Assign the client to implement in his/her daily life and journal the steps to prevent impulsive behavior.

12. Practice decision-making skills in recreational situations. (23)

23. Use physical exercises or games (e.g., rock climbing, Mastermind, model building) to allow the client to practice decision-making skills and emphasize the potential harmful consequences of impulsive actions; ask the client to identify real-life situations in which he/she could apply these skills.

13. Identify the difference between fact and opinion. (24)

24. Explore with the client the difference between fact and opinion, and how assuming an

opinion is fact can lead to impulsive behavior.

14. Keep a journal of impulsive thoughts/feelings and triggers that arise daily. (25, 26)

25. Instruct the client to keep a journal of impulsive thoughts/feelings and triggers that arise daily, recording how they were handled, the outcome of the situation, the desired outcome, and the alternate courses of action that could have been taken to achieve the desired outcome.

26. Process with the client any material in his/her journal of impulsive thoughts, feelings, and triggers that led to negative outcomes.

15. Contact those who have been affected/hurt by impulsive behavior to gain feedback and/or make amends. (27, 28, 29)

27. Instruct the client to list the people who have been negatively affected or hurt by his/her irresponsible behavior and record what actions hurt them and why it was hurtful.

28. Encourage the client to contact, if appropriate, those who have been affected or hurt by his/her thoughtless behavior to gain feedback as to the pain caused and/or make amends.

29. Debrief with the client any contact he/she made with those affected or hurt by his/her irresponsible behavior and support or redirect him/her as necessary.

16. Implement new conflict communication skills and receive feedback. (30, 31, 32)

30. Describe and model for the client several conflict communication skills (e.g., double-sided reflections, partially agreeing, agreeing with a twist, "I" statements) that could improve his/her

communication and prevent impulsive responses.

31. Facilitate the client's skill rehearsals for three new communication skills, utilizing his/her own recent situations where better communication skills would have improved the outcome.

32. Review the client's implementation of new conflict communication skills in daily life, reinforce success and redirect for failure.

—. _____   —. _____

_____   _____

—. _____   —. _____

_____   _____

—. _____   —. _____

_____   _____

DIAGNOSTIC SUGGESTIONS:

ICD-9-CM	_ICD-10-CM_	_DSM-5_ Disorder, Condition, or Problem
312.34	F63.81	Intermittent Explosive Disorder
312.30	F91.9	Unspecified Disruptive, Impulse-Control, and Conduct Disorder
314.01	F90.1	Attention-Deficit/Hyperactivity Disorder, Predominately Hyperactive/Impulsive Presentation
301.50	F60.4	Histrionic Personality Disorder
301.7	F60.2	Antisocial Personality Disorder
301.9	F60.9	Unspecified Personality Disorder
_____	_____	_____
_____	_____	_____

INADEQUATE SOCIAL SUPPORT/ SOCIAL ISOLATION

BEHAVIORAL DEFINITIONS

1. Inability to establish and maintain meaningful, pro-social, peer support group.
2. Social support network composed entirely of people involved with crime.
3. No participation in pro-social groups, organizations, or activities.
4. Absence of close friends or confidants.
5. Hypersensitivity to perceived disapproval, rejection, or criticism.
6. Passive avoidance of any conflict leads to an absence of relationships.
7. Pattern of persistent interpersonal conflict and/or personal isolation.
8. Highly anxious in social situations.
9. Overly aggressive in social situations.

—. _____
    _____
—. _____
    _____
—. _____
    _____

LONG-TERM GOALS

1. Develop a meaningful and reliable pro-social network that shares and supports a healthy lifestyle and self-respect.

2. Terminate relationships with everyone who is involved with criminal behavior.
3. Increase a sense of ease and confidence in various social situations.
4. Improve ability to effectively express personal opinions, desires, and feelings without antagonizing or alienating others.
5. Develop essential social skills necessary to communicate in a constructive manner.
6. Find a balance between personal time alone and interpersonal interactions with others.

—. _____
_____
—. _____
_____
—. _____
_____

SHORT-TERM OBJECTIVES

THERAPEUTIC INTERVENTIONS

1. List the specific thoughts, feelings, and attitudes that are associated with engaging in social interactions. (1)

1. Instruct the client to list the specific thoughts (e.g., "I'm going to make a fool of myself"), feelings (e.g., anxiety, fear), and attitudes (e.g., only weak people need friends for support, social interactions are a waste of time) that are associated with engaging in social interactions.

2. Reframe each of the thoughts, feelings, and attitudes that represent obstacles to making new friendships. (2)

2. Assist the client in formulating several ways to positively reframe each of the thoughts, feelings, and attitudes that represent obstacles to making new friendships.

3. Identify what you are willing to give and what you need from a social relationship. (3)

3. Explore the client's expectations of social interactions, outlining what he/she is willing to give (e.g., honest interaction, support,

four hours per week) and what he/she needs (e.g., sharing of interests, acceptance, support, availability) from a social relationship.

4. Verbalize short-term goals related to modifying social situation. (4)

4. Assist the client in detailing short-term goals (i.e., within six months) related to modifying his/her social situation (e.g., what relationships to terminate, how to improve social skills, where to meet pro-social people, what relationships to strengthen, what social activities or groups to join).

5. Participate in a cognitive behavioral social skills training group. (5)

5. Refer the client to a cognitive behavioral, social skills training group.

6. List the benefits and negative consequences of social isolation. (6)

6. Brainstorm with the client a list of the benefits (e.g., time to myself, not having to explain anything to anyone, not having to worry about what others think) and the negative consequences (e.g., lack of support, no one to turn to for help, boredom) of social isolation.

7. Describe any suicidal impulses that may accompany isolation. (7)

7. Explore with the client any suicidal impulses associated with isolation, taking the necessary steps to determine the strength of his/her suicidal ideation and to arrange any required supervised care (see Depression/Suicidal Ideation chapter in this *Planner*).

8. Balance time spent between social and solitary activities. (8)

8. Instruct the client to describe in writing how he/she could balance time spent between social and solitary activities; monitor the implementation of

this plan, reinforcing success and redirecting for failure.

9. Describe the depth and nature of all friendships and acquaintances (if any), noting the needs met by criminal relationships. (9, 10)

9. Assist the client in creating a sociogram of all friends or acquaintances (if any); place an asterisk next to those involved in criminal behavior.

10. Explore with the client needs that are being met with peer-related criminal behavior that could be met with pro-social relationships (e.g., camaraderie, support, excitement).

10. Identify, practice, and implement strategies for distancing self from criminal peers. (11, 12, 13, 14)

11. Teach the client strategies (e.g., setting clear boundaries, telling peers his/her goal of avoiding criminal behavior, assertively saying no) for distancing himself/herself from criminal peers.

12. Role-play with the client the use of the new distancing techniques; provide him/her with positive feedback for effort, as well as suggestions for improvement in implementation.

13. Assign the client to choose one deviant friend or acquaintance that he/she feels comfortable distancing himself/herself from and implement the new distancing techniques with that person.

14. Debrief with the client about how new distancing techniques worked with the chosen person; provide positive reinforcement and feedback for improvement.

11. Evaluate past attempts to establish pro-social friendships. (15)

15. Explore the client's past attempts to establish and maintain meaningful, pro-social friends and

acquaintances; evaluate what went wrong and how the client can make and replace old patterns with new social skills.

12. Learn and practice healthy communication and active listening skills and learn how they can be improved over time. (16, 17, 18)

16. Brainstorm with the client various communication styles and techniques (e.g., aggressive, anxious, passive, avoidant).

17. Assist the client in identifying the composition of the various communication styles he/she tends to use in routine interactions.

18. Teach the client the fundamental skills of communication (e.g., asking open-ended questions, using "I" messages, affirming the speaker with eye contact and nodding, reflecting the feelings behind the communication, summarizing the content, and eliciting self-motivating statements) and how to implement these skills in everyday communication.

13. Verbalize and implement the essential steps for effectively expressing and receiving criticism. (19, 20, 21, 22)

19. Instruct the client in a technique for expressing a complaint or providing criticism (e.g., specifically decide what the issue is; decide if he/she should express anything; when, to whom, and what should be said; state complaint and suggested solution in a friendly, respectful manner; ask for reaction; indicate he/she understands others' view; discuss alternative solutions; reach agreement).

20. Use role-playing, modeling, and behavioral rehearsal to

apply the effective, assertive technique for expressing complaints and criticism to the client's real-life situations.

21. Instruct the client in a technique for responding to complaints or criticism (e.g., listen carefully to the complaint, ask for more information, decide if the complaint is justified, decide if he/she should accept or deny responsibility and what should be done, respectfully express his/her view and suggested solution, ask for the other person's view).

22. Use role-playing, modeling, and behavioral rehearsal to apply the assertive technique for responding to complaints and criticism to the client's real-life situations.

14. Identify and replace negative or anxiety provoking self-talk associated with social interactions. (23, 24)

23. Assist the client in listing negative or anxiety providing self-talk associated with social interactions (e.g., "I always say foolish things"; "No one is interested in anything I say"; "I have nothing to offer"; "No one listens, anyway").

24. Brainstorm positive "reframes" for anxiety-provoking self-talk and encourage implementation of positive self-talk in social interactions (e.g., "I do have something to offer," "I am good enough to be listened to," "Sometimes I can have interesting things to say or an interesting perspective to offer").

15. Implement the use of quick "anxiety reducers" techniques in the face of social anxiety. (25)

16. Increase involvement with other pro-social people, activities, and structured groups. (26, 27, 28, 29)

25. Teach the client some quick "anxiety reducers" (e.g., breathing deeper, counting, using pleasant imagery); encourage and monitor their implementation, reinforcing success and redirecting for failures.

26. Advise the client to make efforts to get more involved with other pro-social people; suggest activities that might facilitate that process (e.g., joining a community or church group, inviting someone from work to a recreational activity, become a volunteer, take an educational class).

27. Ask the client to attend three different clubs, groups, or organizations (e.g., 12-step groups, church or faith community, sports, or fitness groups) to initiate contact with pro-social people; direct the client to stay involved for at least nine consecutive weeks to give himself/herself a chance to build relationships.

28. Encourage the client to practice new social skills with other members of a club, group, or organization in an effort to develop new friends and acquaintances.

29. Debrief with the client about how new techniques worked; provide him/her with positive reinforcement for effort and feedback for improvements.

17. Evaluate progress made on short-term goals related to

30. Evaluate with the client progress made on short-term

improving social support and decreasing isolation. (30, 31)

goals set at the beginning of treatment, providing feedback as appropriate.

31. Assist the client in resetting new short-term goals related to improving social support and decreasing isolation.

__. _____   __. _____
    _____   _____
__. _____   __. _____
    _____   _____
__. _____   __. _____
    _____   _____

DIAGNOSTIC SUGGESTIONS:

ICD-9-CM	*ICD-10-CM*	*DSM-5* Disorder, Condition, or Problem
300.23	F40.10	Social Anxiety Disorder (Social Phobia)
300.4	F34.1	Persistent Depressive Disorder
296.xx	F32.x	Major Depressive Disorder, Single Episode
296.xx	F33.x	Major Depressive Disorder, Recurrent Episode
300.21	F41.0	Panic Disorder
300.22	F40.00	Agoraphobia
309.81	F43.10	Posttraumatic Stress Disorder
301.82	F60.6	Avoidant Personality Disorder
301.20	F60.1	Schizoid Personality Disorder
301.0	F60.0	Paranoid Personality Disorder
301.22	F21	Schizotypal Personality Disorder
_____	_____	_____
_____	_____	_____

INTIMATE RELATIONSHIP CONFLICT

BEHAVIORAL DEFINITIONS

1. Inability to establish and maintain a meaningful intimate relationship.
2. History of perpetrating physical, emotional, or psychological abuse in an intimate relationship.
3. Involvement in several intimate relationships at the same time.
4. History of explosive, aggressive outbursts in reaction to relationship conflict, leading to assaultive acts or destruction of property.
5. Hypersensitivity to perceived disapproval, rejection, or criticism that causes communication breakdowns.
6. Passive avoidance of conflict and irritations that contribute ultimately to the collapse of a relationship.
7. A pattern of allowing self to be victimized in abusive relationships.
8. Inability to communicate wants/needs to an intimate partner.
9. Relationship stress triggers involvement in substance abuse or criminal behavior.

—. _____
_____

—. _____
_____

LONG-TERM GOALS

1. Establish and maintain a meaningful intimate relationship.
2. Improve self-awareness and understanding of own behavior and contribution to relationship stress.
3. Communicate needs or wishes in a constructive manner.
4. Learn effective, pro-social problem-solving skills to deal with inevitable relationship stress.

5. Learn to identify precursors to violence as a perpetrator or a victim, and means to de-escalate the tension.

—. _____
   _____

—. _____
   _____

SHORT-TERM OBJECTIVES

1. Describe past intimate relationships, whether conflictual or not. (1)

2. Identify issues that lead to conflict in intimate relationships. (2, 3)

3. Identify the dysfunctional patterns in intimate relationships that need to be modified to make healthy relationships possible. (4, 5, 6)

THERAPEUTIC INTERVENTIONS

1. Instruct the client to describe past intimate relationships, whether conflictual or not.

2. Explore with the client the causes of past or present conflicts in intimate relationships.

3. Confront the client's attempts to minimize his/her poor management of behavior, to project blame on to others, or to discount his/her contribution to relationship conflict.

4. Explore the client's dysfunctional patterns in the nature of his/her intimate relationships (e.g., moving from one relationship to another quickly, always being involved with an abusive partner, discontinuing relationships without cause).

5. Encourage the client to verbalize short-term goals (attainable within six months) related to how he/she will modify his/her intimate relationships to make them more meaningful, healthy, and respectful.

4. Identify what needs are met by having multiple intimate partners and the pros and cons associated with that practice. (7, 8)

6. Assist the client in listing the components of a meaningful, ideal intimate relationship.

7. Explore with the client what needs are met by him/her having multiple intimate partners, guiding this exploration toward the components of a pro-social, healthy and supportive relationship.

8. Brainstorm the pros (e.g., excitement, variety, ego boost) and cons (e.g., lack of honesty and trust, increased risk of STDs, shallowness of relationship) of having multiple intimate partners.

5. Participate in a cognitive behavioral social skills training. (9)

9. Refer the client to a cognitive-behavioral, social skills training program.

6. Identify interpersonal communication style and techniques. (10, 11)

10. Brainstorm with the client various communication styles and techniques (e.g., passive, passive-aggressive, aggressive, assertive).

11. Assist the client in identifying the composition of the various communication styles he/she tends to use in routine interactions.

7. List the advantages and disadvantages of maintaining versus improving communication style and techniques. (12, 13)

12. Assist the client in identifying and prioritizing specific goals for improving his/her interpersonal communication skills.

13. Process with the client the decisional balance (e.g., pros and cons) for his/her present interpersonal communication style versus implementing a more healthy, assertive style.

8. Learn and practice healthy communication and active listening skills. (14, 15, 16, 17)

14. Teach the client the fundamental skills of active listening (e.g., asking open-ended questions, affirming the speaker with eye contact and nodding, reflecting the feelings behind the communication, summarizing the content, and eliciting self-motivating statements) and how to implement these skills in everyday communication.

15. Use role-play, modeling, and behavioral rehearsal to teach the client several conflict communication skills (e.g., double-sided reflections, partially agreeing, agreeing with a twist, "I" statements) that could improve his/her communication.

16. Use role-play, modeling, and behavioral rehearsal to teach the client active listening skills, showing how they are apt to vary within the four classic interpersonal styles (e.g., passive, passive-aggressive, aggressive, and assertive).

17. Assign specific exercises from an established curriculum and workbook for teaching the client effective communication skills (e.g., *The Prepare Curriculum* by Goldstein; *Reasoning and Rehabilitation* by Ross, Fabiano, and Ross; *Controlling Anger and Learning to Manage [CALM] Program* by Winogron, VanDieten, and Gauzas; *Anger Workout Book* by Weisinger; *Criminal Conduct and Substance Abuse Treatment* by Wanberg and Milkman).

9. Verbalize a greater understanding of the principal elements of assertiveness versus passivity or aggression. (18, 19)

18. Teach the client the differences between passive, passive-aggressive, aggressive, and assertive styles of interpersonal communication that minimally includes: tactics associated with each style; short-term consequences; and long-term consequences associated with each style.

19. Ask the client to read a book on assertiveness (e.g., *Your Perfect Right* by Alberti and Emmons; *Asserting Yourself* by Bower, Bower, and Bower; *Managing Assertively* by Burley; or *The Assertiveness Workbook* by Paterson).

10. List the relationship consequences that are most likely to result from passive, passive-aggressive, and aggressive, interpersonal styles. (20, 21)

20. Assist the client in generating a list of relationship consequences most likely to result from passive (e.g., not being heard, not getting one's needs met, feeling put upon), passive-aggressive (e.g., not getting one's needs met, frustration, not being able to be clear about needs), and aggressive (e.g., getting one's needs met at the cost of someone else's, losing a relationship, upsetting the other person and oneself) interpersonal communication styles.

21. Guide the client in a brainstorming session that identifies the common benefits resulting from assertive communication skills (e.g., get needs or desires met, promotes understanding, clarifies feelings to others, establishes boundaries for self and others).

11. Implement assertive ways of communicating wants and needs in daily interaction. (22)

22. Facilitate a role-play with the client using assertive ways of communicating wants and needs; encourage the client to implement assertive communication in his/her daily life, monitoring and reinforcing success, and redirecting for failure.

12. Verbalize the difference between fact and opinion and how assuming opinion is fact can create conflict. (23)

23. Explore with the client the difference between fact and opinion, and how assuming an opinion is fact can lead to conflict (e.g., "You slammed the door because you are an angry person and you don't respect me"); ask the client to cite times when he/she has made an assumption of opinion as fact.

13. Report on attempts to see the other person's point of view. (24)

24. Role-play with the client seeing and stating another's point of view using active listening skills, like reflection (e.g., "You feel a lack of respect because I slammed the door"); assign the client to apply this skill in his/her daily life, journaling the situation and the consequences.

14. Cite instances when different levels of closeness or separateness were implemented based on mutual need satisfaction. (25)

25. Teach the client that in relationship, different degrees of closeness and of separation are needed at different times and that verbalizing his/her needs is a way to prevent conflict or misunderstanding; encourage implementation of this sensitivity.

15. Verbalize and implement the essential steps for effectively expressing criticism or complaints to another person. (26, 27, 30)

26. Teach the client a technique for expressing a complaint or providing criticism (e.g., specifically decide what the issue is; decide if he/she should

express anything; when, to whom, and what should be done; state complaint and suggested solution in a friendly manner; ask for reaction; indicate he/she understands others' view; discuss alternative solutions; reach agreement).

27. Use role-playing, modeling, and behavioral rehearsal to teach the client to apply the effective, assertive technique for expressing his/her complaints and criticism to real-life situations.

30. Review the client's implementtation of giving and receiving complaints and criticism in his/her daily life; reinforce success and redirect for failure experiences.

16. Verbalize and implement the essential steps for effectively receiving a complaint or criticism from another person. (28, 29, 30)

28. Instruct the client in a technique for responding to complaints or criticism (e.g., listen carefully to the complaints, ask for more information, decide if the complaint is justified, decide if he/she should accept or deny responsebility and what should be done, express his/her view and suggested solution, ask for other person's view).

29. Use role-playing, modeling, and behavioral rehearsal to apply the assertive technique for responding to complaints and criticism to real-life situations.

30. Review the client's implementation of giving and receiving complaints and criticism in his/her daily life; reinforce

success and redirect for failure experiences.

17. Implement the use of anger-reducing techniques. (31, 32, 33)

31. Assist the client in developing and prioritizing an inventory of their anger triggers (activating issues or antecedent events).

32. Teach the client the steps of the complete AMBC anger cycle that includes: (1) the activating issue or Antecedent, (2) Mental process of forming self-statements, (3) Behavior or physical responses, (4) Consequences (see *The Prepare Curriculum* by Goldstein); role-play positive self-talk to improve step two.

33. Teach the client simple quick techniques (e.g., breathing deeply, counting backward, imagining pleasant scenes, manipulating a worry stone) for immediately reducing tension and anger elevations in a variety of situations; encourage implementation of these techniques, reinforcing success and redirecting for failure.

18. Verbalize and implement constructive ways to cope with internal or external triggers for relationship conflict. (34, 35, 36)

34. Assist the client in listing common internal (e.g., hunger, tiredness) and external (e.g., conflict at work, traffic) triggers that create relationship conflict or stress.

35. Provide the client with a selection of reading material on the topic of managing anger and conflict (e.g., *The Verbally Abusive Relationship* by Evans, *The Relationship Rescue Workbook* by McGraw, *The Eight Essential Steps to Conflict Resolution* by Weeks).

36. Brainstorm with client constructive ways of dealing with conflict triggers and resulting stress (e.g., taking a time out, communicating feelings or thoughts without acting on it, taking a walk); encourage implementation of these techniques, reinforcing success and redirecting for failure.

19. Evaluate progress on short-terms goals set at the beginning of treatment. (37, 38)

37. Evaluate and provide feedback to the client progress on short-term goals set at the beginning of treatment.

38. Assist the client in setting short-term goals related to engaging in, improving or maintaining an intimate relationship.

__. _____   __. _____

_____   _____

__. _____   __. _____

_____   _____

DIAGNOSTIC SUGGESTIONS:

ICD-9-CM	_ICD-10-CM_	_DSM-5_ Disorder, Condition, or Problem
312.34	F63.81	Intermittent Explosive Disorder
309.0	F43.21	Adjustment Disorder, With Depressed Mood
309.24	F43.22	Adjustment Disorder, With Anxiety
300.4	F34.1	Persistent Depressive Disorder
300.00	F41.9	Unspecified Anxiety Disorder
311	F32.9	Unspecified Depressive Disorder
311	F32.8	Other Specified Depressive Disorder
309.81	F43.10	Posttraumatic Stress Disorder
301.20	F60.1	Schizoid Personality Disorder
301.81	F60.81	Narcissistic Personality Disorder
301.9	F60.9	Unspecified Personality Disorder
301.7	F60.2	Antisocial Personality Disorder
_____	_____	_____
_____	_____	_____

MORAL DISENGAGEMENT

BEHAVIORAL DEFINITIONS

1. Maintains personal values that are supportive of frequent, serious, and persistent criminal activity.
2. Frequently rationalizes or justifies antisocial behavior through emphasis on extenuating circumstances.
3. Employs denial, projection, or euphemistic language to portray reprehensible behavior more favorably.
4. Bases assessments of personal conduct on "good intentions" rather than actual hurtful behavior.
5. Minimizes personal responsibility by making comparisons to the more severe antisocial behavior of others.
6. Consistently minimizes the impact of personal antisocial behavior on others.
7. Chooses not to be held accountable to conventional norms, mores, laws, and ethical standards.
8. Distorted self-image that emphasizes either a completely negative or completely positive identity.
9. Little or no maintenance of pro-social values.
10. Completely egocentric viewpoints on almost everything.

—. _____

_____

LONG-TERM GOALS

1. Adopt and consistently support pro-social values and behaviors that are beneficial to the community, family, and others.
2. Develop skills and techniques for monitoring and interrupting morally "neutralizing" self-talk.

3. Become less egocentric and better able to accept the perspectives of others.
4. Discover new potential for making conventional contributions to society.

—. _____

_____

SHORT-TERM OBJECTIVES

THERAPEUTIC INTERVENTIONS

1. Participate in a complete psychological assessment that includes a criminogenic risk/need assessment. (1)

1. Refer the client to a complete psychological assessment that includes a criminogenic risk/need assessment (e.g., Level of Service Inventory [LSI-R] by Andrews and Bonta, Correctional Offender Management Profiling for Alternative Sanctions— COMPAS by Northpointe).

2. Cooperate with further assessment and/or treatment referrals as recommended by the evaluation. (2, 3, 4)

2. Administer to the client a psychopathy assessment instrument (e.g., Psychopathy Checklist-Revised [PCL-R] by Hare); refer him/her for an in-depth evaluation if his/her scores indicate a significant problem exists.

3. Refer the client for additional assessments and/or treatment as indicated by the criminogenic needs (e.g., Alcohol or Other Drugs [AOD], Anger Management, Criminal Peers) based on the assessment completed (see chapters in this *Planner* for further information under each of these headings).

4. Refer the client to a cognitive restructuring or skill-building treatment program (e.g.,

3. Complete self-assessment instruments to explore criminal attitudes and thinking styles. (5, 6)

4. Brainstorm and establish five short-term goals for modifying criminal attitudes, thinking styles, and criminal behavior. (7)

5. Describe the history and effects of criminally and morally deviant behavior. (8, 9)

6. Acknowledge the use of strategies to displace or diffuse responsibility for and consequences of your actions. (10, 11, 12)

Criminal Attitude Program by Simourd, Counter-Point by Van Dieten and Graham, Cognitive Living Skills by Ross and Fabiano).

5. Administer to the client a self-assessment instrument to explore criminal attitudes and thinking styles (e.g., Criminal Sentiment Scale—Modified [CSS-M] by Shields and Simourd, Psychological Inventory of Criminal Thinking Styles [PICTS] by Walters, Pride in Delinquency Scale by Shields and Whitehall).

6. Debrief with the client and provide objective, normative feedback on the self-assessment instruments he/she has completed.

7. Using the results of the evaluation, assist the client in setting five short-term goals for modifying criminal attitudes, thinking styles, and criminal behavior.

8. Explore the client's history of criminally and morally deviant behavior.

9. Explore with the client the negative effects of his/her actions on the victims of his/her criminal and immoral actions.

10. Explain to the client that moral justifications (the government takes from us, I'm just robbing money that is federally insured), palliative comparisons (I'm just Robin Hood, evening out things) and euphemistic

labeling (I didn't rape her, I just showed her a good time) are all ways of diffusing responsibility of one's actions by minimizing the reprehensible conduct.

11. Explain to the client that minimizing (it wasn't that bad), ignoring (there weren't any consequences to anyone for my actions) or misconstruing (he didn't black out because I hit him, I only tapped him lightly) the consequences of the client's actions is a way of diffusing the detrimental effects of those actions.

12. Explain to the client how dehumanizing (she's a whore anyway, how would she care) or vilifying (he deserved it because of what he's done) the victim displaces responsibility of his/her actions.

7. Identify which strategies of displacing or diffusing responsibility and consequences are most often personally used. (13, 14)

13. Instruct the client to identify which of the ways of displacing or diffusing responsibility and consequences are most often used by him/her.

14. Using the client's own description of deviant behavior, assist him/her in identifying which ways he/she uses to displace or diffuse responsibility or consequences; confront attempts to avoid responsibility.

8. Implement cognitive techniques to counter each of the ways of displacing or diffusing responsibility or consequences. (15, 16)

15. Assist the client in brainstorming pro-social reframes (e.g., I am responsible for my actions; my actions affect others; everyone, no matter who they are, deserve to

be respected) for each of his/her ways of displacing or diffusing responsibility or consequences; encourage the client's implementation of these reframes, reinforcing success and redirecting for failures.

16. Teach the client to implement a thought-stopping technique (e.g., thinking of a stop sign and then a pleasant scene, or snapping a rubber band on the wrist) that cognitively interferes with distorted cognitive messages that displace or diffuse responsibility and fuel deviant behavior.

9. Verbalize an understanding of the relationship between thoughts, feelings, attitudes, values, and beliefs. (17, 18)

17. Teach the client the relationship between thoughts, beliefs, feelings, and actions (see *Cognitive Therapy of Personality Disorders* by Beck and Freeman).

18. Assign the client reading from different curricula that explore the relationship among thoughts, feelings, attitudes, values, and beliefs (e.g., Criminal Attitude Program by Simourd; Counter-Point by Van Dieten and Graham; Cognitive Living Skills by Ross and Fabiano; The Prepare Curriculum by Goldstein; Reasoning and Rehabilitation by Ross, Fabiano, and Ross; Criminal Conduct and Substance Abuse Treatment by Wanberg and Milkman).

10. Acknowledge the importance of living within social mores and laws. (19, 20)

19. Explore the client's attitudes and beliefs regarding respect for the rule of law; point out the disorganization and

anarchy that results from disregard for mores and law.

20. Assign the client reading from a selection of books on morals, values and empathy (e.g., *Getting Real* by Campbell; *Empathy and Moral Development: Implications for Caring and Justice* by Hoffman; *Values Clarification: The Classic Guide to Discovering Your Truest Feelings* by Simon, Kirschenbaum, and Howe; *What Matters Most: The Power of Living Your Values* by Smith); process concepts learned.

11. Identify feelings, attitudes, beliefs, and values that support criminal behavior and displace or diffuse responsibility for actions. (21, 22)

21. Assist the client in identifying his/her feelings (e.g., hate, distrust, lack of empathy), attitudes (e.g., narcissism, victim, no one cares about me so I don't care about anyone else), beliefs (e.g., since life is futile anyway, might as well screw my life up now; everything is stacked against me), and values (e.g., individuality, selfishness, any means justifies the end) that support criminal behavior and displacing or diffusing responsibility of one's actions.

22. Assist the client in identifying his/her narcissistic tendency to view all mores and laws as subject to his/her approval or acceptance (see Narcissistic-Unprincipled chapter in this *Planner*).

12. Complete a self-administered assessment instrument that measures selfishness and narcissistic tendencies. (23)

23. Administer to the client a validated instrument to assess selfishness and narcissism (e.g., Selfism by Phares and Erskine,

or Paulhus Deception Scales by Paulhus); provide him/her with an objective interpretation and feedback (normative) of the scores he/she attained.

13. Verbalize an understanding of narcissism and grandiosity and their causes. (24, 25, 26)

24. Explain to the client the dynamics of narcissism and grandiosity and how it serves to fill a vacuum in his/her self-concept.

25. Provide the client a range of materials (e.g., cardboard, scissors, glue, tape, string, magazine pictures, found objects such as bones, feathers) and instructions in building a personal mask that hides true feelings and identity.

26. Discuss with the client the various functions a mask serves and how a mask might be a metaphor for narcissism and grandiosity.

14. Implement skills that communicate understanding another's point of view. (27, 28)

27. Teach the client active-listening social skills necessary to communicate understanding of another's point of view (e.g., asking open questions, reflections, affirming the speaker with eye contact and nodding, summarizing the content); role-play these skills with the client and provide the client with feedback.

28. Assign the client to implement active listening social skills in his/her life; debrief on implementation.

15. Acknowledge the far-reaching negative impact of crimi-nogenic attitudes and beliefs and criminal behavior. (29, 30)

29. Teach the client about the interdependence of all creatures (e.g., systems theory) and how his/her actions can have

wide-ranging effects from affecting family to affecting society generally.

30. Explore with the client the rights of family, community, and others that are being violated with the attitudes, values, and beliefs that support criminal behavior and avoid responsibility.

16. Verbalize an understanding of how shallow feelings, no remorse, and no empathy are alike and different. (31, 32)

31. Define shallow feelings (e.g., glib, superficial, charming, and sentimental), no empathy (e.g., total lack of understanding for other's feelings), and no remorse (e.g., no conscience or feelings of guilt) using examples.

32. Teach the client how shallow feelings, no empathy, and no remorse are similar (all three allow the client to escape any responsibility for his/her actions), but different (they target different levels of feeling and responsibility from a superficial understanding to a complete disregard).

17. Acknowledge that human relations are critical in order to meet basic human emotional needs. (33, 34)

33. Teach the client the difference between human wants (e.g., money or power) and human needs (e.g., security, love, affirmation) and how wants can be met without any empathy or remorse (e.g., killing for money), needs cannot be met without increasing ability for empathy and responsibility.

34. Ask the client to write a paper that explains how human relationship that involves empathy, depth of feeling, and

18. Identify and replace criminogenic self-talk to lead to more pro-social behavior. (35, 36, 37)

responsibility are necessary to meet basic human emotional needs.

35. Instruct the client to list distorted, criminogenic self-talk (e.g., I should assault him before he assaults me, I have a right to do whatever I want since this is a free country) that supports criminal behavior and that inhibits seeing another's point of view.

36. Explore with the client the ways that criminogenic self-talk might be related to problems with a need to have control over others, a need for power, or lack of empathy (e.g., making the issues related to power, feelings, and control unconscious and therefore "invisible").

37. Assist the client in brainstorming positive reframes of criminogenic self-talk to lead to more pro-social behavior; instruct the client to practice using these reframes in his/her life and provide feedback on its implementation.

19. Select and implement a method for making a contribution to society. (38, 39)

38. Explore with the client different venues and methods (e.g., voluntary community service; volunteering at farmer's markets, museums, hospitals, or humane society; utilizing pro-social skills to help others—teaching adolescents auto-body work, helping the elderly, or providing computer skills training) for making conventional contribution to society.

39. Assist the client in selecting a method (that is pro-social, does not increase his/her risk for criminal behavior, does not put the community at risk) for making a contribution to society for at least four hours per week for the next four weeks; process this experience with the client and the use of skills learned; provide feedback as appropriate for continuing the activity for three months.

20. Retake a self-assessment to explore criminal attitudes and thinking styles. (40)

40. Administer to the client a self-assessment instrument to explore criminal attitudes and thinking styles (e.g., Criminal Sentiment Scale—Modified [CSS-M] by Shields and Simourd, Psychological Inventory of Criminal Thinking Styles [PICTS] by Walters, Pride in Delinquency Scale by Shields and Whitehall); compare test results to pretreatment results to check for progress and determine areas for more focused treatment.

__. _____   __. _____

_____   _____

DIAGNOSTIC SUGGESTIONS:

ICD-9-CM	_ICD-10-CM_	_DSM-5_ Disorder, Condition, or Problem
312.34	F63.81	Intermittent Explosive Disorder
301.7	F60.2	Antisocial Personality Disorder
301.81	F60.81	Narcissistic Personality Disorder
301.9	F60.9	Unspecified Personality Disorder
_____	_____	_____
_____	_____	_____

NARCISSISTIC—UNPRINCIPLED

BEHAVIORAL DEFINITIONS

1. Exaggerates self-importance in a grandiose manner, resorting to outright lies to inflate his/her self-image if that seems expedient.
2. Has feelings of entitlement, believing that ordinary rules that apply to others are inapplicable to him/her.
3. Deficient conscience, unscrupulous, and amoral.
4. Does not maintain loyalties, and will, if the opportunity arises, exploit a trusting other.
5. Is fraudulent and deceptive, and often is a con or a charlatan.
6. Is arrogant and is contemptuous and/or vindictive toward victims of his/her exploitive endeavors.
7. Is indifferent to the welfare of others, and lacks empathy for their feelings.
8. Is domineering, exercising high levels of control in relationships.

—. _____

   _____

—. _____

   _____

LONG-TERM GOALS

1. Decrease arrogant, contemptuous attitudes and behaviors.
2. Reduce feelings of entitlement and expectations of special treatment.

Most of the content of this chapter (with only slight revisions) originates from N. Bockian and A.E. Jongsma, Jr., *The Personality Disorders Treatment Planner* (New York: John Wiley & Sons, 2001). Copyright © 2001 by N. Bockian and A.E. Jongsma, Jr. Reprinted with permission.

3. Improve empathy, increasing the ability and desire to understand others' feelings.
4. Decrease or eliminate interpersonal exploitation.
5. Reduce or eliminate tendency to denigrate or put down others.
6. Acquire greater discipline and self-control over emotions, especially anger and rage.

—. _____
_____

—. _____
_____

—. _____
_____

SHORT-TERM OBJECTIVES

1. Express comfort with the therapeutic relationship, either verbally or nonverbally, and openly share difficulties and concerns. (1, 2)

2. Establish a trusting relationship with the therapist. (3, 4, 5, 6)

THERAPEUTIC INTERVENTIONS

1. Express empathy for the client's difficulties (e.g., feeling constrained, angry, or frustrated).

2. Assist the client in developing a list of specific dissatisfactions he/she is presently experiencing (e.g., conflicts with the law, relationship conflicts).

3. Avoid appearing weak or soft in the eyes of the client, by refraining from directly asking the client about his/her feelings and emotions early in the treatment.

4. When appropriate, comment on the client's facility with deception and lying, noting that he/she will be able to "con" the therapist at least some of the time. Process the pros and cons of being deceptive toward therapist (see _Cognitive Therapy of Personality Disorders_ by Beck and Freeman).

5. If the client shares feelings, vulnerabilities, or admits mistakes, compliment him/her with phrases such as "it took real strength to 'tell it like it is'" and "most people wouldn't have had the guts to admit that—that was impressive."

6. Convey to the client that the purpose of the meetings with the therapist is to evaluate situations that are interfering with the client's success in getting what he/she wants out of life, and to find solutions.

3. Respond appropriately to having limits set in therapy. (7, 8)

7. Set limits with the client regarding basic therapy arrangements (e.g., availability by phone, payment arrangements, meeting times) in response to the client's request for special treatment.

8. Set limits when the client oversteps boundaries and expects special treatment, such as demands for special scheduling or fee arrangements, desires to smoke in the office, or inappropriately touch the therapist, etc. Use these instances to demonstrate to the client his/her cognitive schemas and belief systems, and relate these to areas in which he/she has problems in other relationships.

4. Express understanding of how a belittling statement may be perceived by another person, and how that may harm a desired relationship. (9, 10)

9. When the client devalues the therapist, explore the client's beliefs or fantasies regarding the impact that has on the therapist, or whether the client has even attended to the impact on the therapist; analyze

whether similar interactions may underlie difficulties in other important relationships.

10. Explore with the client the consequences of his/her denigrating, demanding or disrespectful statements, evaluating long-term negative consequences and how they interfere with the client's goals.

5. Each family member/partner reduce interactions within the family that serve to perpetuate the client's denigrating behavior. (11, 12)

11. During a family session, when the client enacts denigrating or exploitive behavior toward a family member, encourage the target person to set limits (e.g., "answer him back and get him to stop!"). Discontinue the intervention when some degree of success has been achieved, and verbally reward both participants (see *Family Therapy Techniques* by Minuchin and Fishman).

12. Explore family interactions that support denigrating behavior (e.g., the client feeling superior to family members), and family members' tolerance of the behavior.

6. State a request in a respectful manner, rather than as a demand or expectation. (10, 13, 14)

10. Explore with the client the consequences of his/her denigrating, demanding or disrespectful statements, evaluating long-term negative consequences and how they interfere with the client's goals.

13. Discuss with the client his/her role models regarding interpersonal conduct from prior generations (e.g., parents, uncles/aunts, grandparents), to gain an understanding of the

origins of the demanding behavior; process the effectiveness and appropriateness of these behaviors in the present circumstance.

14. During a family therapy session, instruct the client and significant other to engage in a dialogue regarding how to make requests in a way that is respectful.

7. Express readiness to attend group therapy. (15)

15. Instruct the client about the way groups operate, and how this may feel unfair to him/her (e.g., that all group members must be given an opportunity to speak, that everyone's problems are considered equally important, and that group members may not always be appreciative or admiring, but usually provide important feedback); process these themes with the client and refer when he/she is ready to participate in group therapy.

8. Each family member/partner reduce interactions within the family that serve to perpetuate the client's behavior. (11, 16)

11. During a family session, when the client enacts denigrating or exploitive behavior toward a family member, encourage the target person to set limits (e.g., "answer back to him and get him to stop!"). Discontinue the intervention when some degree of success has been achieved, and verbally reward both participants (see *Family Therapy Techniques* by Minuchin and Fishman).

16. Assist family members in identifying their behavior that reinforces exploitive behavior

9. Verbalize awareness of long-term disadvantages of conning, deception, and disloyalty to achieve his/her ends. (17, 18)

10. Verbalize realistic, achievable goals rather than grandiose fantasies that lead to perpetual disappointment. (19)

(e.g., significant other agrees to do all chores in the house). Write a behavioral contract that will allow each participant to get his/her needs met more directly (e.g., sharing chores, and using praise and other social rewards to reinforce the behavior).

17. Explore with the client the consequences of his/her exploitive, disloyal, and dishonest behaviors, evaluating long-term negative consequences and how they interfere with the client's goals.

18. Teach how disloyalty leads to a self-fulfilling prophecy that leads to further distrust (e.g., betraying people leads to being betrayed by them).

19. Interpret the underlying grandiosity and disappointment when the client falls short in an effort, connecting the client's affective experience to his/her wishes and needs; help him/her transform it into something realistic (e.g., "when they went with someone else's idea, you felt massively disappointed and deflated; you wanted them to think your idea was wonderful and would save the day, and when they rejected it you felt defeated and empty"). (See *Using Self Psychology in Brief Psychotherapy* by Gardner, and *Speaking in the Interpretive Mode and Feeling Understood: Crucial Aspect of Therapeutic Action in Psychotherapy* by Ornstein and Ornstein.)

11. Engage in a relationship in a cooperative, rather than a controlling or domineering, manner. (20, 21, 22)

20. Discuss relationships in early childhood in which the client was abused or deceived by an important figure; examine the repetition compulsion in the client's behavior toward others now.

21. Employ the family sculpture technique, recreating a situation in which the client was controlling or manipulative; process the meaning of the event with the client and his/her family, and collaborate with them to discover new and more satisfying ways of relating to one another.

22. Challenge the client's all-or-none thinking about dominance by encouraging him/her to think of role models (e.g., sports figures or other leaders) who were successful by virtue of their team play and team spirit, rather than by hostile aggression.

12. Increase expressions of empathy by accurately identifying the feelings of another person and verbalizing understanding of their predicament. (23, 24, 25)

23. Conduct or refer the client to group psychotherapy in order to provide feedback from others regarding his/her behavior, and to develop basic trust and accurate understanding of others.

24. In a psychodrama, group or individual session, the therapist (or a group member) plays the client, and the client plays the person who was hurt or exploited. Continue the intervention until the client achieves emotional identification with the victim.

25. Hold a family therapy session and encourage the client to persist in rewording and reflecting back the communication of the family member, spouse, or partner, until he/she agrees that the communication is accurate.

13. Demonstrate nurturance behaviors. (26)

26. Under close supervision, have the client interact with kittens, puppies, or children, which tend to naturally elicit nurturance; process the experience with the client (see *Interpersonal Diagnosis and Treatment of Personality Disorders* by Benjamin).

14. Express anger in an appropriate fashion, rather than becoming enraged and/or vindictive when feeling wronged, hurt, or belittled. (27, 28)

27. Ask the client to read *Of Course You're Angry* by Rosellini and Worden; *Managing Anger* by Messer, Coronado-Bogdaniak, and Dillon; or *The Dance of Anger: A Woman's Guide to Changing the Patterns of Intimate Relationships* by Lerner; process key ideas.

28. Institute stress inoculation training for anger by preparing the client for situations in which he/she becomes angry, using behavioral rehearsal to establish appropriate responses, and initiating self-rewards for maintaining control (see *Stress Reduction and Prevention* by Meichenbaum and Jaremko).

15. Identify how the masculine role has impacted behavior, and verbalize developing a more flexible gender role. (29, 30)

29. Process the meaning of masculinity to the client (e.g., needing to be strong, dominant, always on top, and to not show feelings or weakness); explore the impact

of these attitudes and actions, and how to create a healthy male identity (see *A New Psychology of Men* by Levant and Pollack). Hold a family therapy session and encourage the client to persist in rewording and reflecting back the communication of the family member, spouse, or partner, until he/she agrees that the communication is accurate.

30. Assign the client to read *Masculinity Reconstructed* by Levant and process the key ideas.

16. Verbally acknowledge, and express regret, that own sexually exploitive behavior (e.g., demanding sex from a subordinate, or misleading someone to obtain sexual gratification) was hurtful to another person. (31, 32)

31. Explore the client's sexual exploitation pattern, emphasizing the painful consequences to his/her victims.

32. Assist the client in identifying and listing the disadvantages of taking advantage of others and suspecting their wanting to take advantage of him/her.

17. Verbalize beliefs that will encourage the maintenance of satisfying long-term relationships. (33, 34)

33. Conduct or refer the client to a structured therapeutic wilderness adventure program (e.g., Outward Bound), taking advantage of the client's action orientation and providing opportunities to learn about trust (see *Interpersonal Diagnosis and Treatment of Personality Disorders* by Benjamin).

34. Explore the client's distorted, negative beliefs regarding intimate relationships (e.g., there is a person who will never disappoint him/her, or that no one is worth the effort since all

people are basically rotten). Challenge the ideas using rational emotive techniques, replacing unrealistic ideas with more flexible and realistic ones (e.g., everyone has faults; any long-term relationship has peaks and valleys; most people have redeeming features).

18. List the difficulties that have been experienced in forming intimate attachments in prior relationships. (35, 36)

35. Validate the client's concerns regarding intimate relationships and express unconditional positive regard (e.g., that the feelings are understandable from the client's perspective).

36. Ask the client to describe any dreams that he/she has had, and discuss themes involving intimacy and connections to others.

19. Cooperate with a referral to a physician to evaluate the need for psychotropic medication to improve mood and/or to decrease irritability. (37)

37. Refer the client to a physician for an evaluation for psychotropic medications; help the client to process costs and benefits of a psychiatric evaluation.

20. Take psychotropic medications as prescribed, and report as to the effectiveness and side effects. (38)

38. Monitor the client's use of medications for compliance with prescription, effectiveness, and side effects; confer with the client's physician about the effectiveness of the medications on a regular basis.

21. Describe feelings of respect for one other person. (39)

39. Challenge the client's all-or-none thinking by asking him/her to recall or imagine instances when an individual was worthy of trust or respect (e.g., a person, just once, did not betray him/her or did him/her a favor with no expectation of anything in return).

22. Verbalize an expectation of average treatment, rather than expecting special treatment or being above the rules in most or all situations. (40)

40. Using Socratic dialogue, challenge the client's feelings of entitlement (e.g., "I should be rewarded by virtue of my superior talent") by gently exploring the supportive evidence (e.g., listing actual accomplishments).

23. Express satisfaction with what he/she has, rather than always wanting more. (41, 42)

41. Ask the client to read *How to Want What You Have: Discovering the Magic and Grandeur of Ordinary Experience* by Miller, and process key points.

42. Explore the client's dreams and fantasies regarding omnipotent power, riches, or control; connect these to current or past relationships, and the ability to engage in collaborative relationships.

__. _____   __. _____
_____   _____
__. _____   __. _____
_____   _____

DIAGNOSTIC SUGGESTIONS:

ICD-9-CM	*ICD-10-CM*	*DSM-5* Disorder, Condition, or Problem
296.xx	F32.x	Major Depressive Disorder, Single Episode
296.xx	F33.x	Major Depressive Disorder, Recurrent Episode
300.4	F34.1	Persistent Depressive Disorder
301.81	F60.81	Narcissistic Personality Disorder
301.7	F60.2	Antisocial Personality Disorder
301.9	F60.9	Unspecified Personality Disorder
_____	_____	_____
_____	_____	_____

PROBLEM-SOLVING SKILL DEFICITS

BEHAVIORAL DEFINITIONS

1. Routinely overlooks and fails to consider all the important factors when responding to problems.
2. Inability to adequately problem solve creates or adds to the problems that significant others must deal with.
3. Often resorts to criminal behavior (e.g., assault, burglary, embezzling) to solve interpersonal, economic, or other problems.
4. Frequently unable to recognize or define problems in sufficient time to avoid having problems evolve into pernicious and seemingly out-of-control situations.
5. Unrealistically relies on magical or wishful thinking to resolve real-life problems.
6. Frequently opts to deliberately avoid addressing problems and critical decisions.
7. Limited decision-making abilities result in frequent self-disapproval and diminished self-concept.
8. Unable to make personal decisions and stick to them.
9. Pattern of personal decision making that results in loss of freedom, income, and social opportunities.

—. _____
_____

—. _____
_____

—. _____
_____

LONG-TERM GOALS

1. Adhere to a proven sequential step process for making good problem-solving decisions.
2. Recognize and appropriately classify problems at the earliest possible stage.
3. Thoroughly investigate problems so that subsequent decisions are based on the best available information.
4. Clearly define and state the essential factors constituting a given problem.
5. Experience progressively better health-related, financial, and social outcomes as a result of better problem solving.

—. _____
_____
_____

—. _____
_____
_____

—. _____
_____

SHORT-TERM OBJECTIVES

1. Describe conflicts that have developed because of ineffective problem solving. (1, 2)

2. List the consequences of effective versus ineffective problem solving. (1, 3)

THERAPEUTIC INTERVENTIONS

1. Explore the client's history of problem recognition, attempts at problem solving, and consequences of ineffective problem solving.

2. Assist the client in identifying his/her ineffective problem-solving approaches (e.g., ignoring or avoiding confronting a problem, becoming aggressive).

1. Explore the client's history of problem recognition, attempts at problem solving, and consequences of ineffective problem solving.

3. Discuss with the client what some of the consequences are

for effective versus ineffective problem solving (e.g., ineffective problem solving leads to: the problem getting worse, lack of control over outcomes, wasting time solving an ill-defined problem, neglecting pertinent information).

3. Formulate a definition of problems that makes if obvious how commonplace they are in everyday experience. (4, 5)

4. Discuss and explore with the client a definition for problems that is both comprehensive and concrete (e.g., problems continuously arise out of everyday life dealings with other people and one's own thoughts and emotions).

5. Teach the client that problems have many nuances, conse-quences, and demands (e.g., problems are varied in duration, intensity, and malignancy; problems cause stress; problems create difficult feelings and thoughts; problems sometimes require action; action is driven by thoughts and feelings; problems often require dealing with other people; problems can create other problems).

4. Identify methods that have been used to determine that a problem exists. (6)

6. Ask the client to list all the different methods he/she has used for recognizing and determining when he/she has a problem on his/her hands (e.g., increased amounts of stress, feedback from others, a feeling of gloom).

5. Sort methods of problem determination into those that arise from internal versus external indicators. (7)

7. Assist the client in sorting internal (e.g., feelings, physical sensations) from external (e.g., signals or messages from

6. List the pros and cons of identifying a problem sooner rather than later. (3, 8)

outside of your body) problem indicators.

3. Discuss with the client what some of the consequences are for effective versus ineffective problem solving (e.g., ineffective problem solving leads to: the problem getting worse, lack of control over outcomes, wasting time solving an ill-defined problem, neglecting pertinent information).

8. Ask the client to list the pros and cons of identifying a problem sooner versus later.

7. List the pros and cons of solving a problem sooner rather than later. (3, 9)

3. Discuss with the client what some of the consequences are for effective versus ineffective problem solving (e.g., ineffective problem solving leads to: the problem getting worse, lack of control over outcomes, wasting time solving an ill-defined problem, neglecting pertinent information).

9. Assign the client to list the pros and cons of solving a problem sooner versus later.

8. Write out the common steps for problem solving that most often assure success. (10)

10. Ask the client to list the ideal steps (e.g., define the problem, identify alternative solutions, list the pros and cons of each alternative through information gathering, decide on the best course, implement a solution, evaluate the outcome) involved in successful problem solving.

9. Describe the differences between fact and opinion. (11, 12)

11. Teach the client the difference between fact and opinion (e.g., in order to solve a problem, it

needs to be defined clearly to avoid confusion regarding what I *think* the problem is [opinion] versus what the problem really is [fact]. Often when presenting a problem, we confuse fact and opinion, or present opinion as fact).

12. Assign the client to identify and record at least three recent occasions when he/she directly observed people having trouble sorting fact from opinion.

10. Identify a set of skills that contribute to good fact finding. (13)

13. Discuss primary fact finding skills that contribute to good fact-finding (e.g., Observation or using the senses to take in what the problem is; Information Gathering or asking questions [Who, What, When, Where, Why] to increase the information we have about a problem to aid in formulating a complete definition of the problem; Remembering or using different techniques to store all the information gathered [mnemonics, taking notes]; Evaluation or sorting the information collected for relevancy, fact, and opinion).

11. Identify personal strengths and weaknesses in fact findings. (14)

14. Assist the client in identifying his/her fact-finding strengths and weaknesses (i.e., which skills are utilized and which are ignored).

12. Describe the impact that pausing to think has on each of the fact-finding skills. (15)

15. Ask the client to write a description for the effect(s) pausing to think would likely have on his/her fact-finding skills (e.g., allows for more complete observation, allows for father more information

regarding the problems and possible solutions, allows time to recall previous similar problems and successful solutions, allows time for evaluating facts versus opinions).

13. Describe how open questions and closed questions are different and what terms tend to prompt or activate one versus the other type of question. (16, 17)

16. Explain the dynamics and differences between open (e.g., leads the other person to give more complete answers that may express his/her thoughts, feelings, and opinions) and closed (e.g., leads the other person to give brief answers without room for feelings and opinions) questions.

17. Teach the client how open and closed questions have common "stems" that instigate an open (e.g., "Tell me about . . . ," "Describe . . . ," "What . . .") or closed (e.g., "Did you . . . ?" "When did . . . ?").

14. Demonstrate the use of open versus closed questions when probing for more information on several different topics. (17, 18)

17. Teach the client how open and closed questions have common "stems" that instigate an open (e.g., "Tell me about . . . ," "Describe . . . ," "What . . .") or closed (e.g., "Did you . . . ?" "When did . . . ?").

18. Use modeling and role-playing to teach the client how to use open and closed questions in various situations to gather information.

15. Demonstrate an understanding of the steps in effective problem solving and implement these steps in daily life. (19, 20, 21, 22)

19. Instruct the client in a recognized model for problem solving (e.g., *Aggression Replacement Training* by Goldstein and Glick; *The Prepare Curriculum* by

Goldstein; *Reasoning and Rehabilitation* by Ross, Fabiano, and Ross) that addresses and elaborates on specific components for the phases of problem solving.

20. Use role-playing, modeling, and behavior rehearsal to teach the client how to implement the sequence of phases or steps for problem solving.

21. Clarify with the client which of the steps in effective problem solving are action steps and which are thinking steps.

22. Assign the client to a group that teaches skills in problem solving.

16. List preconditions that can improve the success rate of problem solving. (23)

23. Discuss and explore with the client various helpful preconditions for problem-solving (e.g., willingness to take responsibility, seek help or learn from mistakes).

17. Demonstrate an understanding of the HALT technique and what influence practicing this technique might have on problem-solving abilities. (24, 25, 26)

24. Teach the client the HALT technique (i.e., if ever Hungry, Angry, Lonely, or Tired, stop and remedy the situation before trying to solve a problem) as an example of a helpful precondition technique for improving problem solving.

25. Review with the client two or three scenarios for each of the four components of HALT (e.g., "what if one was too hungry or had too low blood sugar to concentrate," "what if someone's anger prevented them from identifying a broader range of options) and how each might influence

problem solving or decision making.

26. Ask the client to write a brief, four paragraph paper on how implementing the HALT technique might have a positive impact on problem solving.

18. Maintain a daily log for two weeks that identifies various problems that arise that are challenging. (27, 28)

27. Ask the client to maintain a daily log that identifies the various problems he/she confronts on a day-to-day basis.

28. Review the client's problem log each week and provide him/her with constructive feedback as to implementing effective steps for problem solving.

19. List the potential short- and long-term benefits as well as the potential short- and long-term costs of a decision. (29)

29. Demonstrate how a typical client problem can be analyzed using a decision balance process (e.g., identifying short- and long-term costs versus benefits for a plan of action).

20. Enlist trustworthy friends or family members to act as sounding boards regarding decisions once a week for one month. (30)

30. Ask the client to identify two or three friends or family members whom he/she trusts that could give him/her reasonable feedback on decision making and instruct him/her to review at least one personal decision with each of these friends once a week for a month.

21. Acknowledge using antisocial behaviors to solve problems and describe the negative consequences associated with this pattern. (2, 31, 32)

2. Assist the client in identifying his/her ineffective problem-solving approaches (e.g., ignoring or avoiding confronting a problem, becoming aggressive).

31. Explore the client's pattern of using criminal behavior to "solve" problems rather than using a more effective and adaptive process.

32. Review with the client the significant negative consequences of using antisocial means to solve problems (e.g., legal entanglements, loss of freedom, pain to self and others).

22. List pro-social behaviors that evolve from implementing effective problem solving steps as an alternative to criminal behavior. (33)

33. Review incidents in which the client used antisocial behavior in response to a problem; assist him/her in listing pro-social behaviors that result from implementing the steps for effective problem solving.

23. Solve a classic puzzle and write out the steps for problem solving that were used. (34, 35)

34. Provide the client with a set of five different riddles or mental puzzles (e.g., *The Great Book of Mind Teasers and Mind Puzzlers* by Summers, *Brain Bafflers* by Steinwachs, *Mind Pack* by DeBono, or *The Mammoth Book of Astounding Puzzles* by Serebriakoff) and ask him/her to solve as many as possible, but at least one.

35. Assign the client to list which of the ideal steps (e.g., define the problem; identify alternative solutions, list the pros and cons of each alternative through information gathering; decide on the best course; implement a solution; evaluate the outcome) involved in successful problem solving were used in solving the mental puzzle.

24. Set some concrete goals that can be met within two months regarding improving personal problem-solving skills. (36, 37)

36. Assist the client in setting some reasonable goals for improving problem-solving abilities and skill.

37. Recommend some self-help reading materials for building better problem-solving abilities (e.g., *Step-By-Step Problem Solving* by Chang and Kelly or *Yes or No: The Guide to Better Decisions* by Johnson).

__. _____   __. _____
   _____   _____
__. _____   __. _____
   _____   _____
__. _____   __. _____
   _____   _____

DIAGNOSTIC SUGGESTIONS:

ICD-9-CM	*ICD-10-CM*	*DSM-5* Disorder, Condition, or Problem
300.4	F34.1	Persistent Depressive Disorder
312.34	F63.81	Intermittent Explosive Disorder
301.7	F60.2	Antisocial Personality Disorder
V62.89	R41.83	Borderline Intellectual Functioning
317	F70	Intellectual Disability, Mild
_____	_____	_____
_____	_____	_____

PSYCHOSIS

BEHAVIORAL DEFINITIONS

1. Experiences bizarre (implausible) or nonbizarre (i.e., involving situations that occur in real life) delusions.
2. Psychomotor functioning is impaired (e.g., marked decrease in reactivity to the environment, catatonic behavior, unusual mannerisms, or grimacing).
3. Illogical and disorganized speech (e.g., incoherent, tangential, vague, or repetitive speech).
4. Experiences hallucinations (e.g., auditory, olfactory, visual, or tactile).
5. Demonstrates blunted or inappropriate affect.
6. Withdrawal from involvement with external world and preoccupation with egocentric ideas and fantasies.
7. Extreme aggression toward the external world based in irrational delusional thought and/or uncontrollable hallucinations.

—. _____
   _____
—. _____
   _____
—. _____
   _____

LONG-TERM GOALS

1. Control or eliminate debilitating psychotic symptoms and return to highest level of effective functioning.
2. Increase ability to cope with severe stressors that might precipitate a psychotic break.

3. Improve awareness and understanding of psychosis.
4. Interact with others without defensiveness or aggression.

—. _____

_____

—. _____

_____

—. _____

_____

SHORT-TERM OBJECTIVES

THERAPEUTIC INTERVENTIONS

1. Describe the history and current status of the psychotic symptoms. (1, 2)

1. Explore the client's experience of psychotic symptoms.

2. Coordinate psychological testing to assess the extent and the severity of the client's psychotic symptoms.

2. Cooperate with a short-term placement in a psychiatric facility. (3, 4)

3. Assess the client's level of risk to himself/herself and others, and his/her ability to care for his/her own basic needs.

4. Refer and arrange for involuntary commitment to a secure psychiatric facility if the client is deemed harmful to himself/herself, others, or is unable to care for his/her own basic needs.

3. Cooperate with a complete psychiatric evaluation and comply with treatment and/or medication recommendations. (5, 6)

5. Refer the client for an immediate evaluation by a psychiatrist regarding his/her psychotic symptoms and a possible prescription for antipsychotic medication.

6. Monitor or arrange for the supervision of the client's medication compliance, effectiveness, and side effects.

4. Comply with a move to a supervised or assisted living situation. (7, 8)

7. Arrange for the client to remain in a stable, supervised situation (e.g., crisis adult foster care [AFC] placement or a friend's/family member's home).

8. Monitor the client's adjustment to the supervised living situation; move him/her to a more structured, secure psychiatric setting, if necessary.

5. Initiate and engage in a therapeutic process (individual and/or group therapy). (9)

9. Refer the client to a therapeutic process (supportive individual and/or group therapy, depending on the needs of the client, temperament and available resources); process the experience.

6. Describe stressors that may have precipitated the psychotic break. (10, 11)

10. Explore with the client the stressors and feelings around the stressors that may have precipitated the psychotic break.

11. Explore with the client any unresolved grief or anger issues that may be contributing to internal conflict that triggers psychotic symptoms.

7. Identify healthy ways of coping with stressors before they become severe. (12)

12. Assist the client in identifying ways of responding to the stressors before they become severe (e.g., seeking assistance from others, escaping from the stressful situation, practicing relaxation exercises, engage in a distraction activity).

8. Change or make necessary environmental adjustments so as to reduce the feeling of threat or stress. (13, 14, 15)

13. Assist the client in making any environmental adjustments to reduce the feeling of threat or stress (e.g., changing neighborhoods, limiting or enhancing contact with family,

arranging for regular visits from a caseworker).

14. Utilize caregivers with whom the client is familiar as much as possible to avoid anxiety in the client regarding interacting with strangers.

15. Maintain a regular schedule of activities for the client to establish a routine that is predictable.

9. Replace the irrational beliefs that contribute to the psychotic symptoms with reality-based beliefs. (5, 16, 17)

5. Refer the client for an immediate evaluation by a psychiatrist regarding his/her psychotic symptoms and a possible prescription for antipsychotic medication.

16. Assist the client in reviewing and inventorying some irrational beliefs or descriptions that contribute to the psychotic symptoms (e.g., I am being hunted down and therefore have to strike out at anyone who comes my way).

17. Differentiate for the client the difference between self-generated delusional beliefs and the reality of the external world.

10. Formulate, in writing, several alternatives or ways to counter irrational beliefs. (18, 19, 20)

18. Assist the client in the restructuring of irrational beliefs by reviewing reality-based evidence and misinterpretation; ask him/her to write down the reality that counters the delusional beliefs.

19. Encourage the client to seek frequent reality testing to challenge his/her distorted beliefs (e.g., compare his/her cognitions with the experience

of trusted caregivers, friends, and family).

20. Facilitate a brainstorming inventory of alternatives to counter irrational beliefs that contribute to the psychotic symptoms (e.g., check reality with a trusted person, being consistent with taking medications, accept mental illness as the cause of irrational beliefs).

11. Report diminishing or absence of hallucinations and/or delusions. (5, 6, 21)

5. Refer the client for an immediate evaluation by a psychiatrist regarding his/her psychotic symptoms and a possible prescription for antipsychotic medication.

6. Monitor or arrange for the supervision of the client's medication compliance, effectiveness, and side effects.

21. Reinforce any control over, diminishing or absence of hallucinations and/or delusions.

12. Read about ways that other people have coped with psychosis. (22, 23)

22. Provide the client with a selection of reading options on the topic of mental illness (e.g., *Seduction of Madness* by Podvoll; *Change Your Brain, Change Your Life: The Breakthrough Program for Conquering Anxiety, Depression, Obsessiveness, Anger, and Impulsiveness* by Amen; or *Overcoming Destructive Beliefs, Feelings and Behaviors* by Ellis).

23. Process with the client what he/she has learned through the reading of educational material on mental illness.

13. Establish a regular sleeping, eating, personal hygiene, and exercise pattern. (24, 25)

24. Teach the client the importance of maintaining healthy sleeping, eating, personal hygiene, and exercise pattern.

25. Follow up with the client about his/her progress in maintaining a healthy sleeping, eating, personal hygiene, and exercise pattern.

14. Implement healthy assertive communication skills that support the expression of thoughts, feelings, and needs. (26, 27, 28)

26. Explore with the client his/her history of lack of assertiveness in expressing his/her thoughts, feelings, or needs.

27. Instruct the client in healthy assertive communication skills (e.g., feelings talk, listening skills, asking for help, refusing request).

28. Review the client's implementation of assertive communication skills in daily life; reinforce success and redirect for failure.

15. Gradually return to highest possible level of functioning and accept responsibility and caring for own basic needs. (29, 30)

29. Monitor the client's daily level of functioning (e.g., social interactions, personal hygiene, reality orientation and appropriate affect) and give feedback that either redirects or reinforces his/her progress.

30. Continually monitor the client's possible decompensation that would lead to him/her engaging in aggressive behavior that would be harmful to himself/herself or others.

—. _____
   _____
—. _____
   _____

—. _____
   _____
—. _____
   _____

DIAGNOSTIC SUGGESTIONS:

ICD-9-CM	ICD-10-CM	DSM-5 Disorder, Condition, or Problem
297.1	F22	Delusional Disorder
298.8	F23	Brief Psychotic Disorder
295.90	F20.9	Schizophrenia
295.70	F25.0	Schizoaffective Disorder, Bipolar Type
295.70	F25.1	Schizoaffective Disorder, Depressive Type
295.40	F20.81	Schizophreniform Disorder
296.xx	F31.xx	Bipolar I Disorder
296.89	F31.81	Bipolar II Disorder
296.xx	F32.x	Major Depressive Disorder, Single Episode
296.xx	F33.x	Major Depressive Disorder, Recurrent Episode
301.22	F21	Schizotypal Personality Disorder
301.7	F60.2	Antisocial Personality Disorder
_____	_____	_____
_____	_____	_____

SELF-CONCEPT DEFICITS

BEHAVIORAL DEFINITIONS

1. Inability to identify own positive traits or achievements.
2. Poor self-image leads to association with low-achieving peers.
3. Uses criminal behavior in an attempt to impress others.
4. Powerful fear of rejection or criticism contributes to a difficulty saying no to others.
5. Repeated critical or reproachful statements about self with a pessimistic outlook on own abilities or future.
6. Extreme lack of self-confidence in abilities that inhibits initiating new activities or seeking pro-social, successful friends.
7. Avoids interpersonal interaction due to view of self as inferior, socially inept, inadequate, or personally unappealing.
8. Unrealistic evaluation of self that leads to inappropriately high goals resulting in failures that reinforce feelings of inadequacy.

—. _____
   _____
   _____
—. _____
   _____

LONG-TERM GOALS

1. Develop a consistent, positive self-image.
2. Develop healthy, positive cognitive patterns about self and the world.
3. Increase the ability to self-soothe, self-regulate, and evaluate self in a fair manner.
4. Develop a sense of abilities and self-worth that is based in reality.

—. _____
_____
—. _____
_____

SHORT-TERM OBJECTIVES

1. Describe the view of self, including positive and negative traits. (1)

2. Participate in a group therapeutic process to explore and develop self-esteem. (2)

3. Read material to learn self-esteem building techniques. (3)

4. Describe the mask that is used to hide the real self. (4, 5)

THERAPEUTIC INTERVENTIONS

1. Explore the client's view of himself/herself, asking him/her to list his/her positive and negative traits.

2. Refer the client to a group therapeutic process that supports and develops self-esteem and self-worth; monitor and process the client's progress.

3. Provide the client with a selection of reading materials to learn techniques to improve his/her self-concept (e.g., *Overcoming Low Self-Esteem* by Fennell, *Self-Esteem* by McKay and Fanning, *Maximum Self-Esteem* by Minchinton); process information gained through reading.

4. Discuss with the client the various functions a mask serves and how masks might be a metaphor to distort the presentation of himself/herself.

5. Provide the client with a range of materials (e.g., cardboard, scissors, glue, tape, string, magazine pictures, found objects such as bones, feathers) and instructions in building a personal mask.

5. Identify the costs and benefits of having a limited or distorted view of self. (6)

6. Explore with the client what common costs (e.g., inadequacy, not initiating or accomplishing anything, diminished spontaneity or genuineness) and benefits (e.g., precipitates support from others, protective camouflage, avoidance or delay of responsible action) of having a limited or distorted view of himself/herself.

6. List the ways that automatic thinking might be related to problems related to lack of power, lack of control and diminished ability to initiate new tasks. (7, 8)

7. Instruct the client in the fundamental dynamics and relationships between thoughts, beliefs, feelings, and actions and how automatic thinking is manufactured.

8. Teach the client how automatic thinking leads to believing he/she has a lack of power (e.g., "No one listens to me"), a lack of control (e.g., "Nothing I do makes a difference"), and a lack of ability to initiate new tasks (e.g., "I'll never be successful at anything I try").

7. Identify and replace negative self-talk present in automatic thoughts. (9, 10)

9. Assist the client in reviewing and inventorying some of his/her negative self-talk that supports low self-esteem (e.g., "I am no good," "I can never do things right," "I'm not worthy of praise").

10. Facilitate a brainstorming inventory of possible positive ways to reframe self-talk to support increased positive self-esteem.

8. Contact at least one person daily to receive support. (11)

11. Assist the client in listing at least seven people that are supportive of his/her goal to

increase self-esteem; advise him/her to contact at least one person everyday for support.

9. List positive achievements or qualities and add to this list everyday. (12)

12. Instruct the client to maintain and update daily a list of attributes and achievements that the client encountered in himself/herself and is proud of; review this list weekly with the client, encouraging him/her to consult his/her supportive peers for additions to the list.

10. Implement actions to develop or improve desired characteristics, traits, or abilities. (13, 14, 15)

13. Assist the client in listing characteristics, traits, or abilities that he/she would like to develop or improve that are possible and within reach.

14. Advise the client to set three short-term goals (achievable in three months) related to improving or developing desired characteristics, traits, or abilities.

15. Assist the client in brainstorming ways to improve or strengthen desired characteristics, traits, or abilities; encourage the client to implement the actions that will serve to improve self-image.

11. Describe situations in which it has been difficult to assertively express thoughts, feelings, or needs assertively. (16)

16. Explore the client's history of a lack of assertiveness in expressing his/her thoughts, feelings, or needs.

12. Implement healthy communication skills that support the assertive expression of thoughts, feelings, and needs. (17, 18, 19)

17. Instruct the client in healthy, assertive communication skills (e.g., feelings talk, "I" statements, listening skills, asking for help, refusing request).

18. Use modeling and role-playing to teach the client several

conflict resolution skills (e.g., double-sided reflections, partially agreeing, agreeing with a twist) that could improve his/her communication; utilize recent situations where better communication skills would have improved the outcome.

19. Review the client's implementation of new conflict resolution and assertiveness skills in daily life; reinforce success and redirect for failure.

13. Increase involvement with other pro-social people and activities to practice communication and esteem skills. (20, 21, 22, 23, 24)

20. Advise the client to make efforts to get more involved with other pro-social people; suggest activities that might facilitate that process (e.g., joining a community or church group, inviting someone from work to a recreational activity, become a volunteer, take an educational class).

21. Advise the client to explore three different clubs, groups or organizations (e.g., 12-step groups, church or faith community, sports, or fitness groups) in three weeks to initiate contact with pro-social people.

22. Direct the client to select and become involved in one club, group, or organization of interest (e.g., sports league, church, charity organization, AA/NA) for at least nine consecutive weeks to give himself/herself a chance to build relationships from a stronger sense of self-worth.

23. Encourage the client to practice new assertive social skills with other members of a club, group, or organization in an effort to develop new friends and acquaintances.

24. Debrief the client about how the assertiveness techniques worked; provide him/her with positive reinforcement for effort and feedback for improvements.

14. Implement relaxation techniques to reduce social anxiety. (25)

25. Teach the client simple, quick relaxation techniques to use when experiencing social anxiety (e.g., breathing deeply, counting backward, imagining a pleasant scene, manipulating a worry stone).

15. Review goals set to improve or develop self and receive feedback on progress. (26)

26. Review with the client and provide feedback on his/her progress made on the short-term goals; reinforce success and redirect for failure.

—. _____   —. _____

_____   _____

DIAGNOSTIC SUGGESTIONS:

ICD-9-CM	_ICD-10-CM_	_DSM-5_ Disorder, Condition, or Problem
300.4	F34.1	Persistent Depressive Disorder
296.xx	F32.x	Major Depressive Disorder, Single Episode
296.xx	F33.x	Major Depressive Disorder, Recurrent Episode
301.9	F60.9	Unspecified Personality Disorder
301.82	F60.6	Avoidant Personality Disorder
301.6	F60.7	Dependent Personality Disorder
_____	_____	_____
_____	_____	_____

SELF-DEFEATING BEHAVIOR PATTERNS (non-AOD)

BEHAVIORAL DEFINITIONS

1. Inability to manage urges, impulses, and cravings and remain abstinent from self-defeating behaviors (e.g., loss of temper, gambling, dysfunctional family interaction, sexual acting-out, poor health habits, isolating socially, shoplifting, noncompliance with medication).
2. Verbalizes a commitment to abstain from self-defeating behaviors but has no plan, strategy, or specific skills for achieving this goal.
3. Increased frequency of engaging in self-defeating behaviors when feeling down, sad, angry, scared, embarrassed, or bored.
4. Feels social pressure when around others who are involved in self-defeating behaviors.
5. Increased frequency of engaging in self-defeating behaviors after fights and arguments with others or after being criticized by someone else.
6. Positive emotions, testing personal control and/or feeling bad physically frequently threatens or undermines commitment to abstain from self-defeating behavior.
7. All or nothing attitude toward changing self-defeating behaviors, results in self-loathing and disgust when slips or minor set-backs are experienced.
8. Little or no lifestyle balance in terms of the amount of obligations or "shoulds" fulfilled as opposed to the amount of gratifications of "wants."
9. Ceases utilizing established and effective strategies, methods, and skills to abstain from self-defeating behaviors.
10. Chronic difficulties managing stress contribute to an on-going cycle of relapse into self-defeating behavior.

—. _____

_____

—. _____

_____

LONG-TERM GOALS

1. Terminate self-defeating behavior and replace it with healthy habits.
2. Develop a set of realistic plans, strategies, and skills for abstaining from self-defeating behaviors and utilize these strategies in everyday living.
3. Build and maintain more supportive social relationships that support abstinence and behavior change goals.
4. Develop a more flexible and resilient self-concept that allows for setbacks in behavior change, but fosters on-going self-improvement.
5. Learn skills for coping with urges, impulses, and cravings for self-defeating behaviors and for reframing their unrealistic outcome expectancies.
6. Learn and implement specific techniques and skills for successfully coping all major high-risk situations relevant to remaining abstinent from self-defeating behavior.

—. _____

_____

—. _____

_____

SHORT-TERM OBJECTIVES

1. Identify the specific self-defeating behavior patterns that are engaged in. (1)

THERAPEUTIC INTERVENTIONS

1. Explore the self-defeating behavior patterns that the client engages in (e.g., loss of temper, gambling, dysfunctional family relations, sexual acting-out, poor health habits, isolating socially, shoplifting, noncompliance with medication).

2. Cooperate with a complete psychological assessment and comply with any further assessments or treatment recommendation. (2)

2. Refer the client for a complete psychological assessment and for additional assessments and/or treatment as indicated (see Chemical Dependence, Anger Management, and Criminal Peers chapters in this *Planner* for further information).

3. Verbalize an understanding of the stages that people go through when changing behavior. (3)

3. Explain to the client the stages of change model for modifying self-defeating behavior (e.g., precontemplation, contemplation, determination, action, maintenance, relapse; see *Changing for Good* by Prochaska, Norcross, and DiClemente).

4. Identify what progress has been made in the process of change that has many stages. (4, 5, 6)

4. Explore with the client his/her past efforts at changing his/her self-defeating behavior, current attitude toward the behavior and intention to change this behavior.

5. Assist the client in determining what stage of change he/she is in (e.g., precontemplation, contemplation, determination, action, maintenance, relapse; see *Changing for Good* by Prochaska, Norcross, and DiClemente).

6. Based on the stage of change, respond appropriately to the client (e.g., if in the precontemplation stage, provide education to raise awareness and doubt; if in the contemplation stage, explore ambivalence about behavior change; if in the determination stage, help determine an action plan; if in the action stage,

support the client with following through the action plan; if in maintenance, help develop a relapse prevention plan and support other areas of life; if in relapse, facilitate the client's re-entry into the change process).

5. List the positive benefits and negative consequences of changing the behavior, as well as the positive benefits and the negative consequences of not changing the behavior. (7)

7. Conduct a benefits and consequences analysis with the client, exploring with the client the positive benefits and the negative consequences of changing the behavior, as well as the positive benefits and the negative consequences of not changing the behavior.

6. List four short-term goals related to desisting the self-defeating behavior. (8)

8. Assist the client in setting four short-term goals related to changing the self-defeating behavior.

7. Verbalize an understanding of the process of relapse. (9, 10, 11)

9. Explain to the client the process of relapse that minimally includes triggers, high-risk situations, seemingly unimportant decisions, lapse, and relapse.

10. Provide the client with a selection of reading material on relapse prevention (e.g., *Surviving Addiction Workbook* by Daley, *Relapse Prevention: Cognitive and Behavioral Interventions* by Daley and Marlatt, *Hope and Recovery: A Twelve-Step Guide for Healing from Compulsive Sexual Behavior* by CompCare, *Relapse Prevention: Maintenance Strategies in the Treatment of Self-Defeating Behaviors* by Marlatt and Gordon).

11. Teach the client what can be learned from relapse in that it provides valuable information about what works and what does not work to terminate self-defeating behavior.

8. List the high-risk situations and triggers for the self-defeating behavior that lead to relapse. (12, 13)

12. Assist the client in compiling a written list of his/her triggers (e.g., attitudes, thoughts, negative emotions, interpersonal conflict) for relapse.

13. Assist the client in compiling a written list of his/her high-risk situations (e.g., parties, being with criminal peers, substance abuse) for relapse.

9. Implement skills to deal with triggers and high-risk situations. (14, 15, 16, 17)

14. Use role-play, modeling, and behavior rehearsal to teach the client relapse prevention skills (awareness, acceptance, avoiding high-risk situations, coping with triggers, using a supportive network, keeping priorities, using positive self-talk); provide feedback as necessary.

15. Teach the client skills for managing thoughts that trigger self-defeating behavior (e.g., thought stopping, taking thoughts to court, reframing); use role-play to apply these skills to the client's daily life.

16. Teach the client skills for managing feelings that trigger self-defeating behavior (e.g., recognizing feelings, accepting feelings, sharing feelings); use role-play to apply these skills to the client's daily life.

17. Use role-play and modeling to teach the client skills to manage interpersonal conflict (e.g., setting boundaries, implementing refusal skills) that can trigger relapse of the self-defeating behavior.

10. List the steps involved in gaining knowledge from a relapse. (18)

18. Teach the client how to learn from a relapse (e.g., evaluate what happened, the causes, what information does it provide for the next time, remake a plan using this information, renew commitment, take action).

11. Identify and replace the specific dysfunctional self-talk that reduces self-efficacy for desisting the self-defeating behavior. (19, 20)

19. Assist the client in listing his/her negative self-talk that inhibits or obstructs beginning the process of abstaining from self-defeating behavior (e.g., "I can't do it"; "It's not worth it"; "I don't deserve the help").

20. Brainstorm with the client positive reframes for his/her negative self-talk that would support abstaining from self-defeating behavior (e.g., "I can do it"; "I deserve to do this for myself"; "It is possible").

12. Identify the components of a balanced lifestyle and list activities that need to be added to achieve balance. (21, 22, 23, 24)

21. Explore with the client what a balanced lifestyle means (being able to manage and enjoy different aspects of life); assist him/her in identifying the variety of life roles and activities he/she could engage in to avoid relapse into self-defeating behaviors.

22. Instruct the client to list "shoulds" (obligations) and "wants" (desires) in different

areas of his/her life (e.g., physical, emotional, spiritual, employment, peers, education, financial) on two sides of a page.

23. Explain to the client how lifestyle imbalance occurs using the analogy of a seesaw, if one side (obligations an desires) outweighs the other; point out the high-risk of relapse associated with this condition.

24. Instruct the client to generate a list of pleasant activities (or desires) that he/she could engage in to increase lifestyle balance and satisfaction.

13. Journal daily about what triggers or high-risk situations were faced, the corresponding self-talk engaged in and what coping strategies were used. (25, 26)

25. Instruct the client to journal daily about what triggers and high-risk situations were faced, negative self-talk engaged in, the corresponding positive reframes used, coping strategies implemented, and outcome.

26. Using the client's journal of daily triggers and high-risk situations he/she encountered, explain to him/her the importance of being aware of Seemingly Unimportant Decisions (SUDs) that are often the beginnings to a relapse (e.g., sitting at a casino bar thinking that I can handle resisting gambling, waking up in the morning feeling well and thinking that I can go the rest of the day without my medication).

14. Increase social network supportive of relapse prevention. (27, 28)

27. Explore with the client his/her current social network and brainstorm ways to increase

his/her positive social network that would be supportive of relapse prevention.

28. Assist the client in identifying potentially supportive people and how to directly ask them for help.

15. Review progress made on goals set at the beginning of treatment and set new goals as necessary. (29, 30)

29. Review with the client progress made on goals set at the beginning of treatment and provide the client with feedback.

30. Assist the client in setting new short-term goals for changing self-defeating behavior.

—. _____   —. _____

   _____   _____

—. _____   —. _____

   _____   _____

DIAGNOSTIC SUGGESTIONS:

ICD-9-CM	_ICD-10-CM_	_DSM-5_ Disorder, Condition, or Problem
307.50	F50.9	Unspecified Feeding or Eating Disorder
312.34	F63.81	Intermittent Explosive Disorder
312.31	F63.0	Gambling Disorder
312.32	F63.81	Kleptomania
312.30	F91.9	Unspecified Disruptive, Impulse-Control, and Conduct Disorder
300.23	F40.10	Social Anxiety Disorder (Social Phobia)
V61.10	Z63.0	Relationship Distress with Spouse or Intimate Partner
301.82	F60.6	Avoidant Personality Disorder
301.83	F60.3	Borderline Personality Disorder
301.7	F60.2	Antisocial Personality Disorder
_____	_____	_____
_____	_____	_____

SEXUALLY DEVIANT BEHAVIOR

BEHAVIORAL DEFINITIONS

1. Involvement in the criminal justice system due to charges of criminal sexual conduct or assault.
2. Exposure of genitals to an unsuspecting stranger.
3. Acts of frottage involving touching or rubbing against a nonconsenting person.
4. Observing an unsuspecting person who is naked, disrobing, or engaging in sexual activity.
5. Sexual activity with a prepubescent child.
6. Abuse of alcohol and/or other drugs associated with deviant sexual arousal.
7. An attitude of sexual entitlement that leads to sexually deviant behavior.
8. Low impulse control especially as related to deviant sexual behavior.

—. _____

_____

—. _____

_____

LONG-TERM GOALS

1. Eliminate sexually deviant behavior.
2. Terminate attitude of sexual entitlement.
3. Terminate the abuse of alcohol and other drugs.
4. Decrease the frequency of impulsive behavior related to deviant sexual arousal.

—. _____
_____
_____

—. _____
_____

SHORT-TERM OBJECTIVES

1. Acknowledge the presence of sexual deviancy in own life and describe how it is demonstrated. (1, 2)

2. Cooperate with and complete a sexual deviancy risk assessment evaluation that includes a clinical interview with validated assessment tools. (3)

3. Comply with treatment and/or medical monitoring recommendations that result from the evaluation. (4)

THERAPEUTIC INTERVENTIONS

1. Explore with the client the presence of sexual deviancy in his/her life and how it is demonstrated.

2. Confront the client's attempts to minimize his/her deviant sexual behavior, to project blame onto others, to vilify the victim, or to discount the harmful consequences.

3. Refer the client for, or conduct a complete risk assessment evaluation that includes a clinical interview with validated objective assessment tools (e.g., Static 99 developed by the Canadian Government, Minnesota Sex Offender Screening Tool—Revised [MnSOST-R] by Epperson, Level of Service Inventory [LSI] by Andrews and Bonta, Adult Substance Use Survey [ASUS] by Wanberg, Psychopathy Checklist—Revised [PCL-R] by Hare); provide feedback regarding test results to the client and other involved professionals.

4. Refer the client for more in-depth evaluation, if indicated, in related areas (e.g., alcohol/drug, anger management, psychopathy).

4. Cooperate with electronic monitoring, day reporting, or no-contact orders as recommended. (5)

5. Refer the client for electronic monitoring, day reporting, no-contact orders, or other behavior containment interventions, if indicated by the risk assessment results (greater the risk, more the containment); monitor for compliance and provide feedback to other involved professionals.

5. Comply with an evaluation of the nature and strength of deviant sexual arousal using a Penile Plethysmograph or Abel Assessment Instrument. (6)

6. Refer the client for an evaluation of deviant sexual arousal using a Penile Plethysmograph (PPG) or Abel Assessment Instrument (Abel); provide feedback to the client and to other involved professionals.

6. Enroll and engage in a cognitive behavioral skills training conducted in a group setting. (7, 8)

7. Refer the client to a cognitive behavioral skills training conducted in a group setting or multisystemic therapy; monitor for compliance and progress.

8. Meet regularly with other professionals involved in the case (e.g., victim advocate, treatment provider, probation/parole officer, polygrapher) to keep them informed of assessment results and treatment progress, to ensure comprehensive management of the client, and to reduce splitting by the client.

7. Register as a sex offender and comply with HIV testing and/or DNA testing requirements. (9)

9. Instruct the client to register as a sex offender and monitor his/her compliance with HIV testing and/or DNA testing requirements.

8. Verbalize an understanding of where the deviant arousal comes from (Antecedents), how it manifests (Behavior),

10. Explain to the client the ABCs of behavior, minimally describing where the deviant arousal comes from

and what results (Consequences) are likely to be produced by it. (10, 11)

9. Identify and replace thinking errors associated with deviant arousal. (12, 13, 14)

10. Implement through-stopping techniques to interrupt distorted cognitive messages associated with sexual deviance arousal and behavior. (15)

(Antecedents), how it manifests (Behavior), and what results (Consequences) are likely to be produced by it.

11. Teach the client the relationship between thoughts, attitudes, feelings, and beliefs and how they are the antecedents to behavior.

12. Assist the client in identifying his/her thinking errors (e.g., nobody will find out; nobody will be hurt; the victim is asking for it; I am entitled to do whatever I want; everyone else deserves it; if it feels right, then it is right) associated with his/her deviant arousal and help him/her recognize the relationship of these thoughts to deviant behavior.

13. Assist the client in listing reframing statements (e.g., I am responsible for my actions; it is not okay to hurt others) for each of his/her sexual deviance thinking errors.

14. Instruct the client to maintain a written log of thinking errors encountered, the context they were encountered in, and the reframes used; process the content of the journal material.

15. Teach the client to implement a thought-stopping technique (e.g., thinking of a stop sign and then a pleasant scene, or snapping a rubber band on the wrist) that cognitively interferes with distorted cognitive messages that fuel deviant behavior; monitor the use of the

technique, reinforcing success and redirecting for failure.

11. List the costs and benefits of changing the prevailing personal sexual deviancy pattern as well as the costs and benefits for not changing the pattern. (16)

16. Assist the client in listing the costs (e.g., loss of preferred sexual behavior) and benefits (e.g., legal, safer, healthier lifestyle) of changing the prevailing personal sexual deviancy pattern as well as the costs (e.g., entrenchment in the criminal justice system) and benefits (e.g., maintaining the preferred sexual behavior) for not changing the pattern.

12. Formulate, in writing, several ways to reframe each of the feelings or attitudes that represent obstacles to modifying deviant behavior. (17, 18)

17. Assist the client in listing the specific moods (e.g., doubt, resistance), feelings (e.g., reluctance, fear), and attitudes (e.g., I don't have to do this; No one can make me change) that hold him/her back from achieving or making progress with successfully modifying deviant behavior.

18. Instruct the client to formulate, in writing, several alternative ways to reframe each of his/her moods, feelings, or attitudes that represent obstacles to modifying deviant behavior.

13. Acknowledge the harmful effects on the victim of the sexually deviant actions. (19, 20)

19. Assist the client in listing the negative, harmful effects of his/her actions on his/her victim, confronting any effort by the client to vilify the victim, attribute blame to the victim, or minimize the consequences of his/her actions on the victim.

20. Explain to the client that the protection of victims or potential victims from unsafe and unwanted contact with the

client outweighs the needs/desires of the client.

14. Write a clarification letter to the victim, taking responsibility for the assaultive behavior. (21)

21. Instruct the client to write a clarification letter to the victim, taking full responsibility for the assaultive behavior; review the letter with the client, encouraging any effort to take responsibility for his/her actions and correcting any effort to evade or project blame.

15. Pay ordered restitution to the victim(s) of sexual offending behavior. (22)

22. Monitor payment of restitution by the client to the victim as ordered by the criminal justice system.

16. Rehearse and implement constructive ways of responding to high-risk situations for sexually deviant behavior. (23, 24, 25, 26)

23. Develop with the client an inventory of high-risk situations for precipitating him/her engaging in sexually deviant behavior (e.g., viewing pornography, attending sex peep shows, cruising neighborhoods for sexual satisfaction, engaging in deviant fantasizing).

24. Taking into consideration the client's dynamic risk factors (e.g., low self-control, substance abuse, criminal peers) from assessments, brainstorm with him/her constructive ways of responding to his/her high-risk situations (e.g., thought-stopping using a rubber band, distancing from criminal peers, contacting a person supportive of his/her goals).

25. Role-play with the client using constructive methods of responding to high-risk situations for sexually deviant behavior.

26. Review and reinforce the client's implementation of coping strategies to deal with high-risk situations.

17. Monitor and record progress on implementing a relapse prevention plan, including high-risk situations encountered, skills used, and outcomes of each situation. (27, 28)

27. Develop with the client a relapse prevention plan that minimally includes how to cope with his/her high-risk situations, as well as thinking and feeling triggers for urges and arousal.

28. Instruct the client to record progress on his/her relapse prevention plan, high-risk situations encountered, skills used, and outcomes of each situation; review and reinforce the client's progress on the relapse prevention plan.

18. Acknowledge that human relations are critical in order to meet basic human emotional needs. (29, 30)

29. Teach the client the difference between human wants (e.g., money or power) and human needs (e.g., security, love, affirmation).

30. Assign the client to write a paper that explains how human relationships are necessary to meet basic human emotional needs.

19. List positive and negative methods for trying to get human emotional needs met. (31)

31. Assign the client to list several fundamentally different methods (e.g., coerce, manipulate, trade off, persuade, collaborate, reciprocal kindness and respect, inspire) for obtaining what he/she needs emotionally from other people.

20. Develop a pro-social system supportive of your goals to reduce deviant behavior. (32)

32. Assist the client in developing a pro-social system supportive of his/her goals to reduce deviant behavior.

21. Complete a reassessment using validated assessment tools and

33. Reassess the client using validated assessment tools (e.g.,

PPG or Abel Assessment Instrument. (33, 34, 35, 36)

Static 99 developed by the Canadian Government, Minnesota Sex Offender Screening Tool—Revised [MnSOST-R] by Epperson if the client has been recently released from prison, Level of Service Inventory [LSI] by Andrews and Bonta, Adult Substance Use Survey [ASUS] by Wanberg, Psychopathy Checklist—Revised [PCL-R] by Hare).

34. Reassess the client using a PPG and Abel Assessment Instrument.

35. Provide the client with an objective interpretation and normative feedback on the assessments completed.

36. Reinforce the client for any progress made between the first assessment and the reassessment.

DIAGNOSTIC SUGGESTIONS:

ICD-9-CM	_ICD-10-CM_	_DSM-5_ Disorder, Condition, or Problem
302.4	F65.2	Exhibitionistic Disorder (Exhibitionism)
302.81	F65.0	Fetishistic Disorder (Fitishism)
302.89	F65.81	Frotteuristic Disorder (Frotteurism)
302.84	F65.52	Sexual Sadism Disorder
302.82	F65.3	Voyeuristic Disorder (Voyeurism)
302.2	F65.4	Pedophilic Disorder
302.9	F65.9	Unspecified Paraphilic Disorder
312.30	F91.9	Unspecified Disruptive, Impulse-Control, and Conduct Disorder
303.90	F10.20	Alcohol Use Disorder, Moderate or Severe
304.30	F12.20	Cannabis Use Disorder, Moderate or Severe
304.20	F14.20	Cocaine Use Disorder, Moderate or Severe
304.00	F11.20	Opioid Use Disorder, Moderate or Severe
301.20	F60.1	Schizoid Personality Disorder

301.82	F60.6	Avoidant Personality Disorder
301.22	F21	Schizotypal Personality Disorder
301.9	F60.9	Unspecified Personality Disorder
301.7	F60.2	Antisocial Personality Disorder
_____	_____	_____
_____	_____	_____

TIME MANAGEMENT PROBLEMS

BEHAVIORAL DEFINITIONS

1. Inability to manage time in order to meet personal obligations.
2. Routinely fails to meet deadlines, make appointments, or follow through on things in a timely manner.
3. Inability to adequately anticipate time needed to accomplish tasks, projects, or goals.
4. Fails to prioritize obligations in order to ensure that all necessary ones are completed before less important ones.
5. Frequently overextends self, making it impossible to meet obligations in a timely manner.
6. Lack of time management abilities result in frequent self-disapproval and diminished self-concept.

—. _____
_____

—. _____
_____

—. _____
_____

LONG-TERM GOALS

1. Ability to manage time efficiently so that personal obligations are met.
2. Develop the skill necessary to prioritize personal obligations.
3. Gain an understanding of personal abilities to avoid becoming overextended and overwhelmed with obligations.

—. _____
    _____
—. _____
    _____

SHORT-TERM OBJECTIVES

THERAPEUTIC INTERVENTIONS

1. Describe a history of inability to manage time and the consequences of such inabilities. (1)

1. Explore the client's history of an inability to manage time and the consequences he/she has experienced due to poor time management.

2. Discuss the pros and cons of not adhering to a time management schedule. (2)

2. Have the client discuss what he/she sees as the pros (e.g., more flexibility, avoid responsibility) and cons (e.g., failure to meet deadlines, not dependable) of not adhering to a time management schedule.

3. List the costs and benefits of changing the prevailing personal pattern of poor time management as well as the costs and benefits of not changing the pattern. (3)

3. Assign the client to list in writing the costs and benefits of changing versus not changing the prevailing personal pattern of not managing time efficiently or effectively.

4. List the common steps and strategies for time management that most often assure success. (4, 5)

4. Explain effective strategies to improve time management abilities (e.g., carry a day planner with them, developing a detailed daily schedule, prioritize tasks).

5. Teach the client the ideal steps (e.g., prioritize obligations, realistically estimate time to accomplish tasks, adhere to schedule, evaluate) involved in successful time management.

5. Attend a time management training class. (6)

6. Assign the client to attend some form of time management training, skill-building programs or classes.

6. Read material about time management. (7)

7. Provide the client with appropriate workbooks and other reading materials (e.g., *Getting Things Done: The Art of Stress-Free Productivity* by Allen, *7 Habits of Highly Effective People: Powerful Lessons in Personal* Change by Covey, *Time Management from the Inside Out: The Foolproof System for Taking Control of Your Schedule—and Your Life* by Morgenstern, *The Art of Doing Nothing: Simple Ways to Make Time for Yourself* by Vienne and Lennard) relevant to providing information regarding time management skills and strategies.

7. Identify past successful and unsuccessful attempts to manage time in a more constructive manner. (8)

8. Ask the client to share his/her past attempts to manage time in a more constructive manner, exploring attempts that were both successful and unsuccessful.

8. Assess reasons past attempts were either successful or unsuccessful and write out new strategies for improving time management based on assessment. (9, 10)

9. Assist the client in assessing reasons some of the past attempts at time management were successful, whereas others were unsuccessful.

10. Have client write out new strategies for improving time management based on feedback and assessment.

9. Make a list of all personal obligations that are required to be met. (11)

11. Instruct the client to make a list of all personal obligations he/she has that are required to be met.

10. Prioritize personal obligations in terms of importance. (12, 13)

12. Teach the client how to prioritize obligations based on level of importance (e.g., deadlines, needs versus wants) to help ensure that the most important obligations are met before less important ones.

13. Ask the client to prioritize his/her list of obligations; placing what he/she sees as the most important obligation at the top of the list and continuing to do so until entire list has been numbered.

11. Receive feedback about how well the personal obligation task list has been prioritized and then rework list to include feedback. (14, 15)

14. Review the client's list of personal obligations, providing him/her with feedback about how well the list has been prioritized.

15. Have the client rework list based on feedback.

12. Identify a situation where unrealistic expectations were formed regarding how long it would take to accomplish a task, including the consequences of such unrealistic expectations. (16)

16. Assign the client to describe a situation where he/she developed unrealistic expectations of how long it would take to accomplish a task, making sure he/she includes the consequences of such unrealistic expectations.

13. Estimate how much time is required to accomplish each personal obligation task. (17, 18)

17. Teach the client how to estimate the amount time it will take to accomplish tasks (e.g., consider the scope of task, review similar experiences, allow for transition or off-task time) to help ensure that realistic time lines are formed.

18. Assign the client to estimate how much time he/she thinks each task on his/her personal obligation list will take; review

his/her estimated times, making sure the estimates are realistic.

14. Based on the prioritized list and estimated times, develop a daily schedule that can be followed to meet the personal obligations. (19, 20)

19. Assign the client to develop a daily schedule based on his/her list of obligations.

20. Review the client's daily schedule with him/her, providing him/her with positive reinforcement regarding effort as well as feedback about how to improve schedule.

15. Commit to following the newly developed schedule for one week. (21)

21. Solicit the client's commitment to following the newly developed schedule for one week.

16. Maintain a time management journal, keeping track of challenges, accomplishments and failures. (22)

22. Assign the client to maintain a time management journal, including challenges, accomplishments, and failures he/she has experienced.

17. Modify time management schedule based on personal experience and feedback. (23, 24)

23. Debrief with the client about how well he/she was able to stick to the weekly time management schedule, providing him/her with positive reinforcement for successes as well as feedback for improvements.

24. Ask the client to incorporate feedback into schedule and commit to following the schedule for at least one month, while maintaining a journal about the experience.

18. Debrief and receive feedback on a weekly basis about how well efforts to manage time are going. (25)

25. Meet with the client weekly to discuss progress of managing time and meeting obligations in a timely manner; provide him/her with positive support, as well as suggestions for improvement.

__. _____   __. _____
     _____   _____
__. _____   __. _____
     _____   _____
__. _____   __. _____
     _____   _____

DIAGNOSTIC SUGGESTIONS:

ICD-9-CM	*ICD-10-CM*	*DSM-5* Disorder, Condition, or Problem
308.3	F43.0	Acute Stress Disorder
309.24	F43.22	Adjustment Disorder, With Anxiety
300.02	F41.1	Generalized Anxiety Disorder
300.3	F42	Obsessive-Compulsive Disorder
301.7	F60.2	Antisocial Personality Disorder
301.82	F60.6	Avoidant Personality Disorder
301.83	F60.3	Borderline Personality Disorder
301.50	F60.4	Histrionic Personality Disorder
_____	_____	_____
_____	_____	_____

UNSTABLE LIVING SITUATION

BEHAVIORAL DEFINITIONS

1. Currently lives in an environment with excessive criminogenic influences (e.g., criminal peers, substance abuse, violence) and is at high risk for relapse.
2. Family members or roommates are involved in criminal behavior.
3. Has a history of frequent moves, conflictual relationships, and repeated unemployment.
4. Currently homeless or lives in community shelters.
5. Depends on others for shelter, food, and clothing.
6. Lives in an environment where there is a high risk of sustaining physical, sexual, or emotional abuse.
7. Failure to make rent, mortgage, or utility payments, leading to a loss of residence.

—. _____

_____

—. _____

_____

—. _____

_____

LONG-TERM GOALS

1. Maintain employment as a legal means of obtaining income and responsibly manage finances for a stable living situation.
2. Change living situation to reduce or eliminate association with those involved in criminal behavior.

3. Manage pro-criminal relationships with roommates or family members by establishing boundaries to reduce risk for relapse or recidivism.

4. Establish a social network that is supportive of pro-social, stable living.

—. _____

_____

—. _____

_____

—. _____

_____

SHORT-TERM OBJECTIVES

1. Describe the current living situation, the benefits and negative consequences associated with maintaining the current living situation versus changing to a more stable living pattern. (1, 2, 3)

2. List any safety concerns present at the current living situation. (4, 5, 6)

THERAPEUTIC INTERVENTIONS

1. Explore the client's current living situation and history of homelessness, frequent moves, unemployment, and dependence on others.

2. Explore with the client the benefits (e.g., no responsibilities, exciting, carefree lifestyle) and negative consequences (e.g., criminal involvement, health-related consequences) associated with the current unstable living situation.

3. Explore with the client the benefits (e.g., a consistent shelter, increased safety) and negative consequences (e.g., too much work or effort, accountability) associated with changing to a stable living situation.

4. Explore with the client any safety concerns (e.g., physical, emotional, or sexual abuse;

violence risk; health-related concerns from substances used in manufacturing drugs) present at the current living situation.

5. Encourage the client to move to a safehouse or shelter to escape immediate safety concerns.

6. Take the necessary steps to report any child or elder abuse; encourage the client to report any adult or domestic abuse.

3. List specific values or beliefs that support continuing to live in the unhealthy living situation. (7)

7. Assist the client in listing his/her specific values (e.g., freedom, unpredictability) or beliefs (e.g., having a stable living situation will tie me down, I deserve to be in an abusive living situation) that support continuing to live in the present unhealthy situation.

4. Outline specific short-term goals for changing current living situation. (8)

8. Help the client outline specific short-term goals for changing current living situation.

5. List criminogenic influences present in current living situation. (9)

9. Explore with the client how his/her current living situation has reinforced a criminal behavior pattern; list the criminogenic factors present (e.g., substance abuse, criminal family members or peers, poverty due to unemployment, violence prevalence).

6. Implement skills to distance self from peers or family members associated with criminal behavior. (10, 11)

10. Use role-play, modeling, and behavior rehearsal to teach the client new strategies (e.g., setting clear boundaries, telling peers his/her goal of avoiding criminal behavior, assertively saying no) for distancing himself/herself from criminal

peers; provide him/her with positive feedback for effort, as well as suggestions for improvement in implementation.

11. Encourage and monitor the client's implementation of assertive setting of boundaries with criminal peers; reinforce success and redirect for failure.

7. Enroll temporarily in a shelter to provide stability while looking for employment. (12)

12. If the client is currently living on the streets, advise and assist him/her in enrolling temporarily in a shelter to provide stability while looking for employment.

8. Review job search strategies and principles others have used successfully. (13, 14)

13. Teach the client effective strategies others have used to upgrade their employment situations (e.g., establishing a job-finding network, developing a focus and direction for better livelihood, rehearsing interviewing skills, cooperating with an employment counselor).

14. Provide the client with appropriate workbooks (e.g., Job Club Counselor's Manual by Azrin and Besalel) and other materials (e.g., Appendices to Integrating Substance Abuse Treatment and Vocational Services TIP, U.S. Department of Health and Human Services) relevant to improving his/her employment search.

9. List all sources of leads for possible chosen job opportunities. (15, 16)

15. Ask the client to participate full-time, for at least 10 consecutive workdays, in a job-finding club; monitor progress and reinforce effort.

16. Assist the client in listing all possible sources of job leads (e.g., local classified ads, job clearing centers, and yellow pages).

10. Contact local employers having potential job-of-choice employment opportunities and solicit a job interview. (17, 18)

17. Encourage the client to contact all local employers having potential job-of-choice employment opportunities and to solicit a job interview.

18. Debrief with the client and offer feedback after each job interview.

11. Identify the top three work high-risk situations (for relapse to AOD or crime) and role-play alternative coping. (19)

19. Teach the client the top three work high-risk situations pertinent to new job situation (e.g., working in close proximity to a liquor store, working long hours, working in a high crime neighborhood) and role-play alternative coping strategies (e.g., refusal skills, problem-solving skills, positive self-talk, consequential thinking) several times for each situation.

12. Enroll in and attend a workshop on successful financial management. (20)

20. Refer the client to a workshop on effective financial management techniques.

13. Review effective house-hunting strategies and principles. (21, 22)

21. Brainstorm with the client about ways that would aid in saving toward a rent deposit (e.g., avoiding carrying great amounts of cash, direct deposit at employment, budgeting living expenses well within income).

22. Review with the client effective house-hunting strategies and principles (e.g., researching housing boards, contacting housing helpers, or equivalent

local housing support group, government subsidized housing projects, apartment rental agencies).

14. Identify which influential criminogenic factors must be avoided in a future living situation. (23, 24)

23. Facilitate a process for the client to prioritize his/her top three criminogenic issues (e.g., high-crime neighborhood, substance abuse, criminal peers, family criminality); explore how these issues can be avoided in the future living environment.

24. Assist the client in outlining a basic list of requirements or qualifications for a living situation, while explaining to the client that some compromises may have to be made.

15. Explore low-income or government subsidized housing opportunities, as well as other pro-social private or government-sponsored housing possibilities. (25, 26)

25. Refer the client to local low-income housing, rent-saver, or government subsidized housing opportunities.

26. Assign the client to research pro-social housing opportunities on housing boards at churches, community recreational centers, county housing authorities.

16. Contact available housing opportunities that have an absence of high-risk factors or criminogenic influences and meet the list of requirements. (27, 28)

27. Assess with the client each housing option based on whether criminogenic influences are absent and basic requirements are met.

28. Assign the client to contact those housing opportunities that qualified based on meeting the basic requirements and the absence of criminogenic influences.

17. Evaluate progress made on short-term goals set at the beginning of treatment. (29, 30)

29. Evaluate with the client progress made on short-term goals set at the beginning of treatment, providing feedback as appropriate.

30. Encourage the client to reset new short-term goals specific to improving current living situation.

__. _____   __. _____
   _____   _____
__. _____   __. _____
   _____   _____

DIAGNOSTIC SUGGESTIONS:

ICD-9-CM	*ICD-10-CM*	*DSM-5* Disorder, Condition, or Problem
309.0	F43.21	Adjustment Disorder, With Depressed Mood
309.24	F43.22	Adjustment Disorder, With Anxiety
309.28	F43.23	Adjustment Disorder, With Mixed Anxiety and Depressed Mood
296.xx	F32.x	Major Depressive Disorder, Single Episode
296.xx	F33.x	Major Depressive Disorder, Recurrent Episode
300.00	F41.9	Unspecified Anxiety Disorder
V62.2	Z56.9	Other Problem Related to Employment
295.90	F20.9	Schizophrenia
298.9	F29	Unspecified Schizophrenia Spectrum and Other Psychotic Disorder
296.xx	F31.xx	Bipolar I Disorder
296.89	F31.81	Bipolar II Disorder
301.0	F60.0	Paranoid Personality Disorder
301.20	F60.1	Schizoid Personality Disorder
310.22	F21	Schizotypal Personality Disorder
301.7	F60.2	Antisocial Personality Disorder

_____ _____ _____
_____ _____ _____

VIOLENT/AGGRESSIVE BEHAVIOR

BEHAVIORAL DEFINITIONS

1. History of violent, aggressive responses out of proportion to any precipitating stressors.
2. History of involvement in the criminal justice system with charges related to violence, assault, menacing, or battery.
3. Uses violence as a means to achieve power and control.
4. Shows a cavalier disregard and no remorse for perpetrating violence or injuring on others.
5. Unreasonably attributes betrayal and/or hostility to others and overreacts aggressively to others accordingly.
6. Has a paranoid quality that leads to projection of own malicious outlook onto others.
7. Has a childhood history of exposure to repeated physical abuse and neglect.
8. Receives reinforcement for violence from peer group and faces possible alienation for nonaggressive behavior.

—. _____
_____

—. _____
_____

—. _____
_____

LONG-TERM GOALS

1. Significantly decrease frequency and intensity of violent, aggressive behavior, including verbal and physical abuse.

2. Improve awareness and understanding of violence: how it is triggered and what its painful consequences are to others.
3. Access and accept a greater range of emotions with increased ability to express these emotions constructively.
4. Develop a repertoire of behavior that makes it possible to achieve reinforcement from nonaggressive behavior.
5. Develop a pro-social network that shares and supports healthy nonaggressive lifestyle and respect for others.

—. _____
_____
—. _____
_____
—. _____
_____

SHORT-TERM OBJECTIVES

THERAPEUTIC INTERVENTIONS

1. Participate in a complete psychiatric evaluation. (1)

1. Refer the client for a complete psychiatric evaluation, including an assessment for a prescription for psychotropic medication to calm anger and/or reduce irrational cognitions associated with paranoia.

2. Comply with taking prescribed medications as recommended. (2)

2. Monitor the client's prescribed psychotropic medications for compliance, effectiveness, and side effects; consult with the prescribing physician, as needed.

3. Complete an objective risk assessment for violent, aggressive behavior. (3)

3. Assess the client using a validated violence or aggression screening instrument (e.g., Propensity for Abusiveness Scale by Dutton, The Abusive Behavior Inventory by Shepard and Campbell, Interpersonal Control and Psychological

4. Enroll and participate in a group therapeutic process for violence and aggression management. (4, 5)

5. Verbalize what triggers aggression (antecedents), how it manifests (behavior), and what results (consequences) are likely to be produced by it. (6, 7, 8)

6. Describe the thoughts, beliefs and feelings that arise after engaging in violent, aggressive behavior. (9, 10, 11)

Aggression Scales by Stets); provide the client feedback on the test results.

4. Refer the client to a group therapeutic process for violence and aggression management (e.g., anger management, domestic violence, victim awareness).

5. Process with the client information he/she learned through the group therapeutic process.

6. Explain to the client the relationship between thoughts, beliefs, feelings, and actions.

7. Instruct the client on the Antecedents, Behaviors and Consequences (ABCs) of aggression and have the client verbalize the triggers for aggression (antecedents), how it manifests (behavior), and what results (consequences) are likely to be produced by it.

8. Provide the client with a selection of reading material about the ABCs of aggression and violence (e.g., *In Control* by Miliken; *Strategies for Self-Improvement and Change* by Wanberg and Milkman; *Aggression Replacement Training* by Goldstein, Gibbs, and Glick).

9. Explore the client's dysfunctional thoughts, beliefs, and feelings that arise after engaging in violent, aggressive behavior.

10. Teach the client how his/her dysfunctional thoughts (e.g.,

they deserved it, that felt good), beliefs (e.g., I did what I had to do; violence is the best high), and feelings (e.g., powerful, high, righteous) reinforce his/her violent behavior.

11. Explain to the client how his/her violent behavior can become repetitive when his/her distorted thoughts, beliefs and feelings offer immediate gratification.

7. List five of the best consequences for self of own anger expression and the five worst consequences. (12)

12. Instruct the client to list five of the best consequences of his/her uncontrolled anger expression and the five worst consequences; process the list for distorted perceptions and lack of empathy.

8. Implement nonaggressive ways of responding to or avoiding triggers for violence. (13, 14, 15)

13. Explore with the client common triggers that provoke violent, aggressive behavior.

14. Brainstorm with the client nonaggressive ways of responding to or avoiding his/her triggers for violent, aggressive behavior (e.g., taking time out; count backward; engage in deep breathing; utilize "stop, look, listen, and think"; practice assertiveness).

15. Role-play with the client the implementation of nonaggressive responses to his/her triggers for aggression; encourage implementation of nonaggressive responses in daily living and monitor progress.

9. Implement alternative, positive, realistic self-talk in response to internal and

16. Assist the client in identifying self-statements that trigger or escalate aggressive responses to

external anger trigger situations. (16, 17, 18)

situations (e.g., I need to show everyone who's boss, I am in control when I react violently).

17. Brainstorm with the client a list of alternative, positive, realistic self-talk to counter self-talk that triggers or escalates violent behavior (e.g., I can resolve this conflict without resorting to violence, I can be assertive without being aggressive).

18. Assign the client to implement realistic self-talk in situations that trigger violent behavior; monitor progress, reinforcing success and redirecting for failure.

10. Acknowledge that healthy human relationships cannot be controlled by violence. (19, 20)

19. Teach the client how healthy human relationships cannot be controlled with violence, but are critical in order to meet basic human emotional needs; point out the need for trust, mutual respect, and empathy.

20. Confront the client on his/her statements that indicate that human relationships can be controlled by violent behavior.

11. Implement healthy communication skills to improve relationships and avoid aggression. (21)

21. Use modeling and role-playing to teach the client healthy communication skills (e.g., starting conversations, engaging in feelings talk, utilizing listening skills, asking for help appropriately, refusing requests,; implementing drink/drug refusal skills).

12. Implement new conflict resolution skills to replace intimidation and violence. (22, 23)

22. Teach the client three new conflict resolution that would improve interpersonal communications skills (e.g., double-sided reflections, stating

the other side, stating needs clearly).

23. Instruct the client to implement new conflict resolution skills; assign the client to make daily recordings of any conflicts experienced or avoided due to interpersonal communication skills and provide him/her with feedback on reported experiences.

13. Identify needs that are being met with peer-approved violent, aggressive behavior which could be met with pro-social behavior. (24)

24. Explore the client's feelings that he/she experiences when pressured by peers to participate in violence or aggressive behavior identifying needs that are being met with peer-approved violent, aggressive behavior which could be met with pro-social behavior (e.g., belongingness, approval, support, inclusion).

14. Identify, practice, and implement new strategies for distancing self from criminal peers. (25, 26)

25. Use modeling and role-playing to teach the client new strategies for distancing himself/herself from criminal peers (e.g., refusal skills, stating his/her goal, making changes in environment and peer group); instruct him/her to implement these new distancing skills learned.

26. Monitor and review the client's implementation of distancing skills, reinforcing success, and redirecting for failure.

15. Verbalize increased feelings of genuine empathy for the pain that has been caused to others. (27, 28, 29)

27. Attempt to sensitize the client to his/her lack of empathy for others by reviewing and listing the negative consequences of his/her aggression on others (e.g., loss of trust, increased fear, distancing, physical pain).

28. Use role reversal techniques to get the client to verbalize the impact of his/her aggression on others.

29. Assign the client to address an "empty chair" in giving an apology for the pain that he/she has caused the victim.

16. Retake an objective risk assessment for violent, aggressive behavior. (3, 30)

3. Assess the client using a validated violence or aggression screening instrument (e.g., Propensity for Abusiveness Scale by Dutton, The Abusive Behavior Inventory by Shepard and Campbell, Interpersonal Control and Psychological Aggression Scales by Stets); provide the client feedback on the test results.

30. Reinforce any gain scores between initial assessment and reassessment.

—. _____
_____
—. _____
_____

—. _____
_____
—. _____
_____

DIAGNOSTIC SUGGESTIONS:

ICD-9-CM	_ICD-10-CM_	_DSM-5_ Disorder, Condition, or Problem
312.34	F63.81	Intermittent Explosive Disorder
297.1	F22	Delusional Disorder
301.0	F60.0	Paranoid Personality Disorder
301.9	F60.9	Unspecified Personality Disorder
301.81	F60.81	Narcissistic Personality Disorder
301.7	F60.2	Antisocial Personality Disorder
_____	_____	_____
_____	_____	_____

VOCATIONAL DEFICITS

BEHAVIORAL DEFINITIONS

1. In need of full-time employment.
2. Not employed full-time at least 50 percent of the past year and/or has never maintained full-time employment longer than one year.
3. Chronically underemployed in positions that provide little or not benefits and pay at or slightly above minimum wage.
4. Currently employed in a work environment with excessive criminogenic influences (e.g., criminal peers, substance abuse, violence) and risk for related relapse.
5. Limited access to job opportunities arising from the requirement to disclose criminal record.
6. Unrealistic expectations regarding the demands of a possible job (e.g., job-required work habits, team participation, and authority interactions).
7. Unrealistic self-expectations and confidence (over or under) regarding performance capability in new job.
8. Chaotic living environment, unstable social relations, illness, or immediate family member illness contribute to vocational conflict.
9. Educational, skills, and learning deficits that represent obstacles to literacy (English or computer), interpersonal skills or minimal mainstream vocational competencies (e.g., basic math).

—. _____
   _____

LONG-TERM GOALS

1. Maintain stable full-time employment in a pro-social work environment.

2. Develop a set of realistic job-related expectations regarding job performance requirements and the ability to meet these requirements.
3. Acquire necessary self-discipline skills to perform full-time work in a punctual, consistent, and productive manner.
4. Realistically acknowledge personal vocational aptitudes, current skills and deficits, and what the related career opportunities are.
5. Learn how to manage existing criminogenic influences in the workplace to reduce the risk for relapse.
6. Identify a concrete, personal set of both short- and long-term vocational goals that reflect a realistic career path.
7. Increase self-presentation and job interview skills for potential employers.

—. _____

_____

SHORT-TERM OBJECTIVES

THERAPEUTIC INTERVENTIONS

1. Identify job search strategies and principles others have used successfully. (1, 2)

1. Explain effective strategies other clients have used to upgrade their employment situations (e.g., establishing a job-finding network, developing a focus and direction for better livelihood, rehearsing interviewing skills).

2. Provide the client with appropriate job search workbooks (e.g., Job Club Counselor's Manual by Azrin and Besalel) and other materials (Appendices to Integrating Substance Abuse Treatment and Vocational Services, 200, TIP by U.S. DHHS) relevant to improving his/her livelihood.

2. Articulate a job search strategy that includes an orderly sequence of events that logically culminates in

2. Provide the client with appropriate job search workbooks (e.g., Job Club Counselor's Manual by Azrin

successfully acquiring a full-time job. (2, 3)

and Besalel) and other materials (Appendices to Integrating Substance Abuse Treatment and Vocational Services, 200, TIP by U.S. DHHS) relevant to improving his/her livelihood.

3. Review and evaluate the client's emerging job search strategy to reality test his/her strengths and weaknesses.

3. Participate in an objective vocational assessment for career aptitudes and preferences. (4, 5)

4. Use clinical interview and/or testing (e.g., Strong Vocational Interest Blank) to assist the client in formulating a self-assessment of his/her job aptitudes, interests, strengths, and preferences.

5. Refer the client to local professional resources for objective vocational testing and assessment.

4. Develop an inventory of career opportunities associated with identified vocational aptitudes (or profile). (5, 6, 7)

5. Refer the client to local professional resources for objective vocational testing and assessment.

6. Review the client's vocational testing results and explore any discrepancies of these results with his/her job search strategy.

7. Provide the client with job classification (types) references to assure he/she incorporates sufficient scope as he/she searches for matches with his/her aptitudes and preferences.

5. List all jobs that appear reasonably interesting and rewarding. (5, 6, 7, 8)

5. Refer the client to local professional resources for objective vocational testing and assessment.

6. Review the client's vocational testing results and explore any discrepancies of these results with his/her job search strategy.

7. Provide the client with job classification (types) references to assure he/she incorporates sufficient scope as he/she searches for matches with his/her aptitudes and preferences.

8. Assist the client in developing an inventory of possible job options that are of interest to him/her.

6. List possible criteria for selecting one job option over another. (9)

9. Discuss examples of useful criteria for narrowing the scope of possible job options (e.g., indoor/outdoor, manual/service/information processing, artsy/mechanical).

7. Prioritize job selection criteria and review all interesting job possibilities to determine top priority job or career options. (9, 10)

9. Discuss examples of useful criteria for narrowing the scope of possible job options (e.g., indoor/outdoor, manual/service/information processing, artsy/mechanical).

10. Assist the client in prioritizing his/her job preferences for the job search process.

8. Screen most interesting job options against identified vocational aptitudes and eliminate any that are completely incongruent with aptitudes and strengths. (4, 5, 11)

4. Use clinical interview and/or testing (e.g., Strong Vocational Interest Blank) to assist the client in formulating a self-assessment of his/her job aptitudes, interests, strengths, and preferences.

5. Refer the client to local professional resources for objective vocational testing and assessment.

9. List the specific duties and job requirements for each of the client's preferred top job option priorities. (12)

10. List an inventory of 10 or more negative attitudes toward fitting into a productive work situation, along with remedies for these negative attitudes. (13, 14)

11. Examine the client's job prioritization list for consistency with his/her decided selection criteria and his/her aptitudes.

12. Provide the client with examples of relevant job descriptions that include a listing of duties and responsibilities.

13. Provide the client with examples of negative work-related attitudes and demonstrate the cognitive steps for identifying such attitudes (e.g., for the negative attitude: "They're screwing me" interception points are: *physical* [shortness of breath, stomach tightness]—*feeling* [anxious]—*thoughts* ["not this again"]—*beliefs* ("I'm entitled to better . . . and shouldn't have to submit to this.").

14. Teach the client how to reverse his/her specific work-related negative attitudes (e.g., teach physical relaxation and/or deep-breathing techniques, teach how to identify and label underlying feelings, teach identification of underlying dysfunctional thoughts and beliefs, teach realistic positive self-talk (e.g., "I can get what I want if I work hard for it.").

11. Meet with a peer who is also engages in a job search to allow for mutual support. (15)

15. Identify and designate a "buddy" peer for the client during his/her job search who is also engaged in a new job search strategy.

12. Obtain a current valid Social Security card and driver's license or appropriate photo identification. (16)

13. Arrive punctually at a set time and place to implement the given day's job-finding strategy. (17)

14. List vulnerability to criminogenic influences and how the workplace may present high-risk situations related to these influences. (18, 19)

15. Identify the top three workplace high-risk situations (for relapse to AOD or crime) and role-play alternative coping strategies for each situation. (20, 21, 22, 23)

16. Instruct the client in the specific steps, addresses, and phone numbers necessary to obtain a Social Security card, driver's license, and/or local photo ID.

17. Monitor the client's punctuality for initiating his/her job-finding strategy and present to him/her each week the percent of on-time starts, reinforcing responsible timeliness.

18. Discuss the evidence (e.g., formal assessments, criminal history, other test results) that may help the client better understand what influences tend to lead him/her into criminal behavior.

19. Facilitate a process for the client to prioritize his/her top two crim-inogenic issues; explore how these issues may present them-selves in the work environment.

20. Explain the role of "triggers" and high-risk situations (for relapse to alcohol or other drugs (AOD) or crime) to the client.

21. Help the client identify his/her personal high-risk situations for his/her prevailing criminogenic issues.

22. Use role-playing, modeling, and behavior rehearsal to teach the client coping behaviors for high-risk or trigger situations in the work environment.

23. Encourage the client to solicit feedback from a pro-social buddy as to coping behaviors for high-risk employment situations.

16. List at least three pro-social alternatives to crime or AOD relapse for each top workplace high-risk situations. (22, 23, 24)

22. Use role-playing, modeling, and behavior rehearsal to teach the client coping behaviors for high-risk or trigger situations in the work environment.

23. Encourage the client to solicit feedback from a pro-social buddy as to coping behaviors for high-risk employment situations.

24. Review the client's work-related relapse prevention plan so that there is a clear emphasis on specific pro-social alternatives (e.g., counters, reframes, support).

17. List at least three negative consequences of relapse behavior. (25)

25. Assist the client in identifying the negative consequences of relapse behavior (e.g., loss of job, revocation of parole, prison, family pain).

18. Participate full-time, for 10 consecutive work days, in a job-finding club. (26)

26. Refer the client to a local job-finding club if he/she has significant discrepancies (either above or below expectations) between aptitudes and abilities and entry-level position requirements.

19. Write a six-month job path plan that includes employment search strategies and coping behaviors for high-risk situations. (27)

27. Assign the client to write a six-month employment plan that includes job search strategies and coping mechanisms for high-risk criminogenic influences.

20. Submit job path plan to at least two peers and one professional for feedback and incorporate that feedback into a revised plan. (28, 29)

28. Facilitate the client's use of the buddy system for receiving feedback on networking job options and new methods for presenting himself/herself to employers.

29. Review the client's six-month job path plan to assure reasonable

and concrete goals that are congruent with the client's aptitudes and that account for coping with high-risk situations.

21. Write a "statement of interest" telling potential employers of particular interest in a job and qualifications for it. (30, 31)

30. Teach the client the fundamentals of building a resume and writing a "statement of interest."

31. Review the client's "statement of interest" and resume and help him/her refine them.

22. Formulate a complete resume. (30, 31)

30. Teach the client the fundamentals of building a resume and writing a "statement of interest."

31. Review the client's "statement of interest" and resume and help him/her refine them.

23. Rehearse at least three times a dynamic presentation of self based on "statement of interest" through initial and final stages of a job interview before a group of peers for feedback. (32)

32. Use role-playing, modeling, and behavior rehearsal to teach the client interviewing skills; solicit constructive feedback on these skills between peer "buddies."

24. Learn and practice a statement that acknowledges a substance abuse and criminal history and offer evidence of rehabilitation. (33)

33. Teach the client how to antici-pate employer inquiries regard-ing criminal history and sub-stance abuse and how to reframe criminal and substance abuse recovery history as a strong asset.

25. List all local classified ads, job clearing centers, and yellow pages for possible chosen job opportunities. (34)

34. Help the client organize his/her job prospects and prioritize the contact sequence.

26. Contact all local available employers having potential job-of-choice employment opportunities and solicit a job interview. (35)

35. Coach the client with a list of favorable local employers (that frequently hire offenders) if the job strategy is becoming overwhelming for the client.

27. Debrief interview experiences with peers for support and feedback on how to improve either presentation of self or statement of interest. (36, 37)

36. Debrief the client's (and his/her buddy's if available) initial job search experiences and review his/her documentation of the experience.

37. Reinforce positive efforts of the client's job search including first time experiences, difficult challenges, and achievements with new skills.

28. Utilize specialized job search resources for those with disabilities. (38)

38. Initiate networking through specialized sources for clients that are handicapped.

—. _____   —. _____

_____   _____

DIAGNOSTIC SUGGESTIONS:

ICD-9-CM	_ICD-10-CM_	_DSM-5_ Disorder, Condition, or Problem
309.0	F43.21	Adjustment Disorder, With Depressed Mood
300.4	F34.1	Persistent Depressive Disorder
296.xx	F32.x	Major Depressive Disorder, Single Episode
296.xx	F33.x	Major Depressive Disorder, Recurrent Episode
309.24	F43.22	Adjustment Disorder, With Anxiety
303.90	F10.20	Alcohol Use Disorder, Moderate or Severe
304.20	F14.20	Cocaine Use Disorder, Moderate or Severe
V62.2	Z56.9	Other Problem Related to Employment
301.0	F60.0	Paranoid Personality Disorder
301.81	F60.81	Narcissistic Personality Disorder
301.7	F60.2	Antisocial Personality Disorder
301.9	F60.9	Unspecified Personality Disorder

_____ _____   _____

_____ _____   _____

Appendix A

SAMPLE CHAPTER WITH QUANTIFIED LANGUAGE

CRIMINAL PEERS

BEHAVIORAL DEFINITIONS

1. Currently associates _____ % of the time with friends and acquaintances who are involved in criminal behavior.
2. Verbalizes acceptance of peers' criminal behavior _____ % of the time that he/she has the opportunity to comment.
3. Admires or identifies with others who are pro-crime and sees their lifestyle as desirable as evidenced by _____ _____ times per week.
4. Encouraged and easily influenced by peers to participate in criminal behavior as evidenced by _____ which occurs _____ times per week.
5. Participates in criminal behavior with friends _____ times per week.
6. Willing to protect, cover-up, and accept responsibility for peers' deviant behavior _____ % of the time that the opportunity arises.
7. Verbalizes a sense of loyalty to and identification with a gang _____ times per week.
8. Prior attempts to distance self from criminal peers have been unsuccessful _____ times.
9. Inability to establish and maintain meaningful pro-social peer support group as evidenced by _____ % times spent with pro-social people.

—. _____

_____

—. _____

_____

_____

—. _____

_____

—. _____

_____

LONG-TERM GOALS

1. Significantly reduce or eliminate association with criminal friends.
2. Learn to manage existing pro-criminal relationships by reestablishing boundaries to reduce risk for relapse or recidivism.
3. Develop a greater understanding about peer group; how peers influence and interact with personal behavior to effect lifestyle quality.
4. Develop a meaningful, pro-social support network.
5. Terminate all criminal behavior, even if it results in peer conflict.

—. _____
  _____
—. _____
  _____
—. _____
  _____

SHORT-TERM OBJECTIVES

1. By _____ (enter date) list all friends and acquaintances; placing an asterisk next to those that have been involved in criminal behavior. (1, 2)

2. By _____ (enter date) map all friends and acquaintances according to how frequently interactions with them occur. (3)

THERAPEUTIC INTERVENTIONS

1. Assign the client to list all his/her friends and acquaintances; denoting criminal peers with an asterisk.

2. Review the client's list of peers, exploring his/her feelings and thoughts about the number of pro-crime peers compared to pro-social peers.

3. Instruct the client to draw three concentric rings, each two inches apart, the center a circle representing himself/herself, the next band representing friends and acquaintances seen almost daily, the next band representing those seen almost every week. Insert small circles (with initials) depicting all friends and acquaintances, and

shade each initialed small circle according to how criminally involved he/she is; process this graph's meaning and implication.

3. By _____ (enter date) describe the history and consequences of criminal behavior with peers. (4, 5)

4. Explore the client's history and consequences of his/her involvement in criminal behavior with friends and acquaintances.

5. Ask the client to write an autobiography focusing the history of involvement in and consequences of criminal behavior with friends and acquaintances beginning in childhood or adolescence.

4. By _____ (enter date) list the positive and negative consequences of yielding to peer pressure as defined by _____ . (6)

6. Explain the dynamics of peer pressure to the client (e.g., wanting to fit in) and the positive (e.g., feeling of belongingness, having fun, avoiding conflict) and negative (e.g., going against one's better judgment, getting caught, conflict with peers) consequences of yielding to peer pressure.

5. By _____ (enter date) identify the feelings that are experienced when pressured by peers _____ (specify type of pressure) to participate in criminal behavior. (7)

7. Explore the client's feelings that are generated by being subjected to peer pressure.

6. By _____ (enter date) identify factors that have led to the development of relationships with deviant peers. (8, 9)

8. Teach the client the various factors that can lead to developing relationships with criminal peers (e.g., low self-esteem, desire to belong, curiosity, thrill seeking).

9. Assist the client in generating a list of personal factors that have led him/her to develop relationships with deviant peers; review and process this list, reinforcing the client's increased understanding of himself/herself.

7. By _____ (enter date) list 10 positive and 10 negative consequences of having friends and acquaintances that are involved in criminal behavior. (10)

10. Ask client to list 10 positive (e.g., excitement, adventure, familiarity) and 10 negative (e.g., anxiety, being pressured into criminal behavior, getting caught) consequences of having friends and acquaintances that are involved in criminal behavior.

8. By _____ (enter date) list the costs and benefits of changing versus not changing the prevailing personal pattern of involvement with criminal peers. (11)

11. Assign client to list in writing the costs and benefits of changing versus not changing the prevailing personal pattern of involvement with criminal peers.

9. By _____ (enter date) compare the values, traits, attributes, and attitudes of criminal peers with those of self. (12)

12. Assign the client to list the values, traits, attributes, and attitudes his/her deviant peers possess; review the list, exploring the similarities and differences between his/her values and attitudes and those of his/her friends and acquaintances.

10. By _____ (enter date) identify needs that are being met with peer-approved criminal behavior that could be met with pro-social behavior. (13)

13. Explore the client's feelings that occur when he/she participates in criminal behavior with friends and acquaintances; note if there are needs being met through this behavior that could be met pro-socially.

11. By _____ (enter date) verbalize a resolution of resistant feelings associated

14. Explore the client's feelings about ending his/her relationships with criminal

with ending relationships with friends and acquaintances who are involved in criminal behavior. (14)

12. By _____ (enter date) list the reasons past attempts to end relationships with criminal friends were unsuccessful. (15)

13. By _____ (enter date) identify, practice, and implement new strategies _____ (specify) for distancing self from criminal peers. (16, 17, 18, 19)

friends and acquaintances; process ambivalent or resistant feelings.

15. Explore the client's past attempts to distance himself/herself from deviant friends and acquaintances, assessing the reasons the past attempts were unsuccessful, and identifying triggers (e.g., people, places, things), ambivalence, and unclear boundaries that led to failure.

16. Teach the client new strategies (e.g., setting clear boundaries, telling peers his/her goal of avoiding criminal behavior, saying no) for distancing himself/herself from criminal peers.

17. Role-play with the client the use of the new distancing techniques; provide him/her with positive feedback for effort, as well as suggestions for improvement in implementation.

18. Ask the client the task of choosing one deviant friend or acquaintance that he/she feels comfortable distancing himself/herself from and implement the new distancing techniques with that person.

19. Debrief with client about how new distancing techniques worked with chosen person; provide positive reinforcement and feedback for improvement.

14. By _____ (enter date) implement activities _____ (specify activities and frequency) designed to meet pro-social people. (20)

15. By _____ (enter date) describe ways _____ (specify) to maintain relationships with friends and acquaintances involved in criminal behavior without participating in such behavior. (21)

16. By _____ (enter date) identify high-risk situations that could lead to participating in criminal behavior and develop a written prevention plan for these high-risk situations. (22)

17. By _____ (enter date) review high-risk situations and determine if the primary triggers are social pressure, problems managing emotions, or conflicts with others. (23)

20. Advise the client to make efforts to get more involved with other pro-social people; suggest activities that might facilitate that process (e.g., joining a community or church group, inviting someone from work to a recreational activity, become a volunteer, take an educational class).

21. Assist the client in identifying ways he/she can maintain his/her relationships with some of his/her criminal peers without engaging in deviant behavior (e.g., setting clear boundaries, expressing his/her goal, saying no). However, if the client is unable to prevent engaging in deviant behavior as a result, instruct him/her to distance himself/herself from criminal peers.

22. Highlight with the client some high-risk situations that may lead to relapse (e.g. criminal behaviors, alcohol or other drug use); develop a written prevention plan for becoming involved in deviant behavior in such high-risk situations.

23. Explain to the client how criminal behavior relapse triggers tend to fall into one of three categories (e.g., social pressure, problems managing moods and emotions, or hassles and conflicts with others) and ask him/her to determine which category his/her primary trigger fits into.

18. By _____ (enter date) practice healthy communication skills _____ (specify) to establish boundaries with deviant friends and acquaintances. (24, 25, 26, 27)

24. Teach the client how to establish boundaries with friends and acquaintances using healthy communication skills such as assertiveness techniques, distancing practices, and refusal skills (e.g., saying no; stating needs in a clear, friendly manner; stating complaints in a clear, friendly manner; using "I" messages).

25. Role-play with the client using healthy communication skills (e.g., refusing requests, drug/alcohol refusal skills) to practice establishing boundaries with deviant friends and acquaintances; provide him/her with positive reinforcement as well as suggestions for improvement.

26. Assign the client to choose one criminal peer and practice using new communication skills with that person.

27. Debrief with client about how new communication skills worked with chosen person; provide him/her with positive reinforcement and feedback for improvement.

19. By _____ (enter date) identify personal values, traits, feelings, and attitudes that may be preventing pro-social relationships from developing. (28)

28. Assist the client in identifying personal values, attitudes, and feelings that may be preventing him/her from developing mean-ingful, pro-social relationships (e.g., they won't like me; those people are boring).

20. By _____ (enter date) formulate several ways to reframe each of the feelings and attitudes that represent

29. Assist the client in formulating several ways to reframe each of the feelings and attitudes that represent obstacles to making

obstacles to making new friendships. (29)

21. By _____ (enter date) make a list of the values, traits, attributes, and attitudes that are seen as important to look for when making a new, supportive, pro-social friend. (30)

22. By _____ (enter date) implement new ways _____ (specify) to go about making supportive friendships. (31)

23. By _____ (enter date) evaluate past attempts to establish pro-social friendships, looking at what went wrong and how to replace old patterns with new techniques _____ (specify). (32)

24. By _____ (enter date) attend three different clubs or groups _____ (specify) in three weeks. (33)

25. By _____ (enter date) participate in a club, group, or organization for at least nine

new friendships (e.g., once they get to know me, they will like me; everyone has something interesting to share).

30. Help the client generate a list of values and attitudes that he/she sees as important to look for when making a new, supportive, pro-social friend; highlight the differences between this set of values and attitudes and those values and attitudes associated with his/her criminal peers.

31. Use role-playing, modeling, and behavior rehearsal to teach the client new social skills to be used in making new, supportive friendships (e.g., active sharing, using "I" statement, listening to feedback, asking open questions, listening to nonverbal communication).

32. Explore the client's past attempts to establish and maintain meaningful, pro-social friends and acquaintances; evaluate what went wrong and how the client can replace old patterns with new social skills.

33. Advise the client to attend three different clubs, groups, or organizations (e.g., 12-step groups, church or faith community, sports, or fitness groups) in three weeks to initiate contact with pro-social people.

34. Direct the client to become involved in a club, group, or organization of interest (e.g.,

continuous weeks, using new social skills to initiate and maintain pro-social relationships. (34, 35, 36)

26. By _____ (enter date) remap and compare all friends and acquaintances according to how frequently interactions with them occur. (37)

sports league, church, charity organization, AA/NA) for at least nine consecutive weeks to give himself/herself a chance to build relationships.

35. Encourage client to practice new social skills with other members of a club, group, or organization in an effort to develop new friends and acquaintances.

36. Debrief with client about how new techniques worked; provide him/her with positive reinforcement for effort and feedback for improvements.

37. Instruct the client to draw three concentric rings, each two inches apart, the center circle representing himself/herself, the next band representing friends and acquaintances seen almost daily, the next band representing those seen almost every week. Insert small circles (with initials) depicting all friends and acquaintances, and shade each initialed small circle according to how criminally involved he/she is; reinforce him/her for any difference between the first map drawn and this current map.

—. _____
_____
—. _____
_____
—. _____
_____

—. _____
_____
—. _____
_____
—. _____
_____

DIAGNOSTIC SUGGESTIONS:

Axis I:	300.23	Social Phobia
	301.34	Intermittent Explosive Disorder
	300.4	Dysthymic Disorder
	_____	_____
	_____	_____
Axis II:	301.20	Schizoid Personality Disorder
	301.7	Antisocial Personality Disorder
	301.82	Avoidant Personality Disorder
	301.6	Dependent Personality Disorder
	_____	_____
	_____	_____

Appendix B

BIBLIOTHERAPY REFERENCES

Anger

Carter, L., P. Meier, and F. Minirth (1992). *The Anger Workbook*. Nashville, TN: Thomas Nelson.

Ellis, A., and R. C. Tafrate (1998). *How to Control Your Anger Before It Controls You*. Secaucus, NJ: Carol Publishing Group.

Gentry, W. D. (2000). *Anger-Free: Ten Basic Steps to Managing Your Anger*. New York: William Morrow and Co.

Potter-Efron, R., and P. Potter-Efron (1999). *Letting Go of Anger: The Ten Most Common Anger Styles and What to Do About Them*. New York: Barnes and Noble Books.

Assertiveness Deficits

Alberti, R. E., and M. L. Emmons (1995). *Your Perfect Right: A Guide to Assertive Living*. Vol. I. Atascaderdo, CA: Impact Publishers, Inc.

Bower, S., and G. H. Bower (1991). *Asserting Yourself: A Practical Guide for Positive Change*. Cambridge, MA: Perseus Publishing.

Burley-Allen, M. (1995). *Managing Assertively: How to Improve Your People Skills*. New York: John Wiley and Sons, Inc.

Paterson, R. J. (2000). *The Assertiveness Workbook: How to Express Your Ideas and Stand Up for Yourself at Work and in Relationships*. Oakland, CA: New Harbinger Publications.

Smedes, L. (1996). *Forgive and Forget*. San Francisco: Harper.

Smedes, L. (1997). *The Art of Forgiving*. New York: Ballantine Books.

Authority Conflicts

Boccialetti, G. (1995). *It Takes Two: Managing Yourself When Working with Bosses and Other Authority Figures*. San Francisco, CA: Jossey-Bass, Inc.

Dyer, W. D. (1993). *Pulling Your Own Strings: Dynamic Techniques for Dealing with Other People and Living Life as You Choose*. New York: HarperCollins Publishers, Inc.

Rosen, M. I. (1999). *Thank You for Being Such a Pain: Spiritual Guidance for Dealing with Difficult People*. New York: Three Rivers Press.

Toropov, B. (1997). *The Art and Skill of Dealing with People: How to Make Human Motivation Work for You on the Job*. Oakland, CA: Fine Communications.

Callousness (Lack of Empathy/Honesty)

Hare, R. D. (1993). *Without Conscience*. New York: Pocket Books.

Chemical Dependence

Anonymous, A. (1976). *Alcoholics Anonymous: The Big Book*. New York: Alcoholics Anonymous World Services, Inc.

Benson, H. (1975). *The Relaxation Response*. New York: HarperCollins Publishers.

Cunningham, J. B. (1997). *The Stress Management Sourcebook*. Lincolnwood, IL: Lowell House.

Daley, D. (1998). *Kicking Addictive Habits Once and For All: A Relapse Prevention Guide*. San Francisco, CA: Jossey-Bass Publishers.

Daley, D., and G. A. Marlatt (1997). *Managing Your Drug or Alcohol Problem: Therapist Guide*. San Antonio, TX: Graywind Publications.

Davis, M., E. R. Eshelman, and M. McKay (2000). *The Relaxation and Stress Reduction Workbook*. Oakland, CA: New Harbinger Publications.

Ellis, A. (2001). *Overcoming Destructive Beliefs, Feelings and Behaviors*. Amherst, NY: Prometheus Books.

Fanning, P., and J. O'Neill (1996). *The Addiction Workbook: A Step by Step Guide to Quitting Alcohol and Drugs*. Oakland, CA: New Harbinger Publications.

Fields, R., P. Taylor, R. Weyler, and R. Ingrasci (1984). *Chop Wood, Carry Water*. New York: Penguin Putnam, Inc.

Gorski, T. T., and M. Miller (1986). *Staying Sober: A Guide for Relapse Prevention*. Independence, MO: Herald House.

Gorski, T. T., and M. Miller (1992). *Relapse Prevention Therapy with Chemically Dependent Criminal Offenders*. Independence, MO: Herald House.

Hardiman, M. (2000). *Overcoming Addiction*. Freedom, CA: The Crossing Press.

Harvath, T. A. (1998). *Sex, Drugs, Gambling and Chocolate: A Workbook for Overcoming Addictions*. Atascadero, CA: Impact Publishers, Inc.

Lazarus, J. (2000). *Stress Relief and Relaxation Techniques*. Lincolnwood, IL: Keats Publishing.

Miller, D., and L. Guidry (2001). *Addictions and Trauma Recovery*. New York: W. W. Norton and Co.

O'Hara, V. (1996). *Five Weeks to Healing Stress: The Wellness Option*. Oakland, CA: New Harbinger Publications.

Peele, S., and A. Brodsky (1991). *The Truth about Addiction and Recovery*. New York: Fireside

Schaler, J. A. (2000). *Addiction Is a Choice*. Peru. IL: Caras Publishing Co.

Walker, C. E. (2001). *Learn to Relax*. New York: John Wiley and Sons, Inc.

Childhood Trauma/Abuse/Neglect

Engel, B. (1990). *The Right to Innocence: Healing the Trauma of Childhood Sexual Abuse*. New York: Ivy Books.

Gil, E. (1984). *Outgrowing the Pain: A Book for and about Adults Abused as Children*. New York: Bantam Books.

Golomb, E. (1995). *Trapped in the Mirror: Adult Children of Narcissistic Parents in Their Struggle for Self*. New York: William Morrow.

Pittman, F. (1998). *Grow Up!* New York: Golden Books.

Smedes, L. (1991). *Forgive and Forget: Healing the Hurts We Don't Deserve.* San Francisco, CA: Harper Publishers.

Whitfield, C. (1987). *Healing the Child Within.* Deerfield Beach, FL: Health Communications, Inc.

Consequential Thinking Deficits

Kellner, M. (2001). *In Control.* Champaign, IL: Research Press.

Miller, W., and S. Rollnick (2002). *Motivational Interviewing,* 2nd ed. New York: Guilford Press.

Criminal Peers

Cloud, H., and J. Townsend (2002). *Boundaries: When to Say Yes, When to Say No to Take Control of Your Life.* Grand Rapids, MI: Zondervan.

Yager, J. (2002). *When Friendship Hurts: How to Deal with Friends Who Betray, Abandon, or Wound You.* New York: Simon and Schuster Trade.

Deceitful

Backus, W. D. (1994). *Learning to Tell Myself the Truth.* Minneapolis, MN: Bethany House Publishers.

Bader, E., P. T. Pearson, and J. D. Schwartz (2001). *Tell Me No Lies: How to Stop Lying to Your Partner—and Yourself—-in the 4 Stages of Marriage.* New York: St. Martin's Press.

Depression/Suicidal Ideation

Amen, D. G. (1999). *Change Your Brain, Change Your Life: The Breakthrough Program for Conquering Anxiety, Depression, Obsessiveness, Anger, and Impulsiveness.* New York: Crown Publishing Group.

Anonymous. (1998). *Depressed Anonymous.* Lousiville, KY: Harmony House Publishers.

Carrigan, C. (1999). *Healing Depression: A Holistic Guide.* New York: Marlowe and Company.

Davis, M., M. McKay, and E. Robbins (1997). *Relaxation and Stress Reduction Workbook.* Oakland, CA: Fine Communications.

Leith, L. M. (1999). *Exercising Your Way to Better Mental Health: Fight Depression and Alleviate Stress Through Exercises.* Morgantown, WV: Fitness Information Technology, Inc.

O'Connor, R. (1998). *Undoing Depression: What Therapy Doesn't Teach You and Medication Can't Give You.* New York: Berkley Publishing Group.

Rowe, D. (1996). *Depression: The Way Out of Your Prison*. New York: Routledge.
Yapko, M. D. (1998). *Breaking the Patterns of Depression*. New York: Doubleday and Company, Inc.

Driving-Related Offenses

American Automobile Association (1999). *Responsible Driving*. Columbus, OH: Glencoe/McGraw-Hill.
James, L., and D. Nahl (2000). *Road Rage and Aggressive Driving: Steering Clear of Highway Warfare*. Amherst, NY: Prometheus Books.
Johnson, M. L., O. Crabb, and A. Opfer (1993). *Drive Right*. Reading, MA: Scott Foresman and Company.
Larson, J. A., and C. Rodriguez (1999). *Road Rage to Road-Wise*. New York: Tom Doherty, LLC.
Shorey, J. (2001). *Bullies Behind the Wheel: How Your Reactions to Aggressive Drivers Can Cause Road Rage, or Prevent It!* New York: Singleton Press.

Family Conflict/Alienation

Davis, L. (2002). *I Thought We'd Never Speak Again: The Road from Estrangement to Reconciliation*. New York: HarperCollins.
Illsley, J., and C. Dawson (1998). *Growing Up Again: Parenting Ourselves, Parenting Our Children*. Center City, MN: Hazelden Information and Educational Services.
LeBey, B. (2001). *Family Estrangements: How They Begin, How to Mend Them, How to Cope with Them*. Marietta, GA: Longstreet Press, Inc.
Lieberman, D. (2001). *Make Peace with Anyone: Proven Psychological Strategies to Bring People Together—Now*. New York: St. Martin's Press, Inc.

Family Criminality/Deviance

Engel, B. (1991). *Divorcing a Parent: Free Yourself From the Past and Live the Life You've Always Wanted*. New York: Fawcett Book Group.
LeBey, B. (2001). *Family Estrangements: How They Begin, How to Mend Them, How to Cope with Them*. Marietta, GI: Longstreet Press, Inc.

Financial Management Problems

Gallen, R. (2001). *The Money Trap: A Practical Program to Stop Self-Defeating Financial Habits So You Can Reclaim Your Grip on Life*. New York: HarperCollins Publishers.

Lawrence, J. (2000). *The Budget Kit: The Common Cents Money Management Workbook.* New York: Dearborn Publishing Company.

Orman, S. (2001). *The Road to Wealthy: A Comprehensive Guide to Your Money.* New York: Putnam Publishing Group.

Orman, S. (2002). *Suze Orman's Financial Guidebook: Putting the 9 Steps to Work.* New York: Crown Publishing Group.

Shelton, P. R. (2001). *Long-Term Care: Your Financial Planning Guide.* New York: Kensington Publishing Corporation.

Gender Identification Issues

Bornstein, K. (1997). *My Gender Workbook: How to Become a Real Man, a Real Woman, the Real You, or Something Else Entirely.* New York: Routledge.

Isensee, R. (1997). *Reclaiming Your Life: The Gay Man's Guide to Love, Self-Acceptance, and Trust.* Los Angeles, CA: Alyson Publications, Inc.

Larkin, J. (2000). *A Woman Like That: Lesbian and Bisexual Writers Tell Their Coming Out Stories.* San Francisco, CA: HarperCollins Publishers.

Minchinton, J. A. (1994). *Maximum Self-Esteem: The Handbook for Reclaiming Your Sense of Self-Worth.* Vanzant, MO: Arnford Corporation

Powell, J. (1996). *Why Am I Afraid to Tell You Who I Am?: Insights into Personal Growth.* Allen, TX: Thomas More Publishing.

Taubman, S. (1994). *Ending the Struggle Against Yourself: A Workbook for Developing Deep Confidence and Self-Acceptance.* New York: Penguin.

Impulsivity

Amen, D. G. (1999). *Change Your Brain, Change Your Life: The Breakthrough Program for Conquering Anxiety, Depression, Obsessiveness, Anger, and Impulsiveness.* New York: Crown Publishing Group.

Covey, S. (2000). *The 7 Habits of Highly Effective People.* Philadelphia, PA: Running Press.

Davis, M., M. McKay, and E. Robbins (1997). *Relaxation and Stress Reduction Workbook.* Oakland, CA: Fine Communications.

Hammond, J., R. Keeney, and H. Raiffa (1998). *Smart Choices: A Practical Guide to Making Better Decisions.* Boston, MA: Harvard Business School Press.

Kellner, M. (2001). *In Control.* Champaign, IL: Research Press.

Santoro, J., A. Bergman, and R. Deletis (2001). *Kill the Craving: How to Control the Impulse to Use Drugs and Alcohol.* Oakland, CA: New Harbinger Publications.

Welch, D. (2001). *Decisions, Decisions: The Art of Effective Decision Making.* New York: Prometheus Books.

Inadequate Social Support/Social Isolation

Miller, W., and G. Sparks (2002). *Refrigerator Rights: Creative Connections and Restoring Relationships.* New York: Berkley Publishing Group.

Intimate Relationship Conflict

Alberti, R. E., and M. L. Emmons (1995). *Your Perfect Right: A Guide to Assertive Living,* Vol. I. Atascadero, CA: Impact Publishers, Inc.

Bower, S. A., and G. H. Bower (1991). *Asserting Yourself: A Practical Guide for Positive Change.* Cambridge, MA: Perseus Publishing.

Burley-Allen, M. (1995). *Managing Assertively: How to Improve Your People Skills.* New York: John Wiley and Sons, Inc.

Evans, P. (1996). *The Verbally Abusive Relationship: How to Recognize It and How to Respond.* Avon, MA: Adams Media Corp.

McGraw, P. (2000). *The Relationship Rescue Workbook: Exercises and Self-Tests to Help You Reconnect With Your Partner.* New York: Hyperion Press.

Paterson, R. J. (2000). *The Assertiveness Workbook: How to Express Your Ideas and Stand Up for Yourself at Work and in Relationships.* Oakland, CA: New Harbinger Publications.

Weeks, D. (1993). *The Eight Essential Steps to Conflict Resolution: Preserving Relationships at Work, at Home, and in the Community.* New York: Putnam Publishing Group.

Moral Disengagement

Campbell, S. M. (2001). *Getting Real.* Novato, CA: New World Library.

Hoffman, M. L. (2002). *Empathy and Moral Development: Implications for Caring and Justice.* New York: Cambridge University Press.

Hoffman, M. L. (2002). *Empathy and Moral Development: Implications for Caring and Justice.* New York: Cambridge University Press.

Simon, S. B., H. Kirschenbaum, and W. Howe (1995). *Values Clarification: The Classic Guide to Discovering Your Truest Feelings.* Boston, MA: Warner Books, Incorporated.

Smith, H. W. (2001). *What Matters Most: The Power of Living Your Values.* New York: Simon and Schuster Trade.

Narcissistic—Unprincipled

Levant, R. with G. Kopecky (1995). *Masculinity Reconstructed.* New York: Dutton.

Miller, T. (1995). *How to Want What You Have: Discovering the Magic and Grandeur of Ordinary Experience.* New York: H. Holt.

Rosellini, G., and M. Worden (1986). *Of Course You're Angry.* San Francisco: Harper Hazelden.

Probation/Parole Noncompliance

Alberti, R. E., and M. L. Emmons (1995). *Your Perfect Right: A Guide to Assertive Living,* Vol. I. Atascadero, CA: Impact Publishers, Inc.

Bower, S. A., and G. H. Bower (1991). *Asserting Yourself: A Practical Guide for Positive Change.* Cambridge, MA: Perseus Publishing.

Burley-Allen, M. (1995). *Managing Assertively: How to Improve Your People Skills.* New York: John Wiley and Sons, Inc.

Paterson, R. J. (2000). *The Assertiveness Workbook: How to Express Your Ideas and Stand Up for Yourself at Work and in Relationships.* Oakland, CA: New Harbinger Publications.

Problem-Solving Skills Deficits

Davidson, J. (1995). *The Complete Idiot's Guide to Reaching Your Goals.* New York: Alpha Books.

Vos Savant, M., and L. Fleischer (1991). *Brain Building in Just 12 Weeks.* New York: Bantam Books.

Psychosis

Amen, D. G. (1999). *Change Your Brain, Change Your Life: The Breakthrough Program for Conquering Anxiety, Depression, Obsessiveness, Anger, and Impulsiveness.* New York: Crown Publishing Group.

Ellis, A. (2001). *Overcoming Destructive Beliefs, Feelings and Behaviors.* Amherst, NY: Prometheus Books.

Podvoll, E. (1991). *The Seduction of Madness: Revolutionary Insights into the World of Psychosis and a Compassionate Approach to Recovery at Home.* New York: Harperperennial Publishers.

Self-Concept Deficits

Fennell, M. (2001). *Overcoming Low Self-Esteem: A Self-Help Guide Using Cognitive Behavioral Techniques.* New York: New York University Press.

McKay, M., and P. Fanning (2000). *Self Esteem: A Proven Program of Cognitive Techniques for Assessing, Improving, and Maintaining Your Self-Esteem.* Oakland, CA: New Harbinger Publications.

Minchinton, J. A. (1994). *Maximum Self-Esteem: The Handbook for Reclaiming Your Sense of Self-Worth.* Vanzant, MO: Arnford Corporation

Paulhus, D. (1998). Paulhus Deception Scales (PDS): The Balanced Inventory of Desirable Responding—7. Multi-Health Systems, 65 Overlea Blvd. Ste. 210, Toronto, Ontario, M4H 1P1.

Phares, E. J., and N. Erskine (1984) The measurement of selfism. *Educational and Psychological Measurement. 44,* 597-608.

Self-Defeating Behavior Patterns (non-AOD)

Daley, D. C. (1990). *Surviving Addiction Workbook: Practical Tips on Developing a Recovery Plan.* Holmes Beach, FL: Learning Publications.

Hope and Recovery: A Twelve Step Guide for Healing from Compulsive Sexual Behavior. (1987). Minneapolis, MN: CompCare.

Marlatt, G. A., and J. R. Gordon (Eds.). (1985). *Relapse Prevention: Maintenance Strategies in the Treatment of Addictive Behaviors.* New York: Guilford Press.

Prochaska, J., J. Norcross, and C. DiClemente (1994). *Changing for Good.* New York: William Morrow.

Sexually Deviant Behavior

Gorski, T. (1993). *Getting It Right: Learning the Choices of Healthy Intimacy.* New York: Simon and Schuster.

O'Connell, T. (1993). *Improving Intimacy: 10 Powerful Strategies.* Dennisport, MA: Sanctuary Unlimited.

Stirling Hastings, A. (2000). *From Generation to Generation: Understanding Sexual Attraction to Children.* Gretna, LA: Wellness Institute.

Time Management Problems

Allen, D. (2001). *Getting Things Done: The Art of Stress-Free Productivity.* New York: Viking Penguin.

Covey, S. (2000). *The 7 Habits of Highly Effective People.* Philadelphia, PA: Running Press.

Morgenstern, J. (2000). *Time Management from the Inside Out: The Foolproof System for Taking Control of Your Schedule—and Your Life.* New York: Henry Holt.

Vienne, V., and E. Lennard (1998). *The Art of Doing Nothing: Simple Ways to Make Time for Yourself.* New York: Crown Publishing Group.

Unstable Living Situation

Morgenstern, J. (2000). *Time Management From the Inside Out: The Foolproof System for Taking Control of Your Schedule and Your Life.* New York: Simon and Schuster.

Violent/Aggressive Behavior

Ellis, A., and R. C. Tafrate (1998). *How to Control Your Anger Before It Controls You.* New York: Carol Publishing Group.

Harbin, T. J. (2000). *Beyond Anger: A Guide for Men.* Berkeley, CA: Avalon Publishing Group.

Potter, R. T. (2000). *Work Rage: Preventing Anger and Resolving Conflict on the Job.* New York: Barnes and Noble Books.

Vocational Deficits

Chope, R. C. (2000). *Dancing Naked: Breaking Through the Emotional Limits That Keep You from the Job You Want.* Oakland, CA: New Harbinger Publications.
DeLuca, M. J., and N. F. DeLuca (1999). *Get a Job in 30 Days or Less: A Realistic Action Plan for Finding the Right Job Fast.* New York: McGraw-Hill Professional.
Perlmutter, D. (1992). *How to Get a Good Job and Keep It.* New York: NTC Publishing.
Woititz, J. (1989). *The Self-Sabotage Syndrome: Adult Children in the Work-Place.* Oakland, CA: Health Communications, Inc.

.

Appendix C

RECOVERY MODEL OBJECTIVES AND INTERVENTIONS

The Objectives and Interventions that follow are created around the 10 core principles developed by a multidisciplinary panel at the 2004 National Consensus Conference on Mental Health Recovery and Mental Health Systems Transformation, convened by the Substance Abuse and Mental Health Services Administration (SAMHSA, 2004):

1. **Self-direction:** Consumers lead, control, exercise choice over, and determine their own path of recovery by optimizing autonomy, independence, and control of resources to achieve a self-determined life. By definition, the recovery process must be self-directed by the individual, who defines his or her own life goals and designs a unique path toward those goals.

2. **Individualized and person-centered:** There are multiple pathways to recovery based on an individual's unique strengths and resiliencies as well as his or her needs, preferences, experiences (including past trauma), and cultural background in all of its diverse representations. Individuals also identify recovery as being an ongoing journey and an end result as well as an overall paradigm for achieving wellness and optimal mental health.

3. **Empowerment:** Consumers have the authority to choose from a range of options and to participate in all decisions—including the allocation of resources—that will affect their lives, and are educated and supported in so doing. They have the ability to join with other consumers to collectively and effectively speak for themselves about their needs, wants, desires, and aspirations. Through empowerment, an individual gains control of his or her own destiny and influences the organizational and societal structures in his or her life.

4. **Holistic:** Recovery encompasses an individual's whole life, including mind, body, spirit, and community. Recovery embraces all aspects of

life, including housing, employment, education, mental health and healthcare treatment and services, complementary and naturalistic services, addictions treatment, spirituality, creativity, social networks, community participation, and family supports as determined by the person. Families, providers, organizations, systems, communities, and society play crucial roles in creating and maintaining meaningful opportunities for consumer access to these supports.

5. **Nonlinear:** Recovery is not a step-by-step process but one based on continual growth, occasional setbacks, and learning from experience. Recovery begins with an initial stage of awareness in which a person recognizes that positive change is possible. This awareness enables the consumer to move on to fully engage in the work of recovery.

6. **Strengths-based:** Recovery focuses on valuing and building on the multiple capacities, resiliencies, talents, coping abilities, and inherent worth of individuals. By building on these strengths, consumers leave stymied life roles behind and engage in new life roles (e.g., partner, caregiver, friend, student, employee). The process of recovery moves forward through interaction with others in supportive, trust-based relationships.

7. **Peer support:** Mutual support—including the sharing of experiential knowledge and skills and social learning—plays an invaluable role in recovery. Consumers encourage and engage other consumers in recovery and provide each other with a sense of belonging, supportive relationships, valued roles, and community.

8. **Respect:** Community, systems, and societal acceptance and appreciation of consumers—including protecting their rights and eliminating discrimination and stigma—are crucial in achieving recovery. Self-acceptance and regaining belief in one's self are particularly vital. Respect ensures the inclusion and full participation of consumers in all aspects of their lives.

9. **Responsibility:** Consumers have a personal responsibility for their own self-care and journeys of recovery. Taking steps toward their goals may require great courage. Consumers must strive to understand and give meaning to their experiences and identify coping strategies and healing processes to promote their own wellness.

10. **Hope:** Recovery provides the essential and motivating message of a better future—that people can overcome the barriers and obstacles that confront them. Hope is internalized, but can be fostered by peers, families, friends, providers, and others. Hope is the catalyst of the recovery process. Mental

health recovery not only benefits individuals with mental health disabilities by focusing on their abilities to live, work, learn, and fully participate in our society, but also enriches the texture of American community life. America reaps the benefits of the contributions individuals with mental disabilities can make, ultimately becoming a stronger and healthier Nation.[1]

The numbers used for Objectives in the treatment plan that follows correspond to the numbers for the 10 core principles. Each of the 10 Objectives was written to capture the essential theme of the like-numbered core principle. The numbers in parentheses after the Objectives denote the Interventions designed to assist the client in attaining each respective Objective. The clinician may select any or all of the Objectives and Intervention statements to include in the client's treatment plan.

One generic Long-Term Goal statement is offered should the clinician desire to emphasize a recovery model orientation in the client's treatment plan.

LONG-TERM GOAL

1. To live a meaningful life in a self-selected community while striving to achieve full potential during the journey of healing and transformation.

SHORT-TERM OBJECTIVES

1. Make it clear to therapist, family, and friends what path to recovery is preferred. (1, 2, 3, 4)

THERAPEUTIC INTERVENTIONS

1. Explore the client's thoughts, needs, and preferences regarding his/her desired pathway to recovery (from depression, bipolar disorder, posttraumatic stress disorder [PTSD], etc.).

2. Discuss with the client the alternative treatment interventions and community support resources that might facilitate his/her recovery.

---

[1] From: Substance Abuse and Mental Health Services Administration's (SAMHSA) National Mental Health Information Center: Center for Mental Health Services (2004). *National consensus statement on mental health recovery.* Washington, DC: Author. Available from http://mentalhealth.samhsa.gov/publications/allpubs/sma05-4129/

3. Solicit from the client his/her preferences regarding the direction treatment will take; allow for these preferences to be communicated to family and significant others.

4. Discuss and process with the client the possible outcomes that may result from his/her decisions.

2. Specify any unique needs and cultural preferences that must be taken under consideration during the treatment process. (5, 6)

5. Explore with the client any cultural considerations, experiences, or other needs that must be considered in formulating a mutually agreed-upon treatment plan.

6. Modify treatment planning to accommodate the client's cultural and experiential background and preferences.

3. Verbalize an understanding that decision making throughout the treatment process is self-controlled. (7, 8)

7. Clarify with the client that he/she has the right to choose and select among options and participate in all decisions that affect him/her during treatment.

8. Continuously offer and explain options to the client as treatment progresses in support of his/her sense of empowerment, encouraging and reinforcing the client's participation in treatment decision making.

4. Express mental, physical, spiritual, and community needs and desires that should be integrated into the treatment process. (9, 10)

9. Assess the client's personal, interpersonal, medical, spiritual, and community strengths and weaknesses.

10. Maintain a holistic approach to treatment planning by integrating the client's unique mental, physical, spiritual, and community needs and assets into

5. Verbalize an understanding that during the treatment process there will be successes and failures, progress and setbacks. (11, 12)

6. Cooperate with an assessment of personal strengths and assets brought to the treatment process. (13, 14, 15)

7. Verbalize an understanding of the benefits of peer support during the recovery process. (16, 17, 18)

the plan; arrive at an agreement with the client as to how these integrations will be made.

11. Facilitate realistic expectations and hope in the client that positive change is possible, but does not occur in a linear process of straight-line successes; emphasize a recovery process involving growth, learning from advances as well as setbacks, and staying this course toward recovery.

12. Convey to the client that you will stay the course with him/her through the difficult times of lapses and setbacks.

13. Administer to the client the *Behavioral and Emotional Rating Scale (BERS): A Strength-Based Approach to Assessment* (Epstein).

14. Identify the client's strengths through a thorough assessment involving social, cognitive, relational, and spiritual aspects of the client's life; assist the client in identifying what coping skills have worked well in the past to overcome problems and what talents and abilities characterize his/her daily life.

15. Provide feedback to the client of his/her identified strengths and how these strengths can be integrated into short-term and long-term recovery planning.

16. Discuss with the client the benefits of peer support (e.g., sharing common problems, receiving advice regarding successful coping skills, getting encouragement, learning of

helpful community resources, etc.) toward the client's agreement to engage in peer activity.

17. Refer the client to peer support groups of his/her choice in the community and process his/her experience with follow-through.

18. Build and reinforce the client's sense of belonging, supportive relationship building, social value, and community integration by processing the gains and problem-solving the obstacles encountered through the client's social activities.

8. Agree to reveal when any occasion arises that respect is not felt from the treatment staff, family, self, or the community. (19, 20, 21)

19. Discuss with the client the crucial role that respect plays in recovery, reviewing subtle and obvious ways in which disrespect may be shown to or experienced by the client.

20. Review ways in which the client has felt disrespected in the past, identifying sources of that disrespect.

21. Encourage and reinforce the client's self-concept as a person deserving of respect; advocate for the client to increase incidents of respectful treatment within the community and/or family system.

9. Verbalize acceptance of responsibility for self-care and participation in decisions during the treatment process. (22)

22. Develop, encourage, support, and reinforce the client's role as the person in control of his/her treatment and responsible for its application to his/her daily life; adopt a supportive role as a resource person to assist in the recovery process.

10. Express hope that better functioning in the future can be attained. (23, 24)

23. Discuss with the client potential role models who have achieved a more satisfying life by using their personal strengths, skills, and social support to live, work, learn, and fully participate in society toward building hope and incentive motivation.

24. Discuss and enhance internalization of the client's self-concept as a person capable of overcoming obstacles and achieving satisfaction in living; continuously build and reinforce this self-concept using past and present examples supporting it.

Appendix D

BIBLIOGRAPHY

Abel Assessment Instrument by Abel, G.G. can be found by contacting Abel Screening, Inc., Suite T-30, West Wing, 3280 Howell Mill Road NW, Atlanta, GA, 30327.

Andrews, D.A. & Bonta, J. (1994). *The Psychology of Criminal Conduct.* Cincinnati, OH: Anderson.

Daley, D.C., and Marlatt, G.A. (1992). *Relapse Prevention: Cognitive and Behavioral Interventions.* Baltimore, MD: Williams and Wilkins.

Elliott, D., and Henggeler, S. (1988) *Blueprints for Violence Prevention: Multisystemic Therapy.* Boulder, CO: Center for the Study and Prevention of Violence.

Epperson, D.G. (1995). Minnesota Sex Offender Screening Tool—Revised (MnSOST-R). Minnesota Department of Corrections.

Fisher, J. and K. Corcoran (1994). *Measures for Clinical Practice: A Sourcebook,* Volume 2: Adults. 2nd ed. New York: The Free Press.

Gambrill, E.D. and C.A. Richey (1975). "An Assertion Inventory for Use in Assessment and Research." *Behavior Therapy.* 6, 550-561.

Gibbs, J.C., G.B. Potter, and A.P. Goldstein (1995). *The EQUIP Program: Teaching Youth to Think and Act Responsibly Through a Peer-Helping Approach.* Champaign, IL: Research Press.

Goldstein, A.P. (1988). *The Prepare Curriculum: Teaching Prosocial Competencies.* Champaign, IL: Research Press.

Heaven, P.C.L. (1985). "Construction and Validation of a Measure of Authoritarian Personality." *Journal of Personality Assessment,* 49, 545-551.

Heimberg, RG., E.J. Chiauzzi, R.E. Becker, and R. Madrazo-Peterson (1983). "Cognition Mediation of Assertive Behavior: An Analysis of the Self-Statement Patterns of College Students, Psychiatric Patients, and Normal Adults." *Cognitive Therapy and Research,* 7, 455-464.

Letourneau, E.J. (2002). A Comparison of Objective Measures of Sexual Arousal and Interest: Visual Reaction Time and Penile Plethysmography. *Sex Abuse: A Journal of Research and Treatment.* Vol. 14, No. 3.

Marlatt, G.A., and Gordon, J.R. (Eds.). (1985). *Relapse Prevention: Maintenance Strategies in the Treatment of Addictive Behaviors.* New York: Guilford Press.

Monti, P.M., D.B. Abrams, R.M. Kadden, and N.L. Coney (1989). *Treating Alcohol Dependence: A Coping Skills Training Guide.* New York: The Guilford Press.

Paulhus, D. (1998). Paulhus Deception Scales (PDS): The Balanced Inventory of Desirable Responding—7. Multi-Health Systems, 65 Overlea Blvd. Ste. 210, Toronto, Ontario, M4H 1P1.

Perez, R., DeBord, K., and Bieschke, K. (2000). *Handbook of Counseling and Psychotherapy with Lesbian, Gay and Bisexual Clients.* Washington, DC: American Psychological Association.

Phares, E.J. and Erskine, N. (1984) The Measurement of Selfism. Educational and Psychological Measurement. 44, 597-608.

Rigby, K. (1987). "An Authority Behavior Inventory. *Journal of Personality Assessment,* 51, 615-625.

Ross, R.R., E.A. Fabiano, and R.D. Ross (1986). *Reasoning and Rehabilitation: A Handbook for Teaching Cognitive Skills.* Ottawa, Ontario: Flix Desktop Services.

Simourd, D.J. (1997). The Criminal Sentiments Scale—Modified and Pride in Delinquency Scale: Psychometric properties and construct validity of two measures of criminal attitudes. *Criminal Justice and Behavior, 24,* 52-70.

Simourd, D., and Olver, M. (2002). *The Future of Criminal Attitudes Research and Practice*. Saskatoon, Canada: University of Saskatchewan, Canada.

Van Dieten, M., & Graham, I. (1998). *Counter-Point: A Program For Attitude and Behavior Change*. Ottawa, Canada: John Howard Society of Ottawa-Carleton.

Wanberg, K.W. and H.B. Milkman (1998). *Criminal Conduct and Substance Abuse Treatment: Strategies for Self-Improvement and Change*. Thousand Oaks, CA: Sage Publications.

Winogron, W., M. VanDieten, and L. Gauzas (1997). *Controlling Anger and Learning to Manage (CALM) Program: Guide 2*. Toronto, Ontario: Multi-Health Systems, Inc.